CORPORATE BRANDING
PURPOSE/PEOPLE/PROCESS

Edited by Majken Schultz, Yun Mi Antorini
& Fabian F. Csaba

TOWARDS THE SECOND WAVE OF
CORPORATE BRANDING

CORPORATE BRANDING
PURPOSE/PEOPLE/PROCESS

Copenhagen Business School Press

Corporate Branding

© Copenhagen Business School Press
Printed in Denmark by Narayana Press, Gylling
Cover illustration: Getty Images
Cover design by Morten Højmark
1. edition 2005

ISBN 87-630-0140-3

Distribution:

Scandinavia
DJØF/DBK, Mimersvej 4
DK-4600 Køge, Denmark
Phone: +45 3269 7788, fax: +45 3269 7789

North America
Copenhagen Business School Press
Books International Inc.
P.O. Box 605
Herndon, VA 20172-0605, USA
Phone: +1 703 661 1500, fax: +1 703 661 1501

Rest of the World
Marston Book Services, P.O. Box 269
Abingdon, Oxfordshire, OX14 4YN, UK
Phone: +44 (0) 1235 465500, fax: +44 (0) 1235 4656555
E-mail Direct Customers: direct.order@marston.co.uk
E-mail Booksellers: trade.order@marston.co.uk

All rights reserved. No part of this publication may be reproduced or used in any form or by any means - graphic, electronic or mechanical including photocopying, recording, taping or information storage or retrieval systems - without permission in writing from Copenhagen Business School Press at www.cbspress.dk

Acknowledgements

This book has been written as part of the research project: Corporate Branding – An Organizational Perspective on the Creation and Implementation of Global Corporate Brands. The project ran from 2002-2005 and was co-funded by the Danish Social Science Council as part of the LOK program along with the LEGO® Group and Copenhagen Business School. The Corporate Branding Project was initiated by Professor Majken Schultz, Copenhagen Business School in collaboration with Professor Mary Jo Hatch, University of Virginia. The complete Corporate Branding Research Project has generated a range of different activities both in Denmark and internationally. They include the establishment of an international network of companies involved in corporate branding; in-depth case studies of select companies; co-development of conceptual contributions with practitioners in the field and more classic academic contributions; e.g. articles, teaching cases, talks and course-development.

This book has emerged from the discussions and research activities conducted by the Danish team based at Copenhagen Business School (see www.brandstudies.com). The book includes contributions from Majken Schultz, Yun Mi Antorini, Fabian F. Csaba, Esben Karmark, Pernille Gjøls-Andersen and Kasper S. Andersen. In our development of the book, we have built on and benefited from discussions with our international research partners, Mary Jo Hatch, Phil Mirvis and James Rubin. A special thanks to Phil Mirvis for his extensive comments to chapter 8. Furthermore, we are grateful for the experiences and insights that we have gained from the companies who have participated in our corporate branding research activities. We have learned much from our year-long collaboration with the LEGO Group and are indebted to many people related to the company, in particular, Kjeld Kirk Kristiansen, Poul Plougmann, Francesco Ciccolella, Frank Banke Troelsen, Iben Eiby-Johannesen, Mie Krog, Tormod Askildsen and Jacob McKee. We would also like to thank Kåre Schultz, Mike Rulis and Tina Nørgaard from Novo Nordisk for their support in conducting our case-study of Novo Nordisk, which has served as important inspiration for the conceptual discussions in this book. Finally, we have drawn on the themes and discussions which have taken place in our international network of managers dedicated to corporate branding. In addition to the participants from the LEGO Company and Novo Nordisk®, we especially want to thank Mark

Perry, Nissan™ US; Owen Rankin, Johnson & Johnson©; Stephan Geron, ING Group©; Alberto Andreu and Esther Trujillo Giménez, Telefonica© and Erich Joachimsthaler, VivaldiPartners©.

Although we greatly appreciate the insights and inspiration we have gained from others, the ideas and contributions in this book primarily derive from the many meetings and workshops held in our Danish team. We hope that this joint effort is reflected in recurring concepts, themes and issues spanning the individual contributions in the book, which together constitute our move towards the second wave of corporate branding.

Copenhagen, May 15, 2005

Majken Schultz

Table of Contents

1 CORPORATE BRANDING – AN EVOLVING CONCEPT   9
Majken Schultz, Yun Mi Antorini & Fabian F. Csaba

PURPOSE

**2 A CROSS-DISCIPLINARY PERSPECTIVE
ON CORPORATE BRANDING**   23
Majken Schultz

3 CORPORATE BRANDING AND THE 'CONFORMITY TRAP'   57
Yun Mi Antorini & Majken Schultz

4 A COMMUNAL APPROACH TO CORPORATE BRANDING   79
Yun Mi Antorini & Kasper S. Andersen

PEOPLE

5 LIVING THE BRAND   103
Esben Karmark

6 THE LIMITS OF CORPORATE BRANDING   127
The Application of Branding to Non-Profit Organizations and Places
Fabian F. Csaba

7 CORPORATE BRAND STRETCH   151
Brand Extension in a Corporate Branding Perspective
Pernille Gjøls-Andersen & Esben Karmark

PROCESS

8 CORPORATE BRANDING AS ORGANIZATIONAL CHANGE   181
Majken Schultz

**9 PRINCIPLES FOR THE SECOND WAVE
OF CORPORATE BRANDING**   219
Yun Mi Antorini & Majken Schultz

CHAPTER 1

CORPORATE BRANDING – AN EVOLVING CONCEPT

Majken Schultz, Yun Mi Antorini
& Fabian F. Csaba

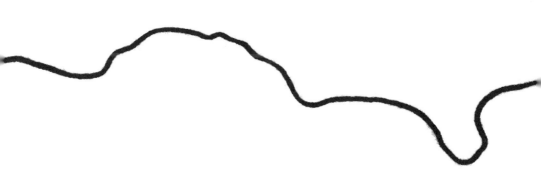

Majken Schultz, Yun Mi Antorini & Fabian F. Csaba

'Who are we'? 'What do we stand for'? 'What do we want to become'? These are some of the universal questions organizations have wrestled with throughout the ages. In a time of rapid technological development, global agendas and changeable market conditions, it has gradually become both more difficult, and far more important, to answer these classic questions.

This book is about corporate branding. The aim of the book is to describe and analyze corporate branding as a strategic and cross-disciplinary process that rethinks questions of identity, purpose, and direction and seeks new answers. We present the view that corporate branding must be understood as a process by which an organization continually asks itself the universal identity questions that can propel it forwards as a competitive and innovative organization. Corporate branding is therefore not so much about finding definite answers to these questions. Rather, it is about finding a path in a changeable and dynamic age that paradoxically requires that the organization develops, while also being able to hold on to its identity.

Even though corporate branding can still be seen as a relatively new field, it is currently in transition between what we call the *first and second waves of corporate branding*.

The *first wave* of corporate branding took shape in the mid 1990s. Authors such as Olins (1988), Aaker (1991), Balmer (1995, 2001), Ind (1997), Keller (1997), de Chernatony (1999), Kapferer (2000), Aaker & Joachimsthaler (2000), Hatch & Schultz (2000, 2001), Gray & Balmer (2001) played a leading role in influencing thought. Contributions derived from such diverse quarters as marketing, corporate communication, organization theory and the visual and graphical tradition. For some authors, the idea of an organization as a brand was an extension of the *product branding approach*, with its focus on brand essence, benefits and individual visual identities. Others were more concerned with positioning corporate branding as a *strategic concept* that fleshed out *how* an organization could formulate an enduring identity that was relevant to its stakeholders. The field of corporate branding basically became divided into two camps. One camp was characterized by a product driven *tactical and visual focus*, while the other camp emphasized corporate branding as a *strategic and integrated* field.

The tactical and visual approach ended up largely dominating both corporate branding literature and practice. It also formed the foundation for what we call the *first wave of corporate branding*. With its focus on tactics and visuality, the first wave of corporate branding was carried forward as a *marketing and campaign driven* approach. As a consequence, responsibility for corporate branding was anchored in the marketing function. While the first wave of corporate branding differed fundamentally from the strategic and integrated approach, both directions did agree that the most important role of corporate branding was to give greater focus to the organization as a force for differentiation.

Many organizations gained experience with corporate branding during the last decade. International brand measuring systems (such as Interbrand and Business Week's annual survey: *The Best Global Brands*) confirmed, time and again, the impact of corporate brands on companies' financial performance. These surveys often ascribed corporate brands such as Disney©, Coca-Cola©, Nike© and McDonald's© a central place as ideal corporate brands. Due to the charisma and broad public exposure of the leaders of these organizations, and the strength of these brands as icons and universal symbols, corporate brands such as these came to stand as practical examples of the approach and practice that characterized the first wave of corporate branding. Their global, outward-looking practices, and often quite considerable marketing budgets, created a feeling of omnipresence.

The significance of corporate branding as a way in which an organization could build relationships with its environment in a strategic and more farsighted manner was often neglected during the first wave, overshadowed by a marketing and campaign approach. Under this approach, corporate branding was therefore established as a field that did not necessarily consider the organization's culture, long-term stakeholder relationships and employee involvement. This situation often locked brand managers and communication consultants into what Kapferer called *clouded cuckoo land* (Kapferer, 2000:60). It usually was not enthusiasm, initiative, or energy that was lacking, but, rather, strategic anchoring and a focus on building long-term relationships with the organization's stakeholders. Slowly but surely, in our opinion, the marketing and campaign approach therefore decoupled the idea of corporate branding from being a practice based in each organization's unique situation, culture and distinctive characteristics. This decoupling often led to the organization being split into the claims: *Who we say we are*, and behaviour: *Who we really are*. In cases where there was a great gap between *superficial promises* and *the substantial performance*, this situation eventually led to perceptions of the organization as lacking in coherence and credibility.

The first wave of corporate branding can be summed up as being driven by the recognition of the fact that the organization itself, rather than its products, was playing an ever increasing role in the organization's differentiation and its relationships with various stakeholders. However, practices associated with the first wave of corporate branding, i.e. the way in which organizations generally thought about and implemented corporate branding, were tied to marketing and campaign thinking. Thus corporate branding came to be more about optimizing the expressiveness of the organization than establishing long-term relationships with its multiple internal and external stakeholders.

Corporate branding basically represents a relatively simple idea, that the organization and everything it stands for is mobilized to interact with the stakeholders the organization wants to reach and engage them in dialogue. However, if one reflects on this perception, it becomes clear that corporate branding, due to its strategic, integrated and longitudinal foundation, is a deeply paradoxical concept. This may be the very reason why the first wave of corporate branding was driven by promises of changes to practice, rather than conceptual development.

When we look back on corporate branding as a concept, it is our opinion that practical issues ended up running ahead of the conceptualization of the idea. In other words, *corporate branding was translated into practice before the conceptual foundation was sufficiently clarified.* The basic questions that ought to clarify and simplify the paradoxical complexity of the concept thus continue to be just as relevant and pressing. For example, what do we mean when we say the organization is a whole that involves and is co-created by many different parts? How can we meet the organization's need for stability, while also meeting the need for flexibility and change? How can the organization build meaningful relationships with its specific stakeholders while also representing a recognizable symbolic universe?

Corporate Branding Myths

Today, more than 10 years after corporate branding was conceptualized, we can see that these questions are still largely unanswered. It is our opinion that the marketing and campaign driven focus has blocked the important conceptual discussion associated with corporate branding as a strategic concept. We also believe that the perception of corporate branding is locked into a number of myths which the marketing and campaign driven focus has given rise to. And we believe that these myths are preventing companies and other organizations from creating effective corporate brands (see figure 1:1):

Figure 1:1 Corporate Branding Myths

Myth 1: Corporate Branding is Like Product Branding - Just at the Organizational Level!

In the classic marketing definition of branding, the concept is associated with identification of a product and differentiation from competitors' products using names, logos, design and other recognizable signs or symbols. Brands are created and supported through effective utilization of the organization's marketing mix. During the first wave of corporate branding, product branding principles often merged with corporate branding principles. This was tantamount to the perception that you could communicate your way to a strong corporate brand. With time, the myth took shape that corporate branding was like product branding. The problem with the myth is that a focus on the organization as a central and enduring differentiating force is lost.

Myth 2: Corporate Branding is 'Owned' by the Marketing Department!

Corporate branding processes were often initiated by top management. Despite this, responsibility for executing and maintaining the corporate brand (in line with the marketing and campaign focus), was often given to the marketing function. Marketing naturally played an important role in communicating who the organization is and what it stands for. But by positioning corporate branding exclusively in the domain of marketing, the risk arose that corporate branding became anchored in a short-term and tactical focus. The problem with this myth is that the organization loses the long-term, strategic focus that characterizes most organizations that manage, year after year, decade after decade, not only to maintain market share but also to demonstrate growth and development that far exceeds that of their competitors.

Myth 3: Corporate Branding is Like a Sugar Coating!

The marketing and campaign approach provided fertile soil for the myth that corporate branding could be likened to a 'sugar coating', i.e. something you could wrap around the organization which did not necessarily relate to what was inside. In such a perspective, vision and values became 'show vision' and 'show values', i.e. something the organization claims to be or strive for, but does not feel committed to. Thus this myth created the perception that you could stage corporate branding. However, when the gap between 'who we say we are' and 'who we really are' became too wide, it often resulted in confusion and mistrust among the organization's stakeholders. The myth that corporate branding is like a sugar coating is a problem because it creates the impression that the organization's 'exterior' and 'interior' do not necessarily have to be aligned.

Myth 4: The Goal of Corporate Branding is to Standardize the Organization's Communication!

Corporate branding was often presented as a tidying up project which aimed to reduce complexity and increase clarity, for example, by standardizing and streamlining the organization's communication. However, we learned from the 'visionary companies' (Collins and Porras, 1994; Collins, 2001) that being consistent in your communication is not essential. It is more important that *all* functions of the organization are loyal to the underlying vision and values that characterize the organization. The problem with this myth is that it creates a limiting framework for the organization's communication, that it locks the organization into tactical details and overlooks the strategic vision of corporate branding, where the goal is to create continual clarity in a changeable environment.

Myth 5: Corporate Branding Automatically Mobilizes the Organization's Employees!

The significance of the role of employees in relation to corporate branding was recognized to some extent, but during the first wave it was considered as a form of involvement and an obligation that virtually arose automatically. This perception still lingers to some extent, and people often claim: *Employees are our most important asset*, and *employees are central to our competitiveness*, without these statements leading the organization to feel an obligation to involve employees in developing and strengthening the corporate brand. The problem with simply assuming that corporate branding automatically mobilizes employees is that the critical insight and knowledge that employees possess gets lost in the process.

Myth 6: Corporate Branding is Only Relevant for Commercial Organizations!

Corporate branding is generally seen as a commercially-oriented field which has the goal of optimizing an organization's transactions with its environment. This perception has given rise to the myth that the principles of corporate branding cannot be transferred to non-profit organizations. However, the corporate branding concept encompasses principle ideas about identity, purpose and direction that are relevant even to non-commercial organizations. In principle, corporate branding can be transferred to countries and regions, as well as non-profit organizations such as NGO's. This process is well underway, but continues to be hampered by the myth that corporate branding is a commercially-oriented concept.

Moving Towards the Second Wave of Corporate Branding

It is our thesis that corporate branding should be understood as a dynamic concept that is evolving. In our view, this development places corporate branding at a crossroads.

One path continues to build on the marketing and campaign approach to corporate branding. Its focus on tactics and visuality renders the corporate aspect superficial, and corporate branding will ultimately blend into the product branding field. This path therefore leads to the gradual undermining of the concept, and one could expect that the concept will eventually be reformulated to better match the organization's short-term and tactical goals. As this happens, the concept will gain the status of yet another piece of management hype and definitively lose its strategic impact.

The *other path* builds on the experience gained from the first wave. It is characterized by greater and more realistic insight into the many conflicts and complex relationships that exist in relation to an organization and its environment. The cross-diciplinary and dynamic perspective that takes into account aspects of the organization's culture and relationships will come to play an increasing role in this perception of corporate branding. Corporate branding will end up becoming one of the few central and cross-disciplinary concepts that can establish cohesion between the organization's strategy, organization and marketing.

The goal of this book is to take the first step on the path of rethinking corporate branding. Such a process will primarily involve taking up the fundamental questions again. Based on the various experiences of the authors, we will examine corporate branding, theoretically and in practice, from various angles. The goal is to stake out a direction for the second wave of corporate branding that positions it as a *process* through which an organization can continually work out its *purpose* – a purpose that is meaningful to *people* inside and outside the organization.

Organization of the Book

As the subtitle of the book suggests, our efforts to rethink corporate branding are organized around three core dimensions: Purpose, people and process. The first three chapters (two to four) address issues related to purpose, while chapters five to seven discuss various aspects of the people dimension. Chapter eight focuses on the managerial and organizational processes of corporate branding. Finally, we offer a set of principles for the second wave of corporate branding drawing on all the contributions.

Purpose relates to the aims, prospects and premises of corporate branding as a managerial practice in organizations. In order to mature as a management approach or business philosophy, we argue that proponents of corporate branding must acknowledge and exploit the different academic disciplines that have contributed to the development of corporate branding. The challenge in the move to the second wave of corporate branding is to find ways of integrating these disciplines into a coherent and relevant framework for corporate branding. This framework must transcend the influences of each discipline and avoid the traps of an oversimplified conception of branding.

In Chapter 2, Majken Schultz provides a comprehensive theoretical introduction to the disciplinary origins of corporate branding. Schultz examines the development of corporate branding by looking at the different disciplinary fields that facilitate it, and discusses the pitfalls of basing corporate branding on a single disciplinary approach. The chapter proposes an integrative framework (the Corporate Branding Tool-Kit, developed by Mary Jo Hatch & Majken Schultz) for corporate brand analysis, and addresses the challenges and paradoxes involved in balancing the different brand elements. This framework depicts the corporate brand as a key symbol of organizational identity, the meaning and value of which are influenced in equal measure by top management vision, organizational culture and stakeholder images. The framework serves as a common frame of reference for the rest of the book.

Chapter 3, written by Yun Mi Antorini and Majken Schultz, analyzes two of the central motifs in corporate branding: Differentiation and uniqueness. The need for organizations to differentiate themselves is considered, both in theory and in practice, to be one of the main purposes of corporate branding. However, this chapter argues that certain aspects and inherent dynamics in corporate brand management tend to push organizations towards conformism and inadequate differentiation. The authors claim that organizations, contrary to their intentions, often fail to differentiate themselves and fall into what the authors call the *conformity trap*. Drawing on the distinction between an essence-based and relationship-based approach, the authors discuss how organizations may overcome the conformity trap, and propose ways of avoiding falling into it in the first place.

The role of the consumer in brand building is also changing with the move to the second wave of branding. The Internet has made it possible for consumers – across time and space – to negotiate brand meaning with other consumers more openly, and to feed back their viewpoints and experiences to the organization. Increasingly, the notion of consumers as passive recipients of brand meaning and products is being replaced with the notion of consumers as active co-creators of brand meaning and important contributors to the organization's value creation. In Chapter 4, Yun Mi Antorini and Kasper S. Andersen explore how closer integration between organizations and consumers can be achieved. The chapter also discusses how closer integration might affect the corporate brand. The chapter is illustrated using three cases: IKEA®, Jones Soda© and WeightWatchers©. They represent organizations which, to varying degrees and in different ways, have chosen to close the gap between the organization and the consumer.

The people dimension deals with people and the social and cultural processes behind brands. The people dimension is central to corporate branding. In fact, the very notion of applying branding to organizations (and their members), rather than to things or ideas, implies a strong emphasis on people. In contrast to classic product branding, corporate branding acknowledges that branding must work through employees as individuals and members of subgroups within the organization.

Chapter 5 deals with different approaches to the role of employees and organizational culture in corporate branding. *Living the Brand* is one of the most common slogans in corporate branding. It expresses the principle of mobilizing employees in the branding process as active representatives or ambassadors of the brand. However, there have been many indications that 'living the brand' campaigns do not succeed. In Chapter 5, Esben Karmark analyzes the concept of living the brand from two contrasting approaches: A marketing and communications-based approach and an organizational and values-based approach. Karmark demonstrates how the two approaches grant employees different roles and opportunities to act as *living brands*. The chapter draws on case examples from Novo Nordisk, LEGO Group, Bang & Olufsen© and Danisco© to illustrate the two approaches and suggests a third, more reflexive, perspective on the employee as a living brand.

Chapter 6 examines the people dimension and cultural issues at a more abstract level, when corporate branding principles are applied outside the corporate setting to non-profits, nations and other geographic entities. The concept of corporate branding has primarily been based on the strategic challenges for large, for-profit organizations. But what are the limits for the application of corporate brand management? In Chapter 6, Fabian F. Csaba argues that, in principle, corporate branding applies to other types of organisations or phenomena than just corporations. Exploring work on the branding of non-profit organizations and nations, regions and cities, the chapter assesses the influence of corporate branding outside its primary realm. The chapter shows how and why corporate branding has spread to other domains, and illustrates how the principles and techniques of corporate branding have been appropriated outside the corporate context. In considering these issues, the chapter challenges common notions about corporate branding's appropriate domain and cultural influence.

Chapter 7 then investigates the limits imposed by organizational identity and culture in expanding and leveraging corporate brands. The issue of the limits of corporate branding can be approached from a different angle, namely that of brand extensions. Many organizations seek to leverage their brand by expanding the range of activities covered by the corporate brand. Brands like Disney© and Virgin© have set new standards for how brand ideas can be leveraged in new areas outside the core business of the organization. In Chapter 7, Esben Karmark and Pernille Gjøls-Andersen discuss the opportunities and limitations of brand extensions for a corporate brand. In a comparative case study of the Disney and LEGO brands, they argue that brand extensions are closely linked to the organization's culture and identity. Their study suggests that an organization cannot instantly transform itself to a broad umbrella brand, since this requires experience in working with the brand at a higher level of abstraction. The chapter offers a set of proposals for renewing and extending brands without stretching them beyond the constraints of their identity.

The process dimension addresses how corporate branding is realized through processes of strategic and organizational change. Classic branding has largely been dominated by a focus on a 'campaign-like' launch of the brand to internal and external stakeholders. The first wave of branding has often overlooked the organizational and managerial difficulties of implementing corporate branding. In contrast, the second wave of branding includes the organizational change processes needed to create a sustainable corporate brand.

Chapter 8 proposes an analytical framework for understanding the different stages in the corporate branding process. Classic brand management theory has focused on the structural consequences of a corporate brand, i.e. how to construct a brand architecture. But in practice, corporate brands are established and developed over a long time and in interaction with existing cultures and images. This process, just like change management, involves a series of transformations, each with different managerial and organizational challenges. In the final chapter, Majken Schultz argues, on the basis of the experience of different organizations, that the development of a corporate brand consists of five stages defined as 1) Stating; 2) Organizing; 3) Involving; 4) Integrating; and 5) Monitoring. How the stages evolve depends on the particular characteristics and conditions of the organization. The chapter suggests that corporate branding is best considered as a dynamic and cyclical process, and not a simple linear, sequential flow. The chapter advances a dynamic corporate branding model which offers a frame of reference for creating and implementing a corporate brand.

Finally, in concluding the book, we suggest five principles that can serve as inspirational guidelines in the move to the second wave of corporate branding.

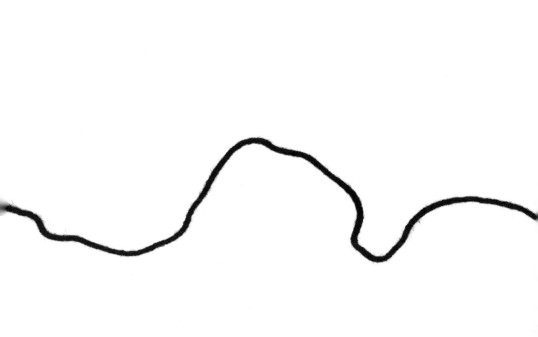

CHAPTER 2

A CROSS-DISCIPLINARY PERSPECTIVE ON CORPORATE BRANDING

Majken Schultz

The chapter examines the development of corporate branding by looking at the different disciplines that have contributed to corporate branding: Marketing, visual identity, organization theory, communication and strategy. The chapter discusses the traps that emerge if corporate branding is based on a single disciplinary approach. It offers an integrative framework - The Corporate Branding Tool-Kit - for corporate brand analysis.

The classic perception and application of branding has been dominated by a product mindset based in the marketing discipline. This model focuses on creating a strong market position for stand-alone products and services, attracting and retaining customers by an optimal marketing mix. More recently, the focus has shifted from a branding of stand-alone products and services to a branding of the organization itself. As stated by Olins, brands are taking over the corporation (2000). Several scholars and practitioners have argued that the classic branding model has been restricting. It is constrained by a narrow external perspective and a single-minded focus on customers that neglects the special conditions for creating brands based in the organization itself (e.g. Aaker & Joachimsthaler, 2000; Kapferer, 2001; Hatch & Schultz, 2001; Olins, 2004). Product brands are detached from the company behind them and relate to consumers as individuals; a corporate brand is founded on an integrated and cross-disciplinary mindset based in the central ideas of who the organization is. It focuses on developing relationships with all stakeholders and engages stakeholders in defining who the organization is – and aspires to be. Not to be perceived as a giant-sized product brand, a corporate brand originates from distinct combinations of symbols, values, and beliefs that are salient to both the organization and its dynamic relationships with internal and external stakeholders (Ind, 1997; Aaker & Joachimsthaler 2000; Hatch & Schultz, 2001; Balmer & Greyser, 2003; Schultz & Hatch, 2003; Olins, 2004; Aaker, 2004).

In a broader theoretical development, corporate branding can be seen as a move towards conceiving more integrated relationships between internal and external stakeholders, linking top management, employees, customers, and other key external stakeholders. As argued by Hatch & Schultz, corporate branding can be conceptualized in the following ways: As alignments between the origin and everyday practices of the organization (organizational culture); where the organization aspires to go (strategic vision); how the organization is perceived by external stakeholders (images); all nested in perceptions of who the organization is (identity) (Hatch & Schultz 2001, 2003). Based in 'who we are as an organization', corporate branding focuses on developing the distinctive features of the organization through managerial and organizational processes. These processes endeavor to express who the company is as an organization and demonstrate how it is different compared with its competitors, all the while making this difference relevant and engaging to its stakeholders.

This chapter argues that corporate branding represents a blending of parallel developments within different academic disciplines. Each discipline points to the need for a more integrated understanding of how corporations express themselves in situations of complexity and change. People involved in managing corporate brands are faced with the pressure to create coherence across organizational functions and business areas in turbulent global markets. The chapter suggests a theoretical framing of corporate branding, which resides in a cross-disciplinary and cross-functional mindset. It points out some of the forces behind the movement as it reaches toward the second wave of corporate branding and shows the traps that are likely to appear if the perception or execution of corporate branding is dominated by one discipline or business function alone. The chapter offers an analytical framework for corporate branding – the Corporate Branding Tool-Kit developed by Mary Jo Hatch and Majken Schultz (Hatch & Schultz 2001, 2003; Schultz & Hatch, 2003), and demonstrates how the Tool-Kit facilitates a simultaneous analysis of both coherence and corporate branding gaps. The dynamics of the Tool-kit and its application is further developed in chapter 8.

From Trademark to Brand

Originally, corporate branding emerged from the notion of 'trademarks.' These trademarks were defined as symbolic markers applied to artifacts, etc. Such marks showed belonging or ownership of the artifacts to specific stakeholders and symbolized the differentiation of these artifacts compared with others compatible artifacts (e.g. this is our symbol, which is different from your symbol!). From burning marks into the hides of cows in the Wild West, to the world's contemporary love affair with designer labels, brands are artifacts that have always been used symbolically to express identity (whether it be that of the product, the company, or the user). Most people associate brands with distinctive names, colors, icons, and shapes: Coke's sinuous bottle or its red can, the Wells-Fargo© stagecoach, or the distinctive four letters of the LEGO or SONY© name, for instance. Thus, companies are taking an interest in how they can claim ownership of distinctive colors, shapes, sounds, smells, and other individual expressions of who they are and what they stand for. Wally Olins has emphasized how these markers of brand ownership have developed over time. Trademarks have facilitated brand awareness and recognition, encouraging consumers to hold special expectations about the promises of the brand – whether it is a promise of special quality, unique experience, or personal identity. In its most simple version, these early assumptions and experiences with trademarks represent many of the forces that are still behind the development of the corporation as a brand (Olins, 2004; Aaker & Joachimsthaler, 2000; Schultz et al. 2000). The central dimensions of corporate branding can be summarized as:

Central Dimensions of Corporate Branding:

- The construction of names, symbols, and experiences, which are perceived as unique to the organization and facilitate recognition and repetition
- Central ideas belonging to the organization that reach out to all internal and external stakeholders
- One organization which stands behind all products, services, and other behaviors
- The expression of promises of distinct quality, substance, emotion, style, or experience, which follow from interaction with the organization
- The creation and re-creation of meaningful distinction towards 'others' in the eyes of stakeholders

In other words, corporate branding enables companies and organizations to step forward and express their distinct identity and heritage towards different stakeholders, while at the same time involving stakeholders in making this difference engaging and relevant. To consumers, the symbolic origin of brands invites them to construct their own identity and meaning, as expressed by former global brand manager of the LEGO Group, Francesco Ciccolella:

- We don't buy products only for what they ARE: A car as a means of transportation or a watch as a measurement of time
- We don't buy products only for what they HAVE: A car with 5 seats and 200 HP or a watch with 99.999% precision
- We buy products for what they MEAN: A Volvo (safety) or a BMW (driving pleasure), a Swatch (informal, young) or a Rolex (lavish luxury, status)

As argued by Olins, the central challenge for brands is to create and maintain the simultaneous experience of belonging and differentiation to stakeholders (Olins, 2004). A brand should be able to create a relevant and meaningful difference to customers measured against other competing alternatives; but it must also attract and involve the many different stakeholders having relations with the brand. The movement towards corporate branding can best be described as a shift from classic branding to corporate branding and includes a number of different dimensions. These dimensions are summarized in table 2:1, which is an extension of Hatch & Schultz's (2003) overview.

Table 2:1 Differences between Classic Branding and Corporate Branding

	Classic branding	**Corporate branding**
Foundation	Individual products are the foundation for most brands	The company or organization is the foundation for the brand
Conceptualization	• Marketing • Outside-and-in-thinking	• Cross-disciplinary • Combines inside-out with outside-in thinking
Stakeholders	Consumers and customers	All stakeholders
Responsible for branding	Marketing and communication functions	All functions driven by top management
Time perspective	Short: product lifecycle	Long: organization lifecycle
Core process	Marketing and communication decide brand promises and marketing/communication mix.	Managerial and organizational processes align the company behind brand identity
Key issues	• Brand-architecture • Brand-positioning • Brand-identity	• Brand as a strategic force • Relations between strategic vision, organization culture and stakeholder image • Brand-alignment
Difficulties	• Difficult to build and sustain product differentiation • Restricted involvement of employees and use of cultural heritage • Limited involvement of stakeholders in communication efforts	• Difficult to align internal and external stakeholders • Difficult to create credible and authentic identity • Difficult to involve different subcultures and shifting stakeholders

The primary reasons for the shift towards corporate branding are based in the changing conditions for competition in the global marketplace along with growing expectations in many societies to legitimate corporate behavior. The costs of sustaining stand-alone product brands have increased in a global marketplace with a dramatic expansion in channels, and it has become increasingly difficult to maintain a generic product differentiation. In contrast, corporate brands expand the parameters of differentiation and enable companies to exploit their unique cultural heritage and identity (Barney 2000; Aaker 2004). Also, corporate branding has developed as a response to increasing stakeholder expectations that companies become more clear, sharp, and coherent when answering who they are as organizations and what they stand for compared with others. Companies have increased their ability to be distinct, involving, and credible when relating to an ever-shifting range of stakeholders. Thus, it is becoming increasingly obvious that corporate branding is not a one-way street, but depends on the ability of companies to create, expand, and engage in meaningful mutual relationships with their different stakeholders.

The shift from classic branding to corporate branding has been summarized by Wally Olins (2004) in his definition: Corporate brand = product/service + emotions + socio-cultural significance. This means that a corporate brand adds the socio-cultural significance to the product brand, which only consists of products with associated emotions. The socio-cultural significance of brands grows with the shift to corporate branding, as many stakeholders are more related to and more involved in corporate brands than they are to stand-alone product brands. Thus, the impact of corporate brands is strongly connected with the social responsibility of corporations and their involvement in community work in the markets where they operate. When a company engages in corporate branding, the emotional connections with stakeholders change from the consumption of stand-alone products and services to affiliations with the company itself. This implies that all of the organization's unique cultural heritage, significant symbols, iconic leaders and societal importance contribute to the foundation for the corporate brand.

Compared with classic branding, the role of employees in particular is much more important to the credibility and the coherence of the brand. Employees are both co-creators of the brand substance and crucial in the delivery of brand promises to external stakeholders. A shift to corporate branding in a company also has implications for the managerial and organizational processes as well as related support structures; the distinctive identity of the corporate brand should be reflected in the ways the whole organization operates. For example, a strong separation between functional areas such as marketing, corporate communication, stakeholder relations, and human resources often take the brand in very different directions. Furthermore, a lack of cross-functional bridging roles or systems often creates turf-wars and insurmountable obstacles in the management of corporate brands.

At first glance, the shift from classic branding to corporate branding can be perceived as a shift from the brand as a visual symbol to the brand as a framing of the relations between the organization and its multiple stakeholders. In my opinion, however, corporate branding represents a much more fundamental development across a range of different academic disciplines. Opposed to the domination of marketing in classic branding, each discipline contributes to the understanding of what corporate branding entails. In combination, these different disciplines facilitate a more comprehensive potential for a second wave of corporate branding. This potential resides in the opportunities for both research and practice to create cross-disciplinary synergies, where different insights and experiences blend and overcome the limitations of any individual discipline. The risk is that each discipline brings along its own set of pitfalls and limitations. And if a single discipline dominates the perception and implementation of corporate brands, this may prevent their creation and development.

Corporate Branding as a Cross-Disciplinary Construct

The shift to corporate branding has been reflected in the theoretical developments within a range of academic disciplines. The impetus appears to be a search for a more integrated, yet complex and dynamic understanding, of how organizations express themselves and engage in simultaneous relations with their multiple stakeholders (Schultz et al., 2000). Figure 2:1 shows key developments within the five academic disciplines that in my opinion have contributed most to the understanding of corporate branding: Marketing, visual identity, communication studies, organization theory, and strategy.

Figure 2:1 Key Concepts from Different Disciplines

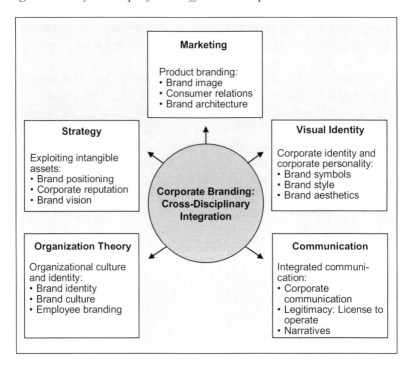

The figure includes both the five disciplines and some of the core concepts which each discipline has introduced in the conceptualization and application of corporate branding.

Furthermore, I argue that conceptualizing and implementing corporate branding within the boundaries of any of the five disciplines will lead to what is labelled corporate branding traps. These occur when dominating concerns within each discipline overshadow the cross-disciplinary synergies unique to corporate branding. The traps related to each of the five disciplines are summarized in figure 2:2.

From Product Thinking to the Organization as Brand

The conceptual origin of 'branding' is located in the *marketing discipline*. But exploding costs in developing and maintaining stand-alone product brands and increasing difficulties in creating and sustaining a meaningful differentiation for individual products have been some of the reasons why companies increasingly seek to build

A Cross-Disciplinary Perspective on Corporate Branding

consumer relations based within the organization itself. More and more companies are operating in a crowded global marketplace. Here the explosion in the number and types of communication channels (e.g. web-based, new media, new types of direct communication) have made it even more expensive and complicated for companies to position their stand-alone products towards ever more sophisticated, aware, and sceptical consumers, who are becoming increasingly tired of classic mass marketing communication. Thus, even global leaders in the area of product branding, such as Unilever© and Nestle©, are making significant reductions in the number of stand-alone product brands. Rather they are engaging in more regional corporate branding strategies, such as Unilever's operations in India branded as Hindulever.

Figure 2:2 Traps from Different Disciplines

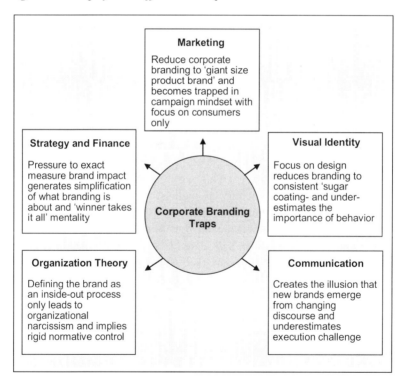

Corporate branding expands the range of *image-building activities*, as the company's own involvement in the creation of the brand opens up

31

a new set of dimensions and attributes, which can be more attractive and engaging to consumers (Ind, 1997; Keller, 2000; Aaker, 2004). For example, corporate branding enables companies to include their social programs and social responsibility activities in the brand, thereby directly involving consumers. Also, corporate branding can use employees and their commitment directly in market communication. This has been done by the US-based Saturn© automobiles. It has used the strong commitment of their employees and their responsible corporate culture in marketing the Saturn car as belonging to a company with a socio-economic impact. Danish Novo Nordisk has encouraged employees to talk to diabetic patients about their experiences in their 'I Wish' campaign. German Volkswagen© has also used the unique heritage of their company to generate new consumer experiences in the creation of their Autostadt, where consumers are invited to participate in the full historical development of the brand. The brand has also been exposed to consumers in new and more experiential ways in the creation of brand stores, making a joint statement of the Volkswagen family of brands (Olins, 2004).

By introducing the concept of *brand architecture*, the marketing discipline has contributed to corporate brand research and practice by offering a complex understanding of the many different types of relations that can arise between consumers and brands. Brand architecture and brand portfolio management address how brand relations can be categorized and extended in a variety of ways. For example, a corporate brand architecture links new generations of HP products to the company, while giving them some space to development their own identity as well. A company like Virgin has been able to extend its brand into new categories of products by using a consistent identity to manage its portfolio (e.g. taking the Virgin brand from music to airlines and jeans) (see Aaker & Joachimsthaler, 2000; Aaker, 2004). Through the shift to corporate branding, companies can further expand their types of connections or 'touch points' with different stakeholders to include relationships that are more driven by the creation of joint experiences with consumers, events, or interactive dialogue. Corporate brands can also – with or without deliberate intention – actively engage consumers as co-creators of the brand through the development of brand communities. Here consumers not only contribute to expand the meaning and symbolic expressions of the brand; they may also contribute to innovations and further development of the services offered by the brand. This kind of contribution is demonstrated by Antorini and

Andersen, showing how adult LEGO users have developed several innovations of LEGO products and product uses (Muniz & O'Guinn 2001, Antorini & Andersen, Chapter 4). Here, one dilemma is that the more the company actively involves consumers in the creation and expansion of the brand, the more difficult it becomes to control and predict the meanings and perceptions of the brand.

The most important *limitations* of a marketing perspective on corporate branding occur when the company as a brand essentially is perceived as a giant-sized product brand. In short, this implies a strong focus on consumers, using massive and efficient market spending to create meaningful and relevant brand associations among consumers. This domination of market communication in reaching consumers is typically executed through the launch of shifting marketing campaigns and has generated what is called a 'campaign syndrome' among managers working with corporate branding. The 'campaign syndrome' implies that brand managers are most concerned with the launch or re-launch of marketing campaigns, expressing the identity and values of the brand. By the same token, brand managers influenced by the 'campaign syndrome' underestimate the managerial and organization implications of embarking on a corporate brand strategy as opposed to launching a new product brand. As argued by Christensen and Cheney (2000), the single-minded focus on the branding campaign has found support in the auto-communicative processes of organizations. Here, brand managers become seduced by the internal effects of the marketing campaigns and by their own ability to appear in the media. Finally, in the pursuit of a unique selling position for the organization, the marketing discipline has focused on creating a brand essence and brand attributes that are expected to attract and seduce consumers instead of grounding the uniqueness of the brand in the heritage and distinct identity of the organization itself.

From 'Logo Merchants' to Brand Aesthetics

Another central discipline which has contributed to the development of corporate branding is the *visual design school*, best known from the concept of corporate identity. Proponents of *corporate identity* aim at creating a unique symbolic universe for the organization by using visual symbols and artefacts such as logos, trademarks, color, packaging, uniforms, architecture, design, house style, etc. The desire among companies to visualize and symbolize who they are and what they stand for has compelled corporate identity experts to go deeper into the 'corporate soul' or 'corporate personality.' Thus, the urge for experts to understand the foundation of what organizations intend to communicate about themselves has created an interest in the values and central ideas to be expressed by the visual identity (Olins, 1989, 2004; Schmitt & Simonson, 1997). The visual identity has often been designed in relation to the strategic development of the brand (e.g. in situations of mergers and acquisitions, strategic repositioning, brand extension into new business areas). But it has also created an interest in the culture behind the development of the personality or identity of the brand, as reflected in the concern with brand histories, such as the Volkswagen story described by Olins (2003).

The visual identity is still needed for enabling stakeholders to *recognize* the majority of corporate brands, although the development of web sites and new types of interactive digital dialogue invite new, more flexible, and customized ways of expressing the symbolic universe of the brand. Thus, new aesthetic opportunities are emerging for many brands, where symbolic elements such as color, sound, and smell are combined and recreated across different media and applications (for example, see the use of smell as described by Lindstrom & Kotler, 2005).

Last, but not least, the visual identity has been used to *explain* the levels and relationships in the architecture of the brand. Take for example the different product areas of FedEx. While all share the lilac FedEx name, each area has its own color code and descriptor: FedEx Express (orange), FedEx Ground (green), FedEx® Freight (red). Reinterpreting the historical origins of their visual identities has been important to many corporate brands because it expresses the unique identity of the brand by references to its aesthetic heritage. This has been particularly relevant to luxury brands, such as Burburry© and Louis Vuitton®, where their revitalization and economic turn-arounds have made strong use of their pools of heritage symbols and histories. Companies outside the fashion industry have also used their visual brand heritage in new and contemporary ways. For example, Bang & Olufsen's reintroduced their classic Bauhaus-inspired logo in the beginning of the 1990s. In the current attempt to strengthen the Georg Jensen© brand, the company is aiming for a more coherent expression of its visual identity in products, communication and retail environment to symbolize the unique historical origin of the company.

More than anything else, visual identity has symbolized both the opportunities and the *limitations* in creating global corporate brands. On the one hand, global brands require global recognition and consistency in their visual expressions. But on the other hand, global brands must also adapt to local cultures, tastes, and preferences in order to create relevance with consumers and other stakeholders. The strong focus on consistency in much corporate branding thinking has been one of the limitations originating from visual identity. This consistency emerges from the experience in many companies that the purpose of visual identity programs has often been to create order and clarity in a fragmented symbolism that has developed over time. Along with the limited strategic and analytical insight among what Wally Olins has labelled the 'logo merchants,' their resolve to be consistent has oversimplified the expressions of their brand. Such oversimplification has often reduced the opportunities for a more complex strategic development of a corporate brand. Furthermore, the visual school has shared some of the weaknesses of the marketing discipline in believing that the brand is first of all shaped by the creative development and launch of visual symbols and other types of aesthetic expressions. Finally, the visual school derives much of its understanding of corporate brand implementation from the execution of design programs, which in most companies is often decided and driven by a small top-management team. The importance of top management for a consistent design program has been extended into the corporate branding process itself, as the branding process has been orchestrated with a top-down mentality. This leaves top management in charge of deciding design programs. A strong top management domination limits the possibility for corporate branding, as corporate branding is a collaborative effort within the organization, requiring dialogue with and among employees in determining the best way to creatively express the brand.

From Fragmentation to Corporate Communication

A third discipline that has contributed significantly to our understanding of corporate branding is *communication studies*. At a more basic level, communication studies has been concerned with how communication processes emerge, proceed, and develop in the relationships between sender and receiver. The fundamental processes of communication studies have been the coding and de-coding of messaging between sender and receiver. The main concern has been how these processes are disrupted and generate situations of miscommunication, auto-communication, or other types of unintended consequences (Christensen & Cheney, 2000; Van Riel, 2000;

Cornelissen, 2004). From having had a dominant focus either on internal organizational communication (e.g. between managers and employees) or communication with external stakeholders, (such as media relations, public relations, corporate advertising), communication scholars have increasingly emphasized the need to create an overall image of the full communication network as it relates to the organization and its various internal and external stakeholders. In particular, the growing field of *corporate communication* has contributed to corporate branding and showed the growing interdependencies between a variety of internal and external stakeholders. Here scholars have argued that – contrary to the classic interest model - the individual corporation may neither be in the center of the communication network nor have full awareness of the communication network in which it is embedded (Argenti & Foreman, 2000; Cheney & Christensen, 2001).

The shift from consumers to all company stakeholders, implied in the move from product to corporate branding, has been reflected within communication studies in the concern for the *social legitimacy* of corporations towards all of their stakeholders. Social legitimacy among all stakeholders is seen as necessary in order for companies to obtain a license to operate within societies and has imposed demands for more transparency and more explicit ethical standards for companies. Thus, corporate branding has required companies to link who they are with how they respond to the growing demands for legitimacy. These demands address everything from corporate governance to an improved documentation of corporate behavior in areas such as environment and social responsibility. This is reflected in the growth of social and environmental reporting, such as the Triple Buttom Line applied by for example Novo Nordisk.

The move towards greater transparency has generated a more holistic way of communicating who the organization is and what it contributes to its various stakeholders. A closer look at the web sites for leading global companies demonstrates the importance of communicating who they are, often in terms of vision, mission, and values. In cyberspace, they also elaborate on the implications of their presence for societies and introduce their special involvement in corporate citizenship and other kinds of responsible activities. Particularly companies operating in high-risk business areas such as the petrochemical industry (e.g. Shell© and BP©) and the pharmaceutical industry have taken the lead in stakeholder communication. Here, Novo Nordisk and Johnson and Johnson are some of the leading companies globally. The return on their efforts is illustrated in their positions in international rankings and receipt of global awards, such as the Dow Jones Sustainability Index (see www.novonordisk.com or www.jnj.com).

Finally, the communication discipline has contributed to the development of new, more *narrative* forms of communicating the central idea of the organization. Here, particularly corporate brands have the opportunity to engage in storytelling about the organization itself – its history, management, and employees (Van Riel, 2000). Such narratives span from storytelling about managerial icons such as Jack Welch or Richard Branson, who through symbolic actions, autobiographies, and their personal exposure communicate who the brand is and what it stands for. At the other end of the scale, companies increasingly use storytelling as ways of creating a more engaging and evocative dialogue between managers and employees and encourage employees to tell stories of their own experiences with the corporate brand (e.g. Shaw, 2000). One of the risks to companies engaged in narrative forms of communication is that the stories about themselves may end up as a narcissistic, self-absorbed exercise rather than meaningful and involving stakeholder communication. Companies may become so seduced by the expression and orchestration of their own values that they neglect the relevance to external stakeholders and become lost in self-reflection (Christensen & Cheney, 2000; Cheney & Christensen, 2001; Hatch & Schultz, 2002).

The strong concern with communication within corporate branding suffers from one overriding *limitation*: Managers and employees are led to believe that organizations are able to communicate or talk themselves into a brand. The strong interest in how organizations talk themselves into being creates the illusion that branding is a question of creating dynamic and explicit interaction between internal and external communication processes. Consequently, corporate communication gives less attention to how the ideas and values of the brand are enacted by organization members in their everyday behavior. 'Walk the Talk' is a challenge which has been neglected by many organizations embarking on a corporate branding strategy, both in relation to the involvement of employees in making the brand live (Karmark, Chapter 5) and with regard to the credibility of the brand towards customers and other stakeholders. This promise-performance gap of corporate branding exceeds the scope of the corporate communication discipline. This much needed link between corporate communication and management/strategy has had the paradoxical implication that the vital concern with how the brand is being enacted and manifested in behavior towards all stakeholders sometimes becomes neglected. Instead the emphasis reflects a single-minded concern with how the brand is being expressed and communicated.

Branding through Identity and Employees

A fourth discipline, which has been my own entry to corporate branding, is *organization theory*. Here, concepts of organizational identity – the perceptions among organizational members about who they are as an organization – have contributed to the understanding of what it means to use the socially constructed 'we' as a foundation for the corporate brand. The construction of organizational identity is similar to individual identity in that it is embedded in social relationships, which include the interrelations between self-definitions and the perceptions among others of who we are (Hatch & Schultz, 2002; see also Cooley, Mead, Brewer & Gardner in Hatch & Schultz, 2004). Based on theories of social and individual identity, Albert and Whetten have argued that organizational identity concerns what is central, enduring, and distinctive to organizational members about who they are as an organization (Albert & Whetten, 1985, see also Whetten & Godfrey, 1998).

The assumption that *organizational identity* is defined in terms of stability and long term durability has particularly been much debated among organization scholars. Scholars sceptical about the enduring nature of identity have argued that organizational identity changes because it is reinterpreted and redefined by organizational members. This ability of organizational identity to adapt to changing environments and shifting perceptions has been labelled 'adaptive instability' by Gioia and colleagues and sometimes has the paradoxical implication that organizations must change to stay the same (Gioia, Schultz & Corley, 2000). One of the key issues in the debate on the enduring nature of identity has been the role of the image concept. The image construct has not been included in Albert & Whetten's conceptualization of organizational identity, but has been put forward by other identity scholars as essential in comprehending the embedded dynamic of organizational identity.

That is why the next step in theories of organizational identity addresses the *interrelations between identity and image*. This implies that members' perceptions of their organizational identity are reinterpreted in the light of reactions and perceptions among external stakeholders of the organization and its claimed identity. Opposed to the definition of the image concept within the marketing discipline, the vast majority of organizational scholars have debated the relations between the self-perceptions among organizational members (identity) and compared these perceptions with members' images of who they believe others think they are (externally construed image).

These definitions have contributed to a strong internal focus within organizational theory, as the image construct only includes perceptions by organizational members opposed to perceptions by external stakeholders. Even though only a few contributions from organization theory have been explicitly related to corporate branding (a few exceptions are Gioia et al., 2000; Balmer, 2001; Hatch & Schultz, 2003; Schultz & Hatch, 2003) theories of organizational identity have had a significant influence on the concept of brand identity. It has done so by emphasizing the relations between internal and external perceptions of who the organization is. Furthermore, organizational scholars have introduced more complexity in the discussion of brand identity. They have pointed out the implications to the company of gaps or discrepancies between identity and image and have given special attention to situations of perceived identity threat (e.g. see studies by Dutton & Dukerich, 1991; Gioia & Thomas, 1996; Elsbach & Kramer, 1996).

The identity concept also has relevance for corporate branding at the individual level of analysis. Here, the search for *individual identity* and uniqueness can been seen as one of the reasons behind the enhanced personal consumption of brands. This makes brands a central provider of self-expressive benefits to individuals, as the individual choice and individual adaptation of brands become a way of expressing one's identity (e.g. as defined by Aaker and Joachimsthaler, 2000). The use of brands to express individual identity relates to individuals as consumers, where, in the words of Wally Olins, brands serve as 'badges of identification.' Brand symbols are transformed by the consumer to satisfy individual needs and sometimes to symbolize their identification with specific brand-driven subcultures or communities (Olins, 2004; Antorini & Andersen, Chapter 4). In principle, this is relevant to both product brands and corporate brands, but the presence and recognition of some corporate brands (all other things being equal) make them more attractive as distinctive 'badges,' such as Nike, Manchester United®, or Prada®

These processes of *identification* are equally relevant to the individual as an employee and in the relationship between employees and the organization. In their role as employees, individuals increasingly search for an organization's identity and values that will support or expand their perceptions of individual identity or personal branding. Here, corporate brands are in a strong position to offer such identity and symbols of identification and – not least – actively involve employees in the co-construction of the identity behind the brand. Belonging to an organization with a value-based foundation creates opportunities for a much stronger identification among individual employees with the brand. But claims about brand identity also provide employees with the opportunity to accept or reject a corporate brand based on its substance. Opposed to product brands, where the attached meanings are often created based on market communication alone, it is much harder for employees to separate the communication related to individual products and services from the company itself. This may influence the ways employees identify or dis-identify with the organization. Particularly in the creation of corporate brands with a strong service dimension, such as financial services, airlines, education, and health care, the attitudes and behavior of employees are crucial to the delivery of and trust in the brand (Ind, 2001; Schultz & Chernatony, 2003; Olins, 2004). Organizational culture, defined as the pattern of meanings and assumptions that guide organizational behavior (Martin, 2002; Schein, 2004), has a dual role in the creation of corporate brands. It serves as a resource of brand heritage and shapes the context for the credibility of the brand. Thus, organizational culture, as manifested through the involvement and support of employees, is a precondition for the delivery of the brand promises.

Furthermore, *organizational culture* has the potential to contribute to a higher degree of complexity – and realism – by understanding how different groups of employees (or shifting constellations of individuals) relate to the brand. Such cultural variation has been defined by the concepts of subcultures and cultural fragmentation (Martin, 2002). Opposed to the discussions of how individuals identify with their organization as an individual process (Ashford & Mael, 1989), the notion of subcultures focuses on how different groups of employees form shared patterns of meaning and behavior, implying that they as subgroups interpret and enact the central ideas of the brand differently. For example, employees from marketing may hold different perceptions of the brand than people working in human resources; manager's perceptions may differ from those of white collar employees; people working in different business units may perceive and express the brand differently, etc. Depending on the nature of these sub-cultural differences and the flexibility of the central ideas of the brands, sub-cultural differences may impact the corporate brand in negative or positive ways. They may range from being a source of fierce struggles for influence on the brand to innovative internal renewal and productive tensions regarding the substance and delivery of brand.

Finally, organization theory has supported the emerging interest in the managerial and organizational implications of corporate branding. The branding literature is full of good advice on how corporate branding ought to be executed and how managers and employees are expected to behave (see for example Davis, 2000). However, this very normative literature provides less knowledge of how corporate branding actually unfolds. The dominating branding field has shown little interest in defining the most important difficulties in making brands work and exposing the pitfalls and setbacks that many branding processes lead to (some exceptions are Balmer, 2001; Schultz & Hatch, 2003; Schultz & Chernatony eds., 2003).

The development towards more flexible and customized forms of management has entailed a shift from a managerial paradigm based on a structure-driven concern with rules and strict economic regulations to a more *value-driven* concern based in the attitudes and perceptions of individual employees. This shift has implied that the ability of the brand idea to engage and involve individual employees has become important for many companies. Involvement in the values and ideas behind the brand helps motivate employees to innovate and adapt the brand to specific markets or customers. Thus, corporate branding also implies a shift towards more inclusive forms of management and transcendence of the limitations found within the different business functions. All of these changes contribute to the creation of a corporate brand, e.g. strategic development, marketing, corporate communications, human resources, and innovation. It is hardly possible to implement the move to corporate branding without significant organizational changes and a reassessment of institutionalized management processes based in the central ideas of the brand. For example, as part of the Novo Nordisk Way of Management, the Novo Nordisk company introduced a team of 'culture facilitators' dedicated to assess the degree to which organizational members enacted the extensive 'codes of conduct' defined by the Novo Nordisk values, practices, etc. These facilitators were given the authority to initiate behavioral changes when needed and follow up accordingly. This illustrates how one company has focused on the everyday behavior of employees as an important dimension in realizing the vision and values of their corporate brand. There is no doubt in my mind that there is a huge and unexploited contribution within the theories of organizational development and change management to corporate branding, which are further addressed here in Chapter 8.

The most obvious *trap* within organization and identity theory's contribution to corporate branding is almost the opposite of the marketing discipline. Contrary to risk of the external domination of consumers within marketing, the risk of organization and identity theory is that the definitions of identity and image become trapped in an internal narcissistic mindset. This narcissism implies that the brand is defined and enacted based only on the perceptions of organizational members and that the needs, interpretations, or feed-back from external stakeholders are being ignored by organizational members (see Christensen & Cheney, 2000; Hatch & Schultz, 2002). Thus, when the image construct is included in organization theory, it typically derives from organization members' interpretations and prejudices toward their images of external stakeholders. This is why image in organizational theory often is defined as externally construed image. When responding to 'images,' organizational members react to their own interpretations of external images rather than to the actual images of the organization held by external stakeholders. At some level, all social actors respond to their perceptions of reality. However, the risk is that organization theory completely neglects how external stakeholders perceive the brand and how these external perceptions affect their relationships with the organization.

From Positions to Strategic Reputation

The last discipline that has had a profound influence on corporate branding is *strategy*. This has been demonstrated both in the development of a more strategic perception of what corporate branding entails and in the growing importance of corporate reputation as a criteria of success for corporate brand management. Last, but not least, the concern with the value of intangible assets generated by the corporate brand derives from an economic-strategic discipline.

The foundation of corporate branding has most often been the search for *strategic differentiation*. The classic notion of differentiation resides in how companies define unique market positions for themselves in a global and competitive marketplace. However, scholars within in the strategy discipline, such as Hamel & Prahalad (1994) have challenged this classic and rather static perception of a market position. Instead of a strategic focus on locating available market positions, these scholars have changed the perception of how market positions are being generated by emphasizing that companies increasingly have to focus on the redefinition of markets themselves. Here, companies should rely more on their own resources, competencies, and capabilities in order to create a visionary redefinition of the marketplace itself. This is exactly what has characterized the most successful and visionary companies studied by Collins and Porras (1994; Collins 2001).

For those reasons, there has been a growing interest among strategists in improving the recognition and valuation of the *competencies and resources* of companies. Furthermore, scholars from the resource-based view have given special attention to the ability of companies to mobilize these resources in the creation of competitive advantage (Barney, 1991, 1996). The strong interest in these more intangible resources has spurred the development of new concepts and models, such as measuring intellectual capital and conceptualizing the dimensions of corporate resources by being valuable, rare, hard to imitate, and highly organized (Barney, 1996; Mouritsen, 2000). Taken together, these concepts have expanded our perception of what constitutes relevant corporate resources or assets. The marketing discipline has also been concerned with the value of corporate brands. Here, the marketing-driven assessment of brand equity has focused on the perceived quality and added value generated by the extra price consumers and other stakeholders are willing to pay for the branded product/service as compared with similar non-branded products. In contrast, the strategic discipline has focused on the value of the resources generated by the company, considering both their content and the company's ability to mobilize these resources in generating value-adding activities.

One of the more recent developments concerning intangible assets is the value of the *corporate reputation*. This is defined as the longitudinal judgement of who the company is and what it stands for among multiple stakeholders (Fombrun, 1996; Fombrun & Van Riel, 2003). It has been demonstrated by multiple studies how corporate reputation not only influences company performance, but also has a profound impact on the long-term credibility and strategic competitiveness of the corporate brand. Corporate reputation has been further refined in relation to a number of dimensions. These dimensions have been suggested in measuring the quality and value of reputation across countries and businesses by the Reputation Quotient. The Reputation Quotient has been applied by the Reputation Institute in the ranking of companies among the general public in the US, Australia, and a growing number of European countries (www.reputationinstitute.com; Fombrun et al, 2000). The dimensions of corporate reputation are defined by the Reputation Quotient as: motional appeal, products, services, financial performance, workplace environment, vision and leadership, and social responsibility (Fombrun & Van Riel, 2003).

As argued by Fombrun & Van Riel (2003), corporate reputation is particularly important for corporate brands, as they are much more invested in their multiple stakeholder relations than product brands. Corporate brands expose their organizational culture and identity in much more direct and transparent ways. The strong focus on corporate reputation has been enhanced by the growing mistrust and scepticism towards companies in the Western part of the world (World Economic Forum Report 2004) that was generated by a series of corporate scandals and a global 'cult of greed' among leading companies and executives. Those experiences have strengthened stakeholders' demands for increasing corporate transparency and expectations that companies become more sincere. In essence, this implies that companies walk the talk and stand behind who they claim to be in their different stakeholder relationships. This pressure has forced companies into more and more situations where they have to care about the credibility of their corporate reputation (Fombrun & Van Riel, 2003). A deliberate move towards corporate branding implies that a company needs to be more serious when making identity claims about who it is and what it is going to deliver to its various stakeholders, as stakeholders have become more aware and attentive.

A global leader such as Shell initiated a comprehensive strategic process in the wakes of the Brent Spar and Nigeria crises in order to re-establish a credible reputation based on the combination of 'Profits and Principles' (Fombrun & Rindova 2000). In spite of this initiative, ten years later Shell was again hit by a new series of scandals, a dramatic decline in market value, and changes in top management after having withheld information on a reassessment of the company's oil-resources. The noble intentions of a more credible corporate brand apparently had limited impact on the identity of the company. It seems that the old organizational culture from Brent Spar, which showed limited respect for external stakeholders and underestimated demands for open and honest information, survived inside the company in spite of very costly campaigns and extensive stakeholder communication. In that sense, the strategy discipline has pointed at central dependencies between the organization identity and corporate reputation. This is supported by perceptions among the general public in several countries, showing that the most essential condition for creating a strong reputation is the perceived authenticity and sincerity of companies (for more see Fombrun & Van Riel, 2003).

The most important *limitations* in the strategic discipline derive from the difficulties in making precise assessments of 'intangible assets.' This is an issue both in relation to the more internal intellectual resources and the external corporate reputation. The focus on assessment has enhanced the need – and pressure – on companies for exact measurements and bench-marking of their internal and external resources in order to monitor the impact, relevance, and development of the corporate brand. Even though there has been an important development in concepts and tools for measurement, the risk is that companies base their strategic decisions on simplistic measurements of ambiguous and contextual attitudes and behaviors among different stakeholders. Such measurements may create illusions of brand efficiency and brand control based on weak premises. At the same time, a strong focus on measurement within companies paves the way for a certain kind of cynicism that shifts focus away from the quality and credibility of the company's behavior to a concern with how one gets the best position in one of the dominant ranking systems. These ranking systems are often driven by media appeal and executive perceptions rather than by profound insights into what generates corporate reputation (such as the Fortune 500's Most Admired Companies and many other local versions). The result of this behavior promotes a 'winner-takes-all' mentality. A supporting example is how much discussion there has been about the implications of the influential *Business Week* ranking of American business schools, as the individual schools start placing their efforts on ranking criteria (e.g. the salary of MBA candidates in their first job) rather than the school's quality in research and education.

Contributions to Corporate Branding Practices

To a large extent, each of the above disciplines is mirrored in the range of business functions or units found within most large companies. Marketing and human resources functions are most related to the marketing discipline and to organizational theory and organizational identity. Both have strong traditions as vital, stand-alone functions in most companies. The emergence of corporate communication functions reflects a shift from a classic, media-oriented public relations function towards a broader perspective on stakeholder management and the inclusion of more proactive forms of corporate communication and corporate citizenship activities (Cornelissen, 2004). The strategy discipline is organized differently depending on the size and scope of the company, which can range from small analytical support staffs to top management to extensive departments for strategic development and corporate reputation or brand management. For example, Johnson & Johnson recently formed a strategic unit dedicated to the management of Brand Equity with a strong strategic focus, while an increasing number of companies form special reputation and/or corporate branding units. Visual identity is the discipline most often outsourced to external professional services such as design, identity, or brand agencies.

Based on their unique conceptual assumptions and traditions, each of the disciplines contributes different types of knowledge, insights, methods, and measurements in the corporate branding practices of companies. The specific execution will obviously differ between companies, but figure 2:3 summarizes some of the most common practices and methods emerging from the five core disciplines of corporate branding.

Towards the Second Wave of Corporate Branding

The development of a corporate brand raises a host of opposing requirements. They have been summarized by Wally Olins's claim that brands have to deliver corporate social responsibility and shareholder value in a stakeholder society while remaining inexpensive and emotionally attractive at the same time (Olins, 2004). Furthermore, particularly corporate brands are faced with expectations of credibility, authenticity, and coherence in a global, multicultural, and turbulent world (Fombrun & Van Riel, 2003). Due to its cross-disciplinary origins, corporate branding on the one hand becomes a shared point of

A Cross-Disciplinary Perspective on Corporate Branding

reference for a number of convergent developments within each of the disciplines; on the other hand, the notion of corporate branding is influenced by strong centrifugal forces, each seeking to bend the concept towards its own point of view. In that sense, aiming at a coherent corporate brand is like squaring the circle. However, I will argue (referring to my work with Mary Jo Hatch) that it is possible to create a framework for corporate branding that both reflects some general perceptions of how corporate brands emerge and develop, yet also allows for the inclusion of the different disciplinary origins of corporate branding.

Figure 2:3 Corporate Branding Practices and Methods

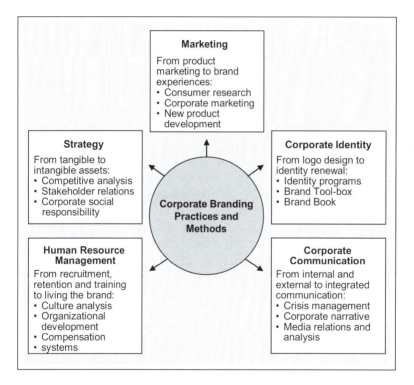

In spite of the complexities of corporate branding, Hatch and Schultz have developed a simple analytical framework, the Corporate Branding Tool-Kit. The kit is based in a relational perception of branding. The Tool-Kit suggests how corporate brands are constituted by the alignment of different elements defined by different stakeholder relationships. It further offers a way to analyze the relations between those elements (Hatch & Schultz 2001, 2002, 2003). The Tool-Kit includes several of the key constructs from the different disciplines contributing to corporate branding and has the ambition to serve as a starting point for a cross-disciplinary understanding and application of corporate branding.

Corporate branding can best be described as the process of creating, nurturing, and sustaining a mutually rewarding relationship between a company, its employees, and external stakeholders. With such a broadly based conceptualization, corporate branding requires a more stable foundation that all organizational members and stakeholders recognize and participate in. Organizational identity provides this foundation within the Corporate Branding Tool-Kit. Every firm develops an identity in the course of conducting its business. This is because it is human nature to personify things with which we have relationships, and companies rely upon scores of human relationships to stay in business. They maintain relationships with employees, customers, suppliers, distributors, investors, creditors, regulators, and special interests groups. The organization's identity emerges from its web of interactions with stakeholders and the firm's accompanying desire to put its best foot forward.

Thus, the starting point for conceptualizing corporate brands is the idea of organizational identity – who are we as an organization – and the relationships that identity invokes not only in relation to external images (who do others think we are?), but also to the historically embedded organizational culture (where do we come from, what are our embedded practices?). The identity of a corporate brand thus emerges in a dynamic way. Part of the dynamic arises from the streams of interactions that take place between a company and its stakeholders, AND from discussions about the company that occur between those stakeholders as they interact with one another. These interactions provide the company with feedback about how the company is being perceived by others. The other part of an organization's identity develops through self-insight, which emerges through competitive analysis and articulation of organizational culture, values, expectations, and desires. Of course, the two parts are not independent, but combine in complex, never-ending rounds of sense making in a way not unlike an ongoing conversation. It is within these identity relationships that people define what the company stands for and what it means to be connected with it. Thus, the fundamental dynamic of a corporate brand is generated from the interrelations between culture, identity, and image and in the tensions between the internal and external stakeholders of the organization. The conceptual foundation for our understanding of corporate branding is within organization theory and organizational identity.

However, we have also strived to include experiences and conceptual contributions from marketing and visual identity in our conceptualization of corporate branding identity, building on both corporate identity (Olins 1989, 2000, 2004) and brand identity (Aaker & Joachimsthaler 2000, Hatch & Schultz 2000). Furthermore, we have expanded the conceptualization of the image construct as defined within organizational theory, where it has been defined as an externally construed image. Instead, we use insights from marketing and corporate communication that enable us to locate the brand within a market and stakeholder context. Contrary to organizational identity, corporate branding also involves a deliberate strategic intent to define the future vision for the corporate brand and to attempt to influence a corporate reputation, something that has been particularly stressed within the strategic discipline. Thus, in debating who we want to become and setting the directions for possible ways of further development or transforming who we are as an organization, strategic vision adds a managerial direction to identity in corporate branding.

We have summarized the four elements of a corporate brand as follows (as cited from Hatch & Schultz 2001, Schultz et al. 2004):

- **Strategic vision** – the central idea behind the company that embodies and expresses *top management's* aspiration for what the company will achieve in the future
- **Organizational culture** – the internal values, beliefs, and basic assumptions that embody the heritage of the company and how these are manifested in the ways *employees* feel about the company they work for
- **Stakeholder images** – views of the organization developed by its *external stakeholders*; the outside world's overall impression of the company including the views of customers, shareholders, the media, the general public, and so on
- **Corporate brand identity** – occurs at the juncture between vision, culture, and image and *defines how 'we' perceive ourselves as an organization. Identity* underpins the corporate brand - partly by the feed-back from stakeholders and partly by 'the organization's self insight. Claims about identity are often stated as core values, beliefs or central ideas

Figure 2:4 illustrates the relations in the basic dynamic of a corporate brand and shows how each of the different stakeholder groups contribute to the brand.

Figure 2:4 The Corporate Branding Tool Kit

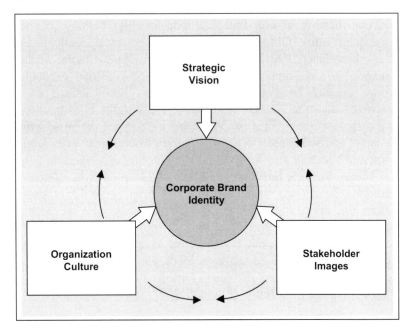

The figure illustrates how the brand is based in the alignment of the different constituting elements: How who we claim to be is related to our everyday beliefs and behavior (identity-culture relation); whether customers experience a coherence between the expectations based in brand promises and their experiences from interacting with the organization (culture-image relation); if the aspirations for the organization communicated by top management are recognized and supported by organizational members (vision-culture relation).

A single-minded focus on brand alignment creates severe limitations. Too much emphasis on consistency between the brand elements and control of their development will restrict the innovative and dynamic adaptation of the brand by stakeholders and prevent their involvement in the development of the brand. In the further development of corporate branding, there is especially a need to improve our understanding of the embedded dynamics that unfold

A Cross-Disciplinary Perspective on Corporate Branding

among the different stakeholders involved in the brand. Furthermore, there is a need to explore the nature and importance of each of the corporate brand relationships, as they shift over time according to the strategic context of the brand. Some of these dynamic perspectives are further developed in Chapter 8.

However, the basic suggestion is that competitive brands with a well-regarded reputation, all other things being equal, will maintain an alignment between the various elements of the brand. Such an alignment should not be perceived as exact consistency, which will prevent the stakeholder involvement necessary to develop the brand. Also, rigid consistency will prohibit the flexibility needed in a multicultural and ever-shifting world. Rather the alignment of a corporate brand should be seen as a longitudinal, large-scale coherence between the identity of the brand and the various practices and perceptions that constitute each of the different brand elements. Such coherence can be generated through a host of different types of development, ranging from temporary equilibrium and convergence in highly turbulent environments to a slower, more emergent development towards increasing situations of alignment.

The Corporate Branding Tool-Kit also invites the analysis and tracking of gaps or disconnections between the different elements of the brand. Such corporate branding gaps may cause both loss of credibility and severe reputation damage. The most general corporate branding gaps are illustrated in figure 2:5.

For example, a *culture-vision gap* emerges when top management wants the company to go to a destination not supported by the employees. The gap usually plays itself out when top management sets an aspiration that is too ambitious for the organization to implement, creating a breach between rhetoric and reality, or if they present an empty imitation of the dominant trends of the time with no connection to the heritage and identity of the company. As a response to a culture-vision gap, management may either choose to revise the strategic vision, bringing it closer to the organizational culture, or, more likely, pay more attention to communicating the vision again and again – in ways that are relevant, concrete, and engaging to employees (see also Argenti & Foreman, 2000). Employees may react with everything from de-motivation to engage in the company to cynicism and obstructive behavior. Likewise, misalignment between a company's image and organizational culture (*culture-image gap*) leads to confusion among customers about what a company stands for. This usually means that a company doesn't practice what it preaches, which will tarnish its reputation among key stakeholders (Fombrun, 1996). For example, this may occur when companies seek to extend their brand into new business areas. Such was the case of the LEGO Group, where their brand extension into games and on-line activities included both the challenge to connect new subcultures (e.g. young programmers) with the LEGO heritage culture, and then align this heritage culture with more 'street credible' images in these new playing fields (Karmark & Gjøls Andersen, Chapter 7). If the gap between culture and image becomes very wide, this may leave customers and other stakeholders in confusion about who the company is and what it stands for.

Figure 2:5 Corporate Branding Gaps

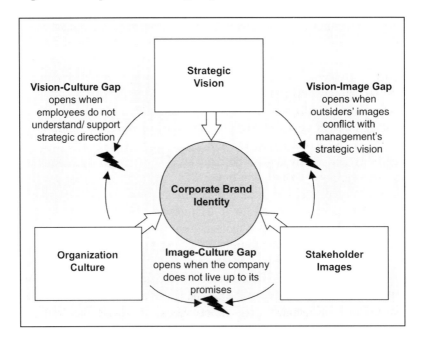

That is why one first possible step in the exploration of corporate branding gaps is to compare employee perceptions of who the company is and how it performs with stakeholder images and their key judgements about the corporate brand. Many companies have improved their ability to create stronger relations directly between employees and external stakeholders, such as in the development of brand communities (Antorini & Andersen, Chapter 4). But often, one remaining challenge is to overcome the widespread turf-mentality, where different business functions feel an exclusive ownership towards specific stakeholders and the entitlement to develop specific ways of interacting with those stakeholders. In cases like these, marketing owns the consumers; human resources owns current and future employees; corporate communication controls the media and other stakeholder relations; strategic units manage alliances, collaboration partners, etc.

Branding Paradoxes

One of the challenges in the move towards the second wave of corporate branding is to strike a balance between the different, paradoxical perceptions of what it takes to create and maintain a corporate brand. Such balance emerges from the paradoxical conceptual points of view held by proponents of the different disciplines. They also refer to the involved managerial and organizational practices because the different disciplines are mirrored in the different business functions contributing to corporate branding. On the one hand, a corporate brand must express central ideas, symbols, and identity claims, which allow stakeholders to recognize and relate to the brand. On the other hand, the brand must be flexible, adaptive, and allow stakeholders to influence the brand as their needs and perceptions change over time and across markets. This balancing act between control and flexibility is expressed in table 2:2 as a set of strategic and organizational concerns, all of which reflect classic tensions within the social sciences.

The argument here is that The Corporate Branding Tool-Kit can facilitate shared reflections and a more conscious balance between a controlling and a flexible form of corporate brand management. This balancing act may overcome the illusions of how ideal corporate brands operate in the hands of top managers and pave the way for more realistic and viable corporate branding processes.

Such realism must include the full range of stakeholders, as developed by Hatch and Schultz (2001, 2003) and acknowledge the paradoxes in the foundation for brand management. The embedded challenges of corporate branding may be perceived as a paradox between a consistent, coherent, unique, and authentic brand versus a flexible, adaptive, and multicultural brand. In my experience, one of the most crucial managerial tasks is to foresee and address such key paradoxes, as they tend to reemerge in all stages of the brand management processes. Furthermore, following the advice from proponents of paradox management (Quinn, 1988; Poole & Van de Ven, 1989), such tensions should be acknowledged and kept alive as part of the corporate brand.

Table 2:2 The Paradoxes of Corporate Branding

Brand dimensions	Corporate branding as consistent control	Corporate branding as flexible adaptation
Brand strategy	To generate and maintain a differentiated market position	To challenge the premises for the market definition and state a differentiated vision for the brand
Visual identity	Unique symbolic recognition	Adaptation to local cultures, markets, and shifting trends
Brand communication	Coherence between internal and external communication	Shifting phases in the corporate branding process with different emphasis on internal and external communication
Brand relations	Relevance and transparency in relation to all stakeholders	Active involvement of stakeholders with different demands and relationships
Brand identity	Authenticity in relation to cultural origin and unique organizational identity	Developing and reinterpreting who we are in shifting conversations with others

In my opinion realizing the cross-disciplinary origin of corporate branding enable managers to gain stronger awareness of the paradoxes embedded in corporate branding. As argued in the corporate branding traps, each of the disciplines offers a limited perspective on corporate branding and finds proponents among the different internal and external stakeholders involved in the brand implementing process. Some stakeholders are based in business functions (typically marketing, human resources and corporate communication), others in staff units (e.g. strategy and investor relations), while others typically are external professionals (identity and brand agencies). Together they represent all the creative tensions needed to build and develop corporate brands. However, the different disciplines also represent a risk of brand destruction and fragmentation, if they turn into hostile or self-contained subcultures/sub-brands with little dedication to the organization as a brand. A cross-disciplinary perspective on corporate branding entails the full range of implications of having the organization as the foundation for the brand. It shifts the managerial focus from a functional concern with marketing and communication to an organization-wide concern with integrating people from different functions and units behind the brand.

No doubt, there are strong forces tearing a corporate brand apart: market complexity and shifting consumer trends create pressure for external adaptation while different subcultures among employees and conflicts between the business functions create obstacles for managing corporate brands. The risk is that corporate brand management becomes too insistent on corporate brand consistency as a way to avoid fragmentation of the brand. These tension-ridden dynamics are part of the existential conditions from which all brands emerge and operate. The paradoxical nature of these tensions implies that they can never be resolved once and for all. In my opinion, acknowledging the contributions from both sides of the branding paradoxes and the shifting balances between them is a starting point for the ongoing management of a corporate brand.

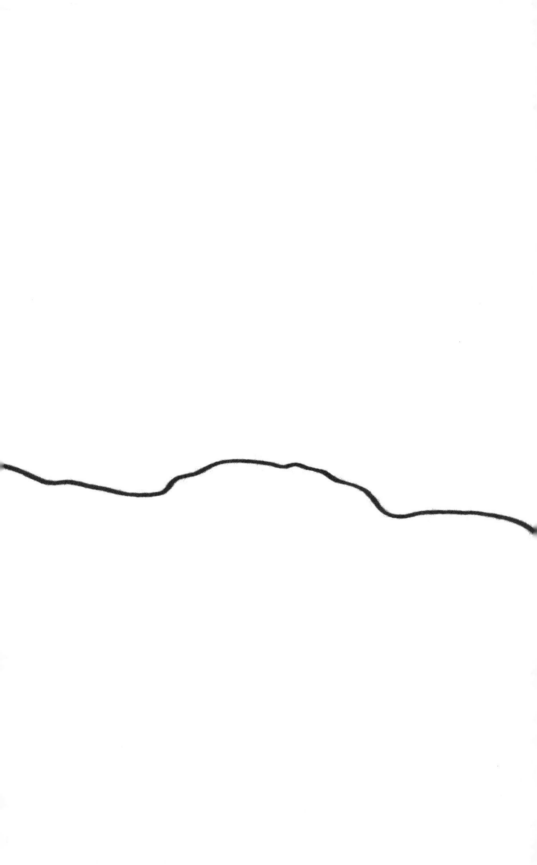

CHAPTER 3

CORPORATE BRANDING AND THE 'CONFORMITY TRAP'

Yun Mi Antorini & Majken Schultz

The need for companies to differentiate themselves is considered, both in theory and practice, to be one of the main purposes of corporate branding. This chapter argues that companies, contrary to their intentions, often fail to appear as differentiated. Instead, they often fall into what the authors call the 'conformity trap'. Drawing on the distinction between an essence-based and a relationship-based approach, the authors discuss how companies might deal with the conformity trap and propose ways of avoiding falling into it in the first place.

'The main idea is that to exist within a social space, to occupy a point or to be an individual within a social space, is to differ, to be different'. (Bourdieu, 1998:9, [1994])

Difference (i.e. 'who am I compared to others?') is essential in order for both people and organizations to exist and operate within a social space. The notion of difference is closely linked to the classic identity debate that has been going on since Descartes (1596-1649) claimed to have proven the existence of the self, i.e. that there is an 'I'. However, in order for this 'I' to exist, it has to stand in contrast to 'the other' and 'the others', that surround the 'I', in what Bourdieu calls the social space. Thus difference is inextricably bound up with the question of, 'who am I?', that is *uniqueness* (i.e. 'what characterizes me alone?').

Most recently, the identity debate has found its way to corporate branding. An argument that is commonly put forward in the corporate branding literature is that if an organization does not know 'who it is', how can the organization's stakeholders know? Questions that regard the identity of the organization are therefore central questions which any strategically thinking organization regularly asks itself and seeks to express via its corporate brand.

If we look at the actual practices that characterize many organizations - the way they define their brand values, and how they express these values through communication and PR - a number of questions arise: Why do many of the processes that aim to help identify and present an organization as unique and differentiated so often produce the exact opposite effect in terms of uniform and clichéd expressions? What is the alternative? i.e. what can an organization do to avoid falling into what we call the 'conformity trap'? These are the central themes that will be discussed in this chapter.

Uniqueness and Differentiation as Themes in the Corporate Branding Literature

The branding literature normally distinguishes between two concepts which permit the organization's uniqueness and differentiation to be described and expressed: Corporate identity and organizational identity (de Chernatony & McDonald, 1992; Balmer, 1995; Ind, 1997; Olins, 2000, Hatch & Schultz, 2000; de Chernatony, 2001; Schultz & de Chernatony, 2002; Aaker & Joachimsthaler, 2000; Schultz & Hatch, 2004; Gjøls-Andersen & Karmark, Chapter 7). Corporate identity is founded in a graphic design tradition and is commonly associated with an aesthetic and visual quest for the organization's 'true', authentic and inherent characteristics, which are also called the organization's brand essence, brand values, and brand personality (Aaker & Joachimsthaler, 2000). Corporate identity is often formulated on the basis of analyses that establish a competitor perspective, for example, an analysis of how Bang & Olufsen's visual identity and overall expression differ from Sony's. Understood this way, corporate identity focuses on 'what is unique about us' in relation to 'them', the competitors.

Organizational identity is conceptually founded in the organization literature and aims to describe and explain how members of an organization define and perceive themselves (Albert & Whetten, 1986; Whetten & Godfrey, 1998; Hatch & Schultz, 2002, 2004). Organizational identity focuses on the processes that create meaning and establish a common perception of 'who we are as an organization'. While corporate identity is typically concerned with the leadership-oriented and visual aspects of corporate branding, organizational identity focuses on the social processes that take place between the members of the organization, and their significance for what are called the central, distinct and enduring characteristics of the organization (Albert & Whetten, 1985).

Brand managers and communication consultants draw heavily on the corporate identity concept because it encapsulates the idea that the organization can visually express its uniqueness in the market and thereby differentiate itself from its competitors in such a way as to attain a special 'position' in the consciousness of consumers and other stakeholders (Trout & Ries, 1981). The corporate identity concept is therefore seen as a way an organization can guide, disseminate and maintain perceptions of what constitutes its unique characteristics. This instrumental foundation explains the importance of corporate branding as a means to attain, for example, cohesion in internal perceptions of the organization, brand loyalty, and not least, increased earnings (Aaker & Joachimsthaler, 2000).

As the basis for an organization's ongoing uniqueness, differentiation occupies a central role in the corporate branding literature, as highlighted, for example, by one of the leading theorists in the field:

'If a brand fails to develop or maintain differentiation, consumers have no basis for choosing it over others. The product's price will then become the determining factor in a decision to purchase. Absent

differentiation, the core of any brand and its associated business - a loyal customer base - cannot be created or sustained'. (Aaker, 2003:83.)

The claimed link between a unique and differentiated corporate brand identity and company earnings is one of the main reasons that, during the last decade, corporate branding has attained a position as an important and prioritized area of an organization's total activities. However, experience has shown that it is often very difficult for organizations to transform their claimed uniqueness into expressive statements that substantially differentiate the organization and distinguish it in ways that are meaningfully perceived by others. We have chosen to call this phenomenon the 'conformity trap'. In this chapter we will explore what causes the 'conformity trap', and what organizations can do to escape it.

Defining the 'Conformity Trap'

The 'conformity trap' describes the reality that *despite* an organization's ambition to present its corporate brand as unique and differentiated, the exact opposite ends up occurring. We maintain that the intrinsic dynamic of the 'conformity trap' not only produces a clichéd expression of the corporate brand, but also locks the organization into ineffective patterns that are difficult to break once they have become evident. We also maintain that the 'conformity trap' prevents the organization from fundamentally expressing who it is and its reason for being.

To support our claims about the existence of the 'conformity trap', we will highlight four independent but prevalent *blind spots* that we have found is often associated with an organization's search for uniqueness and differentiation. These blind spots reflect issues and connections that are often neither recognized nor considered, yet nonetheless - against the organization's will - push it towards the 'conformity trap'. We believe they represent central leadership challenges to the brand managers and communication consultants today. Inspired by the organization theory, we call these blind spots: *the uniqueness paradox, the narcissism dynamic, the leadership monopoly,* and finally, *path dependency.*

- **The uniqueness paradox:** Refers to the paradox that an organization's attempts to isolate and articulate its uniqueness

and differentiation through corporate branding often result in unintentionally clichéd and undifferentiated expressions.
- **The narcissism dynamic:** Highlights the fact that an organization's quest for uniqueness is a practice that borders on narcissism.
- **Leadership monopoly:** Describes the view that corporate branding is often seen as being processes that are 'owned' exclusively by the management. This view not only establishes a leadership monopoly on the right to define the significance and expression of the corporate brand, but also contains the seeds of groupthink, which increases the probability of erroneous decision making, and lastly,
- **Path dependency:** Addresses the issue that corporate branding is often linked to promises to consumers and stakeholders. These promises often commit the management to maintain an existing course even in times that call for change rather than maintenance.

These four blind spots, individually and collectively, explain the dynamics of the 'conformity trap, why it is easy to fall into, and why it can be so difficult to escape from it again.

The 'Uniqueness Paradox'

In the 80s, Martin, Feldman, Hatch and Sitkin (1983) carried out a number of comparative studies of organizational cultures, and what characterizes them and why. They were specifically looking for ways in which cultures manifest themselves in an organizational context. They found that the narratives employees recounted about their organizations largely contained *identical elements and themes and expressed uniform issues and concerns*. In other words, the unique, in terms of the distinct, central and enduring characteristics of an organization, was often expressed in a general and clichéd manner when consciously articulated.

That the 'uniqueness paradox' also operates in a corporate branding context is confirmed by an empirical study carried out by Morsing in 2001, involving 301 Danish organizations. This study shows that the vast majority of organizations define themselves using identical values. Thus the unique characteristics of an organization somehow become the opposite when they are articulated. In relation to corporate branding, this represents a fundamental paradox and problem in the differentiation of the organization.

Martin, Feldman, Hatch and Sitkin (1983) offer a number of possible explanations of why the 'uniqueness paradox' comes into existence. They point out, for example, that the employees' identical narratives express fundamental ongoing conflicts between the interests of the organization and the employees' values. In other words, themes such as hierarchical equality versus inequality, job security versus insecurity, supervision versus lack of supervision over working tasks, etc., are classic organizational conflicts, that in most cases cannot be solved by either employees or the organization alone. Nevertheless, these conflicts are still seen as potentially solvable within the realms of the organization. The fact that these fundamental conflicts are seen as resolvable, but never are resolved, leads to them maintaining a latent presence in the organization as topics that constantly attract attention and discussion. In the tension between the specific conflicts as they unfold and are perceived by the employees, and the simultaneous belief that conflicts can be resolved if there just is a will to do so, narratives arise that turn out to be identical across organizations and employees.

If we relate these observations to corporate branding, they provide a possible explanation for why general (and hence undifferentiated) and clichéd (and hence not unique) corporate brand positions arise, because the dualities that give rise to organizations' inherent and ongoing conflicts are identical for the majority of organizations. Furthermore, one can imagine that other types of conflicts that arise as a result of challenging and demanding market conditions (like government regulations, the reshaping of industry boundaries, increased media-related investments, increased numbers of and more significant private labels, and increased competition for consumer awareness) are basically uniform for most types of organizations operating in the same sector. Finally, as highlighted by institutional theory, organizations typically face the same institutional expectations in the goal of attaining social legitimacy and a 'license to operate'. The fact that organizations employ a number of the same values to express 'who we are as an organization' and 'what we stand for' can thus be explained by the fact that the organization's players are exposed to identical problems and the same institutional pressure at a macro level.

The 'uniqueness paradox' highlights in many ways the complexity within which organizations operate and create meaning. Even though the causes of the 'uniqueness paradox' are often complex and not easy to detect and describe, it is still vital that organizations find ways of breaking the conformity, or at least challenging the way in which conformity is reproduced so that the corporate brand, which constantly operates in the interface between external adaptation and internal integration (Schein, 1992), is not locked into a situation whereby clichéd and undifferentiated values are simply reproduced and built upon.

Uniqueness, Differentiation and Narcissism

As highlighted in the myth of Narcissus, an absorbed quest for one's own identity in combination with an exaggerated fascination with one's self often leads to a gradual but certain isolation from one's social environment. The quest for uniqueness and difference therefore contains the seeds of self absorption and self seduction (Christensen & Cheney, 2000; Hatch & Schultz, 2004). Hence, the more an organization focuses on 'itself' and its own uniqueness, the greater the risk that information and observations that do not 'fit' the organization's self perception will be filtered out. Thus, there is only a small step from the concern with uniqueness and difference to narcissism. From a management perspective, we claim that preoccupation with the unique and the differentiated entails the risk that the organization will develop detached and grandiose perceptions about its own capability, and isolate itself from its environment. The narcissism dynamic hypothesis is therefore that the more intense the pursuit of uniqueness and differentiation, the greater the risk that the organization will become detached from consumers and other stakeholders. Once detached, it becomes difficult for the organization to use its discovered uniqueness in the service of the organization. Thus the organization loses the ability to encapsulate its long-term justification for existence and create relationships with the environment, (Schultz, Chapter 2).

According to two independent and long-term studies (Collins, 2001; Nohria, Joyce & Roberson, 2003) into why certain organizations (identified as visionary and extraordinary) perform better financially over a long period than the majority, these organizations are distinguished by the fact that they constantly fine tune, their strategic direction and focus areas. In contrast to the 'hysterical hyperactive organizations' (Minzberg, 2001 in Richard Norman's book: 'Reframing Business: When the Map Changes the Landscape'), these visionary and extraordinary organizations are able to tackle the challenge of being open and facing externally imposed changes, while at the same time not letting the organization lose itself in endless changes and adjustments. The visionary and extraordinary organizations are also characterized by flat, flexible organizational structures and very ambitious, action-oriented cultures that reward specific results far more than their less successful counterparts. They demonstrate an almost single-minded, yet dynamic focus on the organization's core business, and are characterized by a simple, clear formulation of precisely which types of values the organization creates for end users and other stakeholders. In this perspective, uniqueness and differentiation are constantly being 'negotiated' between the environment's perception of the organization, and the organization's own perception of what it does well and wants to do in the future.

Summing up, a corporate brand's uniqueness and differentiation are typically developed via two different approaches: One approach is *exclusively directed inwards*, and closely linked with self absorption and self seduction. The other approach, that characterizes the visionary and extraordinary organizations, directs the quest for uniqueness and differentiation towards the *relationship* between the environment and the organization's focus on its core business and value creation. In their outward looking yet strongly ambitious and internal focus on progress, development and innovation, these organizations typically escape from self absorption and self seduction.

Corporate Branding as Monopoly on Meaning – the Problem with Groupthink

A management response to the tension that arises in the interface between an organization's external adaptation and internal integration is reflected in the frequently promoted view that corporate branding processes must be initiated and directed by the organization's management (Ind, 1997; Aaker & Joachimsthaler, 2000; Schultz & Hatch, 2001). In other words, an attempt is made to resolve the tension by reducing complexity, with the result that often only a few leading employees participate in the process of defining what is unique and different about the organization and how it is, or should be communicated through the corporate brand. As a result, the power and the right to define what are 'correct' and 'incorrect' perceptions and executions of the corporate brand are distributed between relatively few people. This practice fosters what we call a 'management monopoly' on the corporate brand whereby the management alone decides how perceptions of the organization should develop. In accordance with the corporate identity discussion, corporate branding processes are often seen as a management tool. Like ripples in a pond, corporate branding projects are literally rolled out, first to internal and later to external stakeholders, while the management is assumed to sit at the top and 'pull the strings' to guarantee that the content they have given the corporate brand is disseminated and implanted in the consciousness and subsequent behavior of the employees and other stakeholders. Management tools such as brand books, comprehensive visual programs for the brand's graphical execution, internal training programs, etc., are aimed at supporting this roll out, but also make it difficult for the management to have a flexible and balanced perspective of the perceptions of uniqueness and differentiation that are linked to the formulation and execution of the corporate brand.

In an age where organizations are constantly facing change due to changed market conditions, new technological opportunities and increased competition, it is easy to understand how the myth of the management as 'knowing best' has become firmly established in the corporate branding literature. However, the perception of the management as being primarily 'sense givers' that *dictate* meaning, and not 'sense makers' that *create* meaning in social processes still leads to a number of problems.

As already mentioned, the most central problem is the management's loyalty to the corporate brand, which because of the myth of the management as 'knowing best' can lock the organization's brand approach into ineffective and irrational behavior patterns. This situation is further exacerbated by *groupthink* (Janis, 1972 in Weick, 1979), the phenomenon whereby a close-knit group of – in this case top managers – lock themselves and each other into a common but inappropriate loyalty towards a given conviction about, in this case, the unique and differentiating elements in the corporate brand. Empirical studies of groupthink show that the phenomenon is particularly evident in situations where: 1) The group is subject to stress due to external pressure, 2) the group feels threatened, 3) the group has low self esteem, or 4) the group suffers from internal structural faults such as low morale or weak shared norms (groupthink has been linked to recent business scandals such as Arthur Andersen and Enron). The symptoms of groupthink are described as follows: The group overestimates its own capabilities and develops a closed attitude towards the outside world, which can result in the stereotyping of others, and the group forcing its environment to appear uniform and homogeneous by sanctioning anyone who 'steps outside the line' (Rosander, Stiwne & Granstöm, 1998) or has other convictions. This behavior can lead to the development of even stronger loyalty that gradually results in an increasingly narrow perspective on the surrounding world, including perceptions of the organization's uniqueness, with the potential to ultimately spark a negative spiral of erroneous judgments.

Management monopoly thinking manifested as groupthink represents one of the potential blind spots associated with management work with the corporate brand. However, as discussed earlier, it is essential for the development of a viable corporate brand that it is continually created and fine tuned in interaction with stakeholders such as employees, consumers, etc. In this context, the groupthink phenomenon counteracts the organization's ability to relate openly and inquisitively to its environment, and to actively use input from the environment in the creation of a unique and differentiated corporate brand. As a blind spot, management monopoly thinking thus reduces an organization's ability to utilize its corporate brand as a strategic tool, not just to unite the organization's stakeholders, but also to generate the dialogue that is vital to any organization today.

Corporate Branding as a Promise – the Problem of 'Path Dependency'

As mentioned above, in many cases, the corporate branding process commits management to show loyalty towards a particular perception of the organization's uniqueness and differentiation. This form of loyalty is often a result of path dependency, where choices and decisions made in the past have a critical impact on choices and decisions made in the present. In relation to management's loyalty towards the corporate brand, management risks getting locked into showing loyalty towards a defined brand essence, and values, even though a number of factors clearly indicate that the time has come to question this loyalty. For example: In the 90s, Levi Strauss insisted that their classic model 501 jeans should continue to characterize Levi's brand. This was despite the fact that fashion dictated completely new designs and materials, and that the market had fundamentally changed in that a new generation, which did not wish to share the brand with their parents, had come on the scene and now represented the primary segment. Nonetheless, the management at the time decided that since the 501 model had always defined Levi's brand, it should continue to do so, regardless of what the environment and market happened to think. This decision, which was founded in a 'we have always done it this way and we always will' attitude nearly destroyed Levi Strauss, and the result of the crisis was not only replacement of the management and a total reorganization, but also a new and more complex sub-brand structure that gave the organization the opportunity to break with habit and look at the market in a balanced and multifaceted way.

In times of growth and expansion, management loyalty towards the essence, values and personality of the corporate brand can be both positive and necessary. But when times are tough for an organization, when the market undergoes fundamental changes, as in the case of Levi Strauss, and where unforeseen events occur in the form of declining sales, negative consumer reactions and bad publicity, management loyalty in combination with the myth that the management 'knows best' can trigger the unintended and opposite effect, that the management fails to recognize the realities and is thereby prevented from seeing clearly and acting in response to the new conditions, i.e. 'path dependency'. The paradoxical thing about management loyalty in relation to corporate branding is that it has the potential to be positive and profitable in terms of keeping the organization focused on what it does well, but also the potential to be negative in terms of blindness towards changed market conditions, dissatisfied consumers, disillusioned stakeholders and a chain of bad management decisions which can ultimately be fatal.

Possible Ways to Escape the 'Conformity Trap'

The 'conformity trap' fundamentally challenges the perception that organizations are capable of identifying their own uniqueness, or even capable of articulating and communicating uniqueness in ways that differentiate the organization. The characteristics that are perceived as unique and belonging to the organization alone, are in reality not unique, but clichéd – despite the fact that the organization employees perceive them as unique. In relation to corporate branding, the uniqueness paradox often results in identical and clichéd brand values, creating difficult conditions for differentiation. At the same time, focusing on the organization's uniqueness leads to the risk of producing unrealistic and narcissistic perceptions of the organization's capabilities and relevance. Furthermore, with the manager as the official 'sense giver', conditions for management blindness and groupthink are created, which in turn increases the risk that necessary changes will be blocked, locking the organization into ineffective management and organizational structures and processes. Thus focusing on uniqueness as a means to achieve a differentiated corporate brand carries a number of problems with it.

Does this mean the concepts of uniqueness and difference are superfluous? That they are irrelevant and of no further use in the corporate branding literature? Our answer is 'definitely not'. We believe uniqueness and differentiation are important concepts in the creation of corporate brands. However, we also believe that uniqueness and differentiation, as it is often conceptualized in the corporate branding and marketing literature, is problematic.

Firstly, we assert that the perception of uniqueness and differentiation as *one* brand essence, *one* set of values, and *one* brand personality that can be found 'within' the organization and which have to be 'unveiled' in a definitive and consistent form, expresses a limited and simplistic approach to identity and hence to corporate branding. Rather, uniqueness, as Porras and Collins (1994) and Collins (2001) suggest, is what the organization makes it – in a *dynamic interplay with its environment* (Hatch & Schultz, 2004). The critical thing is not *what* values the organization has, or even whether it has the same values as other organizations; the critical thing is that the organization has values, and that these values result in a particular way of doing things that characterizes this organization alone. In other words, it is what the organization *does* that characterizes it as unique and different, not what it says it is doing or is going to do! Thus if we return to the uniqueness paradox, it is of little significance that the organization articulates identical values. What is more important is that the latent and 'classic' conflict areas that are shared with many organizations are recognized as normal, and that the organization does not search for its uniqueness and difference here alone, but also in its practices and its interactions, i.e. in its relationships with its environment. In this context, practice and interaction are understood as more than just how the organization is perceived by its stakeholders, also conceptualized by the term 'image'. Practice and interaction point to an *action-oriented* and *phenomenologically* based perception of how and why the corporate brand is involved in people's specific consumption and meaning generation.

Uniqueness Revisited – Towards a Relationship-Based Perception of Uniqueness and Differentiation

Uniqueness and differentiation are often founded in what we can call an essence-based approach to corporate branding. The corporate branding literature accordingly positions the brand as a unique and almost untouchable phenomenon that in many ways closes in around itself in its own understanding of 'who we are' and 'what we stand for'. When the environment is considered, it is often in the form of image polls and consumer surveys that reflect what 'they' think about 'us', i.e. as retrospective and static feedback. In order to make the corporate brand more adaptable and flexible, we see it as essential that these perceptions of corporate branding are broadened, including the perception of what uniqueness and differentiation are. We propose that uniqueness and differentiation be founded in a *relationship-based approach to corporate branding* that goes further than the essence-based approach, which only focuses on the 'within'. A relationship-based approach would involve the reflection space in which corporate branding is normally defined being metaphorically 'lifted out' of the organization and 'placed' in the social and cultural environment, so the corporate brand is considered from a broader interactive and hence action-oriented perspective. The central questions are no longer just 'who are we' and 'what do we stand for', as essence thinking often involves, but also, 'what are the characteristics of our relationships?' and 'what do our stakeholders expect of us as an organization?'. It is precisely in the consideration of the surrounding environment that reinterpretations of old truths and historical foundations can take place. As we have touched on, organizations today are strongly dependent on reinterpretations taking place that permit them to adapt and fine tune their behavior so that it fits the environment they operate in.

The new reflexive space for corporate branding includes a focus on both brand essence and brand relationships, and must be seen from a dynamic perspective in which raising awareness of the organization's relationships continually points back to the organization's essence, which in turn points to the organization's relationships, etc. The relationships between the organization and its stakeholders, and the issues they raise, are shown in figure 3:1:

Figure 3:1 The Interaction Between Brand Essence and Brand Relationships

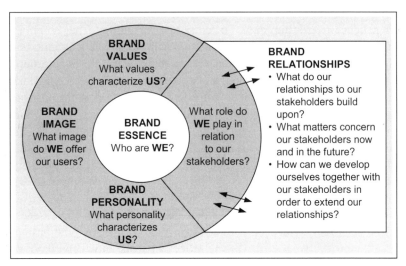

Seen in this light, corporate branding becomes an ongoing cyclical process (Schultz & Hatch, 2003), and from a management perspective, the challenge is not, once and for all, to define a corporate brand with one brand essence, one set of brand values, and one brand personality. The challenge is, instead, to view the corporate brand as an ongoing project of creation, whereby the corporate brand is created in interaction with the environment. Seen this way, it becomes important to view corporate branding as a relationship-based process that opens up to the environment and thus moves corporate branding out of its often inward-looking and sometimes narcissistic focus.

As examples of unique and differentiated corporate brands that apply a relationship-based approach to corporate branding, we will highlight the Italian clothing label, DIESEL® – *'The Haute Couture of Casual'*, and the Swedish clothing group, Hennes & Mauritz©, hereafter H&M, known for *'fashion and quality at the best price'*. In many ways, the clothing industry represents an extreme industry. Changing fashion trends constantly challenge these organizations in terms of design, production and marketing, which in a corporate branding context provide interesting conditions that help explain why some organizations are high up on the social and cultural agenda and other – otherwise 'strong' – brands gradually disappear out of people's consciousness.

Inspired by the 50s optimism and consumerism, in 1991, DIESEL formulated the playful and ironic slogan 'For Successful Living'. Since then, the organization has repeatedly invented new and surprising ways of standing out as different from competing vendors, and as an involved and cultural player that questions and challenges the eternal question of what the 'good life' is and how it can and should be lived. In so doing, DIESEL moves beyond simply being a clothing label, to being part of the culture young people create and identify with. DIESEL's originality derives not only from the way the organization 'gets involved' in it's environment, but also from the way it draws its environment into the organization and transforms impressions and cultural trends into clothing with attitude – i.e. into original clothing expressions. DIESEL's brand essence, brand values and brand personality are, like the organization, in transition, and even though one might expect a fashion clothing label to be capable of reinterpreting its differentiation focal point to some extent, DIESEL is an example of a brand that virtually invites dialogue and the exchange of meaning, and constantly challenges consumers all over the world with very surprising and bold interpretations of 'who we are' and 'what we stand for'.

Another example of a unique and differentiated corporate brand, also taken from the fashion world, is Karl Lagerfeld's design partnership with low price clothing giant, H&M: 'Karl Lagerfeld for H&M'. With this partnership Lagerfeld, who is well-known as one of the big names of haute couture (Chanel®, Fendi®, Lagerfeld®, etc.), challenges the fundamental expectations linked to couture. At the same time, H&M shows itself to be an innovative and unconventional fashion clothing vendor, which does not let itself be limited by its cut-price classification. Lagerfeld himself describes the partnership idea as 'modern', and says that design is no longer a question of price. Through this partnership, both Lagerfeld and H&M are moving the boundaries for what defines an inexpensive clothing label and what defines haute couture, and each is demonstrating in their own way that they are original contributors to the commercial and fashion scene.

Uniqueness and differentiation as practiced by DIESEL, H&M, and Lagerfeld, connects them to the social and cultural agenda. In this way, the relationship-based organizations stand out as innovative pioneers, whose strength lies in continually renewing their corporate brands; and even though these may be copied, they distinguish themselves by being so distinct that any copy will, at best, be a pastiche.

In the next section, we put forward five inputs that focus on corporate branding as a process founded in the relationship-based approach, which can help guide organizations around the 'conformity trap'. We do not profess to have captured and described all the points of view the relationship-based perspective carries with it, nor do we claim to offer a complete framework for how an organization can avoid ineffective corporate branding practices. The aim of what follows is to invite practitioners and academics to reflect on, and challenge in practice, how organizations can escape from the 'conformity trap' and thereby enhance the relevance of corporate branding as a concept for an organization's strategic direction.

Inputs into New Corporate Branding Practices

Input #1: Corporate Branding as CONTINUAL CHANGE – not Maintenance

According to this perspective, the purpose of corporate branding is not, once and for all, to define an organization's uniqueness and differentiation. The organization's interaction with its environment gives rise to demands for change and flexibility that are much too great to permit that. Corporate branding should be viewed as a continual process with alternating periods of stability and change (Gioia et al. 2000; Schultz & Hatch, 2003) to the perceptions the organization associates with its brand. Corporate branding is a cyclical process, where the goal is to make room for both reflection and change, while also permitting consolidation so the organization's quest for cohesive balance (Schein 1992) can be realized – not as a static but as a periodic balance. The path to the relationship-based corporate brand can be found by the organization continually questioning, in interaction with its connections, what it finds unique about 'itself' and as a consequence of this, regularly formulating new proposals for how its uniqueness and differentiation can be reinterpreted and expressed in products, communication and strategy.

Input #2: Corporate Branding as EVOLUTION –
not Revolution

A vast majority of market-leading corporate brands have been owned by the same organization for several decades. 'Old' brands like Gillette© continue to occupy a dominant position in the market for shaving gear, Wrigley's© in chewing gum, Del Monte© in canned fruit, Kellogg's™ in breakfast cereals, Campbell's® in ready-made soups, and Kodak™ in film (Pavitt, 2000). These brands have not achieved their market position overnight, but rather illustrate the fact that corporate branding is not about creating relationships between the organization and stakeholders in a revolutionary manner. Rather, these relationships are created through evolutionary processes, in which the organization gradually recognizes what it is and stands for, and what it is not and does not stand for. Thus corporate branding is a long-term process that is closely related to the organization's culture, and which should therefore not be confused with the organization's tactically oriented day-to-day management.

Input #3: Corporate Branding as INSPIRATION –
not Instruction

According to the relationship-based approach, the primary task of corporate branding is *not to instruct* the organization in its practice; it is to *inspire* the management and employees to continually question and exercise conscious and professional skepticism towards existing practices and perceptions of 'who we are' and 'what we stand for'. Professional skepticism can only be realized if the idea that the management 'knows best' is abandoned and replaced by more democratic and engaging processes that focus more on co-responsibility in all of the organization's functions, and which draw on the organization's shared insights and knowledge about its strengths and weaknesses. Within this democratic zone, the organization must find its uniqueness and differentiation.

Input #4: Corporate Branding as SENSE MAKING –
not Preaching Sense

A characteristic of visionary and extraordinary organizations (Collins, 2001) is that they express the conviction that their future is more dependent on middle management and the dedication and ingenuity of the employees than on top management. With such a perspective it is meaningless to claim that the management 'owns' the right to define the corporate brand more than anyone else. At the same time, drawing on the relationship-based approach, one can claim that the members of the organization, in interaction with the environment, have the role and responsibility to continually fill the brand with meaning, and to unlearn outdated or inappropriate meanings and perceptions. Corporate branding is therefore not about dictating meaning – it is a 'resource' for sense making, whereby the organization finds its authority as a credible and open player by recognizing this connection.

Input #5: Corporate Branding as BROAD-BASED – not Simplified

As we have argued, an organization's distinct, central and enduring characteristics are the subject of ongoing negotiation and discussion between the organization and its stakeholders. In relation to this, the role of a corporate brand is not to monopolize these negotiations and discussions by simplifying and reducing the brand, but rather to make room for complexity and ambiguity. Just as the society around us is complex, the corporate brand is also complex, and rather than seeking simplicity for simplicity's sake, an organization should view its identity as a distillate and a reflection of its complex nature.

Towards Corporate Branding as Relationship

As we implied, drawing on Bourdieu (1998), the justification of an organization's existence is closely linked to 'difference', i.e. to being different from 'the others' that are also fighting to stand out and be seen in the social space. In this chapter we have discussed uniqueness as a way of capturing 'what characterizes us alone?', and differentiation as a way of describing 'who are we compared to our competitors?'. The essence-based approach to corporate branding suggests that uniqueness and differentiation have to be found 'within' the organization, and the behavior of the organization in the social space is thereby determined by what it finds 'within'. In contrast, the relationship-based approach, as we have defined it, highlights the value of more extensively involving the organization's stakeholders in a continual and dynamic process of creating the corporate brand. The differences between the essence-based and relationship-based approach to corporate branding are summarized in the table 3:1.

Table 3:1 From an Essence-Based to a Relationship-Based Perception of Corporate Branding

From: An **essence-based** perception of corporate branding	To: A **relationship-based** perception of corporate branding
The brand's essence, values and personality are **inherent** and have to be **discovered**	The brand's essence, values and personality have to be **developed** – and arise in the **interaction** with the environment
The reflection process takes place internally in the organization	The reflection process is 'lifted out' of the organization and 'placed' in the public space
The corporate brand is 'owned' by the organization and management alone	The corporate brand is created in social interaction
The corporate brand is seen as complete	The corporate brand is seen as a creation process

We believe the relationship-based approach to corporate branding has the advantage that it implicitly entails a tangible and almost trial-and-error approach to the practices the organization attaches to corporate branding. Relationships have to be developed, one could say, earned, and require energy and persistence, as in the example of the partnership between H&M and Lagerfeld. With the relationship-based approach, we also wish to more closely link one of the organization's most important functions – innovation (Drucker, 2001) – to corporate branding, as we believe the connection between corporate branding, relationships and innovation is a seriously overlooked but nonetheless relevant issue in relation to an organization's competitiveness.

In an age that calls for flexibility, adaptation and creativity, corporate branding can and must provide opportunities for organizations to realize their best potential at any given time. We believe this takes place by opening up to the environment in a process of adaptation and learning, which is necessary in order for an innovative and competitive organization to function. By highlighting the significance of the relationship-based approach to corporate branding as central for an organization's differentiation, competitiveness and innovative drive, we are seeking to bring corporate branding up to date with the challenges that face organizations. Thus the relationship-based approach to corporate branding is not reserved for the few, but is, in principle, available to all organizations (Csaba, Chapter 6). Seen in this light, corporate branding offers advantages to all types of organizations, large and small, local and global, and this highlights the fact that the significance of corporate branding extends further and deeper than just the organization's communication. It has once been said that, 'we are born original, but die as copies'. By distancing organizations from the essence-based approach, and by drawing them closer to their connections, we hope that they can avoid falling into the 'conformity trap', and instead develop in ways that create enduring differentiation, competitiveness and innovative drive.

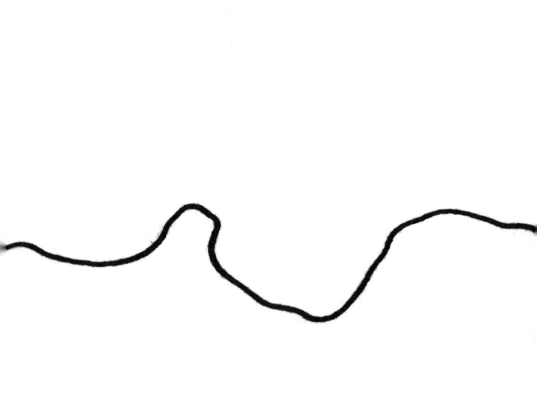

CHAPTER 4

A COMMUNAL APPROACH TO CORPORATE BRANDING

Yun Mi Antorini & Kasper S. Andersen

Increasingly, the notion of consumers as passive recipients of brand meaning and products is being replaced with the notion of consumers as active co-creators of brand meaning and important contributors to an organization's value creation. Drawing on three cases, IKEA, Jones Soda and WeightWatchers, this chapter introduces a *communal approach to corporate branding*. The approach encapsulates the idea of closer integration between the organization and consumer as the key to an organization's competitiveness.

Sergio Zyman, who was the Vice President and Chief Marketing Officer for the Coca-Cola Company up until the mid-90's, very successfully advanced the Coca-Cola brand as a self-assured, dominant, omnipresent, 'all American' brand. Today, Coca-Cola stands as a unified corporate brand characterized by a consistent set of values, visual expressions, and symbols across a variety of markets and consumer segments. Within the marketing and advertising industry, Coca-Cola has become an ultimate symbol of effective and disciplined marketing and branding practices. Until just a few years ago, it was therefore unthinkable that this well-oiled growth and branding machine would ever sputter.

Nonetheless, the constant growth in the Coca-Cola share price of earlier times has given way to significant falls (Fortune, 2004). Even though Coca-Cola continues to be assessed as one of the strongest and most valuable brands in the world (Interbrands, 2005), it is facing tough competition from private labels and national brands on a scale not seen before (Newsweek, 2004). In other words, Coca-Cola's market dominance is being challenged and the company's continuous growth appears to have lost momentum. Many possible explanations have been offered: From management problems and organizational inertia to changing consumer preferences (Fortune 2004). According to the Coca-Cola's website (coca-cola.com), it is necessary that Coca-Cola change and: 'Starts a new chapter', that is more responsive to the fact that consumer expectations of large companies go beyond omnipresence and market dominance. This new chapter includes what Coca-Cola's new CEO, E. Neville Isdell refers to as a *multifaceted, integrated* and *holistic* approach to the way Coca-Cola will interact with its consumers in the future (Isdell, 2004).

In this chapter, we will explore the implications of closer *integration* between organizations and consumers, and what this means for the corporate brand. We are particularly inspired by Isdell, and relatively new concepts such as *co-creation* (Prahalad & Ramaswamy, 2004), that suggests that increasingly consumers and organizations have shared interests in becoming closer integrated, as well as the concept of *brand community* (Muniz & O'Guinn, 2001), that suggests that consumers build communities around branded goods and services.

The Oxford English Dictionary (2005) defines 'integration' as: 'The making up or composition of a whole by adding together or combining the separate parts or elements; combination into an integral whole: A making whole or entire.' In relation to corporate branding, we will introduce the idea of integration through what we call *a communal approach to corporate branding* While product marketing traditionally focuses on product characteristics and advantages, the communal approach to corporate branding focuses on integration between the organization and consumer as the key to an organization's competitiveness. A communal approach to corporate branding thus entails a much greater degree of consumer involvement and closeness than is the case within traditional product marketing.

In the following section, we take a closer look at *why* the consumer has attained this more significant position.

Why Focus on Integration?

The idea of integration reflects a new and different perspective on the competencies an organization draws upon in the battle for market relevance and demand. Prior to 1990 (Prahalad and Ramaswamy, 2004:141), an organization's business units were seen as the source of knowledge and hence competence. In the early 90s, this perception changed, and people began increasingly to see organizations as a portfolio of competencies. From the mid-90s until 2000, attention turned away from the organization. Focus was given instead to an organization's suppliers and partners as vitally important to an organization's competence. After 2000, the perception of competency changed again. Competency building began to be understood as a *whole*, involving the organization, its suppliers and partners, *and* the consumers. In keeping with this understanding, the consumer is seen as an active contributor to the organization's competency building, because the consumer is recognized as an increasingly influential player: 'Now, individually and within groups, consumers can exert considerable influence on how the brand is represented in the marketplace. Firms are faced with the challenge of integrating these consumers into the marketplace process.' (Muniz & O'Guinn, 2005:14). Closer integration with stakeholders is, in other words, currently replacing the classic distinction between 'them' (the stakeholders), and 'us' (the organization).

Two additional trends further explain why the idea of integration is worth focusing on for today's organizations. We call the first trend, *the creating, connected and empowered consumer*. This trend arises from the fact that, over time, technological development has raised the consumer to the level of a creating player, whose knowledge and competence makes him or her capable of more than just consuming. These consumers are often connected with other consumers in interest communities. As a group, they increasingly want to be heard and exercise influence. Closer integration with consumers allow the organization to build closer bonds with and learn from their users, but also to experience what is going on in the marketplace, and how consumption and demand patterns are changing and evolving.

We call the other trend, *branded goods under pressure*. This trend refers to the consolidation taking place among retailers and the associated growth in retailers' private labels. On the American market, private labels now account for 20 per cent of sales, while the figure is 40 per cent on the European market (Boyle, 2003). Private labels are also showing stronger growth than branded goods. This situation is a fundamental threat to the position previously held by (manufacturer) brands. If this battle is to be brought into balance, it is essential that manufacturers of branded goods find a way of getting 'closer to the consumer'. The idea of integration is closely linked with this need.

The Creating, Connected, and Empowered Consumer

The last decade has seen significant technological improvements and greater access to and dissemination of production, information and communication technology. These technological advances have permitted a much greater degree of human interaction across time and space. If one adds to this a generally higher level of education combined with effective global payment systems, a portrait emerges of a consumer who has a wealth of opportunities for getting involved in and having an impact on the value creation process – which was previously the exclusive domain of the organization. This development has created a situation where: 'The hunter [the company] has become the hunted, as informed, connected, and active consumers increasingly learn that they too can extract value at the traditional point of exchange' (Prahalad & Ramaswamy, 2004). Von Hippel (2005) has also described this as the trend towards innovation being democratized, meaning that individual consumers (but also companies) are increasingly able to innovate for themselves.

As a parallel to the political consumer who exercises influence through his or her purchasing choices, we are thus witnessing the appearance of a new type of consumer, which we call the *creating, connected and empowered consumer*.

These consumers typically have great insight into and knowledge of the products and services they consume. This combination of knowledge and insight motivates them, to a greater degree than other consumers, to create new and relevant product solutions which do not exist on the market. Solutions that are beneficial to the individual, but which are also beneficial to other consumers (von Hippel, 1988). One example of this is *Adult Fans of LEGO*, who are connected in a community they have set up themselves. Due to their extensive knowledge of the LEGO building system, these consumers are capable of developing new and exciting LEGO sets and models, as well as new building techniques and software programs that generally improve the experience and handling of the product. Adult Fans of LEGO typically participate in their own online communities, allowing them to distribute ideas, to the benefit of all active members.

This connectedness with other consumers also increases the group's power to influence the company (Muniz & O'Guinn, 2001). For example, Scandinavian Airlines (SAS©) consults the SK-AAL commuter club in Aalborg, Denmark (SK stands for SAS, AAL for Aalborg) before making important decisions about changes to timetables, using new types of planes, or when new products need to be tested (Politiken, 20 January 2005). Similarly, Adult Fans of LEGO explain that their organization in a community with other LEGO fans allows them to communicate special requests to the LEGO Group, which they were unable to do as individual consumers. For example, LEGO fans are interested in buying large volumes of LEGO bricks by weight, in touring the company, in getting information about product launches, and having company representatives participate in Q & A sessions arranged by LEGO fans. The chance of these interests being received with sympathy is increased when a sizeable group of consumers makes the request, rather than individual consumers.

In other words, from an organization's perspective, the consumer has become more than just a consumer. The consumer is increasingly being ascribed a central and more active role. This development has significance for many aspects of an organization, including the role and significance of the corporate brand, which we will return to later in the chapter.

An example of greater involvement by consumers in processes that were previously within the domain of organizations is illustrated by the Brimstone Butterfly band. Brimstone Butterfly has released their debut DVD – bypassing the major record companies. Brimstone Butterfly developed their DVD and video and organized sale and distribution via a volunteer, non-profit, virtual cooperation involving 79 other creative artists from all over the world. Without this cooperation, Brimstone Butterfly would presumably never have reached a real audience, and it also led to the DVD being professionally produced, something which is normally only within the reach of well-known major bands.

Another example is the quite complex but user-friendly LDraw™ software program, designed and developed by Adult Fans of LEGO. LDraw is an open standard for LEGO CAD programs that allow the user to create virtual LEGO models and scenes. You can use it to document models you have physically built, create building instructions just like LEGO, render 3D photo realistic images of your virtual models and even make animations. The possibilities are endless. Unlike real LEGO bricks where you are limited by the number of parts and colors, in LDraw nothing is impossible.' (Ldraw.org). Adult Fans of LEGO provide regular updates and maintain the program. The program allows the user to realize any idea and express it using virtual LEGO bricks. Like Brimstone Butterfly, LDraw has been created by users, with no influence from the organizations that normally handle the design and production of products like this.

Projects like Brimstone Butterfly and LDraw are based on four important premises: 1) Creative zeal!; 2) the availability and broad professional and social exploitation of many forms of production, information and communication technology; 3) an entrepreneurial and constructive knowledge-sharing mentality, whereby the knowledge of all parties increases, the more knowledge is shared, and, 4) the attitude that with joint effort and a broad spectrum of skills, projects that normally cannot be realized via official and traditional channels can actually be achieved. Access to and utilization of new technology that did not exist just five years ago is thus increasing consumer expertise and lifting them out of their role as passive recipients of an organization's messages and products.

As the Brimstone Butterfly and LDraw examples show, consumers are increasingly able to conceive, design, plan and implement complex projects themselves, bypassing traditional institutions and channels. And this is true across industries and product types, as von Hippel (1988, 2001, 2005) and Thomke & von Hippel (2002); Franke & Shah (2003) show in their studies of innovative users.

Branded Goods Under Pressure!

Another equally important trend that is motivating organizations to seek closer integration with consumers derives from the fact that large retail chains such as Wal-Mart, Target and Home Depot have increased their market influence quite significantly. The expansion and growth of these retail chains has, as already mentioned, led to big growth in private labels. Private labels are taking a significant market share, thus putting traditional branded goods under pressure in terms of price and quality. In order to survive in the battle for consumer favor, the private label situation is forcing branded goods manufacturers to focus much more on the end user. Procter & Gamble's CEO, A. G. Lafley, explains:

'Wal-Mart's shopper is our shopper. If you really understand the shopper, you figure out how to increase your share of her wallet, how to encourage her to spend more on your products. That's where the power is – with the shopper. Getting the shopper to spend more comes down to innovation – the critical driver of consumer loyalty – and productivity.' (A. G. Lafley, Fortune, February 21, 2005)

As Lafley indicates, gaining a deeper understanding of the consumer is vital if branded goods manufacturers want their branded goods to have pull effect in the future. In other words, direct relationships with consumers will be increasingly important in order for branded goods manufacturers to develop strong positions in the future that can differentiate them from the chain's private labels.

Whereas in the past organizations have focused on analyzing cognitive properties related to consumer preferences and purchase decision processes, focus is now shifting towards what we might call (based on Lafley's perception) *deep consumer understanding*. Deep consumer understanding focuses on how opinions are shaped, what life themes consumers are preoccupied with, socio-cultural factors, and the relationships the consumer is participating in (Fournier, 1998). The goal of deep consumer understanding is to understand consumption and demand as closely tied up with the consumer's identity, and to understand what issues the consumer is concerned about at a more emotional and psychological level. In the competition with private labels, the products, brands and services of the future will have to build more extensively on deep consumer understanding. Direct interaction with the consumer represents one of the ways an organization can gain access to deep consumer knowledge. And the corporate brand, with its emphasis on values, relationships and culture is seen to have a more appropriate role here than product branding, which focuses on product characteristics and advantages.

Yun Mi Antorini & Kasper S. Andersen

Towards a New Value Creation Paradigm

New technological advances that have provided fertile ground for a creating, connected and empowered group of consumers, together with the increased dependence of branded goods suppliers' on end users, are putting pressure on the traditional value creation paradigm. The traditional value creation paradigm, in which the organization is the primary value-creating player, is currently being replaced by a new paradigm that focuses on the consumer for value creation (Prahalad & Ramaswamy, 2004). Philip Kotler also describes this shift as a transition from the four P's to the four C's, see figure 4:1.

Figure 4:1 From a Seller-Based to a Customer-based View

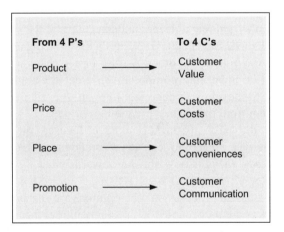

Source: Interview with Philip Kotler: *Kotler's new marketing mantras unplugged*, January 7, 2004 in The Economic Times

Value is no longer understood as something created by the organization alone, but as something that arises in *interaction* between the organization and the consumer, and the consumer and other consumers. Prahalad & Ramaswamy summarize this idea using the concept of co-creation:

'Co-creation converts the market into a forum where dialog among the consumer, the firm, consumer communities and networks of firms can take place. ...Managers must co-shape expectations with consumers.

Finally, consumers have a role in co-shaping experiences with the firm.' Prahalad & Ramaswamy (2004:122).

Co-creation is based on the premise that value is created in interaction between the consumer and the organization. To illustrate what they mean by co-creation, Prahalad & Ramaswamy (2004:5-10) highlight the development that has taken place in the health care industry. Twenty years ago, the doctor was the specialist, exclusively responsible for the diagnosis and subsequent treatment of the patient. Today, the doctor is often just one of many resources in the network the consumer draws upon. Patients consult other patients and patient associations, participate in support groups they have set up themselves, consult other doctors, use alternative treatments, and take the initiative to admit themselves to hospital and be examined. At the same time, the industry is developing methods and products that support the patients' networks and their need to contact specialists (via the Internet), and which help the patient gather and submit data related to their illness. Thus the relationship between patient and doctor is being increasingly founded on co-creation as a solution to health problems, with the patient being responsible, for example, for data collection, which is subsequently analyzed and diagnosed by the doctor.

Co-creation essentially means that the organization and consumer work together to design, develop and implement solutions that create value (also of a financial nature) for both parties. The value created can be distributed to other consumers. This is one of the reasons why Prahalad & Ramaswamy (2004) define the consumer as one of the organization's most important sources of competency.

In the next section we will examine three organizations which have chosen to reduce the distance between the organization and consumer, by integrating with the consumer in various ways. This is followed by a discussion of how we might understand integration and how an organization can create a 'space' for this integration. Finally, we will consider the consequences of closer integration between organization and consumer for the corporate brand.

Practical Examples of Organization and Consumer Integration

We will now take a closer look at three organizations which, in various ways, have taken the first step in the direction of stronger integration between organization and consumer. The first example is Swedish

IKEA. This steadily expanding furniture empire is a good example of an organization that has managed to integrate the consumer by co-creating *values and attitudes*. The second example is the American Jones Soda, which exemplifies a way of integrating the consumer via co-creation of the *product*. The last example is Weight Watchers, which integrates with the consumer via co-creation of a *social community* with the consumer. The examples do not illustrate complete fusion between the organization and consumer. Rather integration exists at certain points, and the examples illustrate different facets of the integration© between organization and consumer.

IKEA – Integration via Co-Creation of Values and Attitudes

'We try not to follow the normal perception of how to do things… We try to do it other ways, and until now, we have succeeded quite well…. We made as many mistakes as we could. It took us a long time to get used to the market.'
(Ingvar Kamprad in USA Today, December 29, 2004)

To use Kamprad's words, IKEA is built upon the idea of doing things differently. And even though it has taken them a long time to get used to the market, the many mistakes have borne fruit for IKEA. Today the chain has 186 stores in 31 countries. IKEA expects to open a further 20 stores in 2005, and their turnover has passed the $15 billion mark (Fortune, 2004). In a recent survey of 2,000 advertising managers, brand managers and academics conducted by the Brandchannel online magazine, IKEA was voted the world's third most influential brand after Apple© and Google©. The same survey ranks IKEA as the leading European brand.

Former Human Resources Manager, Nina Närby, recalls her first meeting with Kamprad at Stockholm Business School:

'Kamprad was completely different from all the other CEOs…They came dressed in business suits and ties, but he came in jeans and sneakers. He seemed like a real human being. What impressed me were the values he talked about.'

IKEA represents an organization that, due to its values, attitudes and actions, breaks with the traditional perception of an organization as apolitical and isolated from social debate. Instead, IKEA exemplifies a way of integrating the consumer that is based upon co-creation of values and attitudes.

In December 2002, IKEA became the subject of intense debate in Denmark when it publicized its new HR strategy. The HR strategy involved adjustments to some of the areas traditionally associated with HR: The introduction of flexible working hours for parents with young children, six weeks holiday for all employees, a longer notice of dismissal period for employees over 40, and the option to work part time as a manager. Other aspects of the HR strategy related to issues that had not previously been on the HR agenda. The decision to abolish both the Christmas party for IKEA's Danish employees and the tradition of giving wedding presents to newly-wed employees in particular provoked a heated debate in the Danish media. With regard to the former, IKEA explained that they wanted to be a workplace for everyone, including people who do not celebrate Christmas for religious reasons. And regarding the abolishment of wedding presents, IKEA argued that they did not wish to signal that it was more 'correct' to be married than single.

It did not take long before IKEA again was in the Danish media. This time, because the organization gave their checkout employees a pay increase of 666 Euros per month, making them the best paid checkout staff in Denmark. IKEA again became the focus of a political debate that was welcomed by the Danish Confederation of Trade Unions (LO), while Danish Commerce and Service (DHS) and competitor, Coop Danmark, were much more critical of the initiative, which they labeled a 'cheap sales trick' (Kommunikationsforum, 2003). Nonetheless, IKEA recently reported improved productivity, better customer service, and a 50 per cent reduction in staff turnover (Fortune, 2004).

Most recently, IKEA, together with SKANSKA, has been in the media spotlight because of their low cost housing project, BoKlok ('live smart'), involving IKEA-designed 'folk homes' which make it possible to live 'beautifully at low cost'. IKEA aims to build 2,000 homes over the next 7 years, making IKEA an active company in the housing market. These homes have already attracted a lot of attention. Not only are they low cost, but they also provide a housing option that meets the needs of middle and low income groups for secure, quality housing with good natural lighting.

IKEA is an organization that has many irons in the fire, and distinguishes itself in many areas with many types of messages. Consistent with this, IKEA Director, Peter Høgsted, describes his leadership style as 'diversity leadership', and the title on his business card is not 'Director', but 'Housing Activist'. The activist is generally known for using alternative and extreme measures to realize his ideas. If we look at all of IKEA's messages and the way they are expressed, we find that IKEA is less concerned about whether it expresses consistent images of itself. What seems to be more important to IKEA is that they are involved in the debates that concern the wider public.

One can justifiably ask what the abolishment of Christmas parties and wedding presents has to do with furniture and IKEA's core business. Perhaps the organization has simply understood the media value of single issues?

IKEA's approach to human resources must naturally be seen as an element in the competition for skilled labor. And this appears to be a battle which IKEA has good odds of success with:

'In a few years, we Europeans must prepare to compete for our labor force. It will become important that commercial enterprises can offer good employment and working conditions. Some have already begun to prepare. Consider IKEA in Denmark, which has been farsighted enough to position itself with good employment conditions.' (Fürstenborg, 2002)

But IKEA's activities must also be viewed in a broader context that goes beyond recruitment and focuses on values and shared attitudes. Together with its consumers, IKEA is co-creating a vision for the conditions which define our general attitudes to life. IKEA furniture and products will come to serve as tokens and symbols for this vision. The vision is about a good working environment, leaving room for diversity, and flexibility. The vision is being realized and gaining ground in step with the specific actions the organization, its employees and consumers are jointly carrying out and supporting.

Jones Soda – Integration via Co-creation of the Product

Jones Soda is a relatively small but rapidly growing American soft drink manufacturer. The organization was founded in 1987 by Peter van Stolk, and has the declared goal of becoming the USA's largest soft drink brand. This might seem ambitious given that Jones Soda currently has a market share of one per cent of the American soft drink market!

Nonetheless, Jones Soda is interesting because the organization is capable of offering the consumer co-created product experiences, which the big brands are either overlooking or are unable to offer.

While the key to profitable earnings on the soft drink market lies in anything but 'custom made' products, Jones Soda is best known for their soft drink which carries labels displaying photographs designed, produced and submitted by consumers. Consumers can also submit electronic 'fortune cookies' and short proverbs that are selected and displayed on Jones Soda's website and on the bottom of bottle caps.

Since 1996, Jones Soda has received several hundred thousand submissions for bottle labels, and some of the latest labels are displayed in a public gallery at jonessoda.com. Jones Soda, together with professional photographers, regularly selects a number of labels that are used on bottles. And should your label fail to be among the lucky winners, if you simply order 12 bottles you can still see your label on a Jones Soda bottle!

The core idea behind Jones Soda resides in the co-creation process between Jones Soda and the consumer. The consumer is given a role in defining the product's appearance, and Jones Soda is given a place in their consumers' worlds. The co-creation process also serves to integrate the user in a common struggle against the major brands with the shared ambition to 'run with the little guy…create some change', which is Jones Soda's slogan. The co-created and tailor-made aspect symbolizes everything the 'big players' cannot do, leaving Jones Soda to represent the original and the authentic.

Jones Soda invites the recipient to take part in a co-creation process which, in our opinion, contributes to creating a dynamic and interesting brand with many facets.

Weight Watchers –
Integration via Co-Creation of Social Communities

In the early 1960's, Jean Nidetch invited friends to her home once a week to discuss the best way to lose weight. This is how Weight Watchers was founded. Forty years later, a million people are gathering each week in groups all over the world, which pay a fixed fee for using Weight Watchers' various products. Based on the principle of self help, the members of these groups support each other and receive advice on losing weight from Weight Watchers consultants. Most recently, Weight Watchers has developed a virtual platform, WeightWahtcers.com, which now attracts millions of users each week.

The focus point is the Weight Watchers POINTS® program, which embodies the Weight Watchers weight loss principles. This program contains a 12 week food plan that promotes weight loss. The Weight Watchers program also involves local meetings, e-tools to help manage the POINTS system, and online facilities such as message boards, recipes, success stories, and expert advice.

However, the remarkable thing about Weight Watchers is the organization's vision, which is: '… for overweight people to help other overweight people lose weight. For who better to advise, inspire and motivate, than a person who, like you, has first hand experience with obesity and weight loss problems' (WeightWatchers.dk). The combination of face-to-face meetings and Weight Watchers' numerous, specialized online message boards, put weight loss – normally an individual problem – into a social context. The overweight person is not alone, but is surrounded by like minded people and specialists with 'first hand experience'. As the following post thread illustrates, weight loss becomes a joint project, where relationship with others plays a vital role and becomes part of the product the consumer is seeking and consuming:

Person A posts: 'I think I am smart. I think I am funny. I am intelligent. So why am I still hating this body that I am in. About 10 years ago I looked pretty good and my self-image was SO high and way up there. Even if things were going bad in my day I still felt great cause I knew that I looked great and people really do treat you differently because of that. Now I feel dumpy and I just can't get myself out of this slump. I am just plain LAZY! HELP! It has been so long since I felt good and I am jeopardizing my marriage 'cause I never want to be intimate 'cause I hate the way I look now. PLSE give me some motivation. Thanks in advance.'

Person B answers shortly afterwards (together with many others): 'Poor baby... be kind to yourself. We 'nice girls' cut other people all kinds of slack in this life and then turn around and beat ourselves up. Do something nice for yourself tomorrow that has nothing to do with food: go get a pedicure, find a good book or movie rental and lose yourself in it for a while, try to get back in touch (if only for a few minutes of this one day) with what makes you happy. Then tackle the body stuff, one day at a time... you're still in there and you are still beautiful.'

Weight Watchers is an example of a type of company that shares many characteristics with a traditional community. A traditional community is characterized by a collective identity, moral responsibility, and a number of traditions and rituals, that bind the community together and give it meaning (Muniz & O'Guinn, 2001).

Weight Watchers functions more as a *facilitator* operating in a social context, founded on the principle of interaction, than a company operating under commercial conditions and focusing on optimizing transactions. Losing weight and keeping it off is a lifelong project for many people. By weaving a social network and a POINTS system under its members, Weight Watchers creates a powerful integration between the consumer and the organization. At the same time, Weight Watchers may gain access to members' recipes and their experiences with successful weight loss, and this information flows to the organization as knowledge that can be converted into new products and services.

Closer Integration between Organization and Consumer Create new Conditions for Corporate Branding

As IKEA, Jones Soda and Weight Watchers all illustrate, close integration between organization and consumer arises because the parties share a common interest area, and because they have a common interest in developing and strengthening this interest area. For example, the consumer might have an interest in promoting special attitudes and values (as in the IKEA example), in better products and greater or more flexible choices (as in the Jones Soda example), or in finding someone to share a personal challenge with (as in the Weight Watchers example).

Conversely, an organization might have an interest in sharing values and attitudes with consumers which make it appear more attractive and distinguish it from competitors who focus more on functional characteristics such as price, product range and location. An organization might also have an interest in co-creating products jointly with consumers in order to create new products and services that generate greater interest and pull effect for the organization's products. Finally, an organization might make community one of its competition parameters, because a community binds consumers more strongly to both the organization and other consumers, building long term loyalty and counteracting competition (Muniz & O'Guinn, 2001).

Such interest fellowships are not necessarily characterized by harmony and consensus. On the contrary, there can be disagreement between the organization and consumer about whether it is reasonable to abolish the company Christmas party (as in the IKEA example), or which labels look best on a Jones Soda bottle.

In this context, Cohen (1985) highlights the capacity of symbols to unite and integrate people. Using the peace symbol, Cohen (1985:18) illustrates how a symbol can unite people who agree that peace is desirable and worth fighting for. However, Cohen's (1985) point is that despite the fact that the symbol unites groups of people, even the most peace-loving group of people can be divided when it comes to the question of how to actually fight for peace, for whom, and so on. In other words, symbols integrate, but do not necessarily ensure long term stability and harmony within the group.

Similarly, the corporate brand is able to unite the organization and consumers in a common understanding of, for example, what IKEA stands for. But it is beyond the scope of the corporate brand, as such, to counteract the fragmentation that can arise between organization and consumer, grounded in disagreement about issues such as whether or not to have a company Christmas party. Focus must be given to other more direct mechanisms. If the goal is long term integration between organization and consumer, this perspective has significance for the perceptions we attach to the corporate brand.

To create the right conditions for continued integration and counteract fragmentation, it will be necessary, in our opinion, to create a 'space' where the organization and consumer can meet. A 'space' where opinions can be exchanged and where disputes about contentious issues can be dealt with. If the goal is greater integration between organization and consumer, it is essential that this takes place via the symbolic dimension of the corporate brand, *as well as* via a specific 'space' that make it possible to put integration into practice. Such a 'space' can be realized using the concept of *brand community*.

A Brand Community as a 'Space' for Consumer Integration

Harley-Davidson©, JEEP®, e-Bay© and LEGO are all examples of brands that have recently established *brand communities*. A brand community is made up of *brand loyalists* (Muniz & O'Guinn, 2001). Brand loyalists often have quite comprehensive knowledge and an interest in knowing more about the brand they use. A brand community represents a 'space', either virtual or face-to-face, where brand users meet to swap experiences and spend time together. Brand communities are typically not bound to geographic locations. They are communities that transcend location, which is only possible because of the Internet.

A brand community unites consumers in ways that are characteristic of traditional communities. In contrast to traditional communities, it is the brand that is the central focus. The brand, or the interests linked to the brand, provide the 'glue' that binds organization and consumer together in a common interest.

Harley-Davidson Motor Company is an example of an organization that has successfully established a brand community (Schouten & McAlexander, 1995, McAlexander & Schouten, 2002). H.O.G.® (the Harley Owner Group®) arranges numerous events all over the world, involving more than 900,000 members in various national and international events, touring rallies, and other events that normally involve airing one's Harley in the company of like minded enthusiasts. H.O.G. offers membership of local chapters, which help connect the Harley owner into a social network that ties them even more strongly to H.O.G. and to other owners. H.O.G. also arranges 'open house' events, so that Harley enthusiasts can witness the production process and get greater insight into the product that means so much to them. Fournier, McAlexander, Schouten, & Sensiper (2000), show in their teaching case, that Harley-Davidson's efforts to get closer to the consumer is paying off in both the short and long term. The organization is gaining insight into what things are important to their consumers, what problems currently exist in relation to using the product, where it is possible to improve the product, and what the organization can do in the future to hold onto these particularly profitable and loyal consumers. Harley owners, on the other hand, are getting the chance to get close to the organization, the local dealer, and other Harley owners. The strength of the Harley-Davidson brand lies not only in the unique associations that define it; it resides just as much in the relationships the organization has with its consumers and the relationships owners have with each other.

In recent times, researchers (Schouten & McAlexander, 1995; Holt, 1995, 2004; Cova, 1997; McAlexander & Schouten, 1998; Muniz & O'Guinn, 2001; Cova & Cova, 2002; McAlexander, Schouten & Koenig, 2002; Muniz & O'Guinn, 2005; O'Guinn & Muniz, 2005) have identified several commercial advantages associated with communities of this type: 1) A brand community attracts and retains an organization's most valuable consumers, i.e. the very involved and loyal consumers; 2) the social processes which take place in a brand community strengthen and develop the consumer's bond with the brand; 3) members of a brand community often act as *brand ambassadors* that 'sell' the brand to other consumers; 4) participation in a brand community protects the brand from competition.

Finally, on the basis of their studies, Muniz & O'Guinn (2001) formulate the hypothesis that a brand community attracts innovative and creative consumers, who develop new and attractive product ideas as a result of their extensive knowledge of products and services. Due to their great knowledge and interest, these consumers often feel they know the brand better than the organization (Muniz & O'Guinn, 2001). They also have a particular interest in preserving perceptions of the brand, what it stands for, and what types of products it is associated with.

The characteristics mentioned can be both an advantage and a challenge to the organization. Preserving perceptions of the brand ensures continuity and stability, but can also counteract new and sometimes necessary interpretations of the brand. For example, BMW's Mini© received widespread criticism from Mini Clubman and Mini Cooper owners (Broderick, Maclaran and Ma, 2003). According to these owners, a 'real' mini is a car that reflects a fun-loving self, a self that is unique and unusual; and a nostalgic self. The BMW Mini was seen as a threat to British design traditions and the fun-loving spirit that characterizes the Mini. The Brand community, made up of Mini Clubman and Mini Cooper owners, expressed their criticism in no uncertain terms on the Internet. Thus potential BMW Mini buyers who 'Google' 'BMW Mini' could come into direct contact with these critics, which could ultimately influence their decision to buy.

In summary, a brand community provides a 'space' in which there is lively debate, and sometimes rumor spreading (O'Guinn & Muniz, 2005), regarding product quality and relevance, brand positioning, and organization credibility. As Muniz & O'Guinn (2005) suggest, it is difficult if not impossible for an organization to ignore these consumer communities. This is especially true for organizations that see the value of a closer integration between organization and consumer. Closer integration places new demands on the organization to be a social player, and the corporate brand plays a vital and central role here.

A Communal Approach to Corporate Branding: Implications

A brand community as a 'space' for integration between organization and consumer goes further than one-to-one marketing and relationship marketing. These marketing principles focus primarily on creating dialog between the organization and individual consumers, and rarely involve as many interaction points as a brand community. The communal approach focuses on the *common* interests between organization and consumer and between consumers, see figure 4:2.

As figure 4:2 shows, both the traditional and the relationship-based approaches to corporate branding have the organization at the centre of the processes and activities linked to the corporate brand. The consumer, as the figure illustrates, is basically seen as a *recipient* of the corporate brand messages and the products that characterize the organization. The components that characterize the corporate brand (the organization's vision, image and culture, Hatch & Schultz, 2001) are defined within the boundaries of the organization, and if the consumer is involved, it is merely as a kind of informant. In contrast, the communal approach sees the corporate brand as part of a co-creation process.

The communal approach gives priority to the consumer-related experience and feelings of affinity the brand provides (Schmitt, 1999). It is the relationship and exchange of meaning between the organization and its consumers that is in focus, see table 4:1. These relationships are based on a shared experience between the organization and consumer of what is important, right, fun, and central, i.e. experiences that build more on culture, rather than, for example, the organization's vision.

In this context, the role of the employee changes from being a service provider (focusing on optimizing the transaction and the actual purchase experience), to being the connection between the organization and the market. The employee becomes a carrier of both the culture that exists in the brand community, and the organization's culture. Thus the employee works in the interface between the organization and the culture of its environment. This central position ensures that the organization constantly receives feedback on the corporate brand's image and identity.

Figure 4:2 Perspectives on Corporate Branding seen from a Company's Point of View

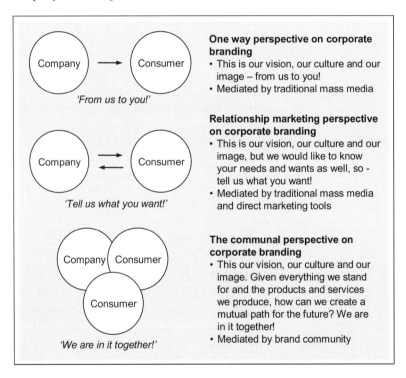

From a corporate branding perspective, the communal approach means that it is no longer enough that an organization stands for something and differentiates itself in the consumer's awareness. With a focus on social relationships, co-creation and culture, brand communities provide a 'space' where the organization can meet with consumers, and where consumers can meet other consumers. In this context, corporate branding is all about interacting with consumers and supporting and strengthening the links consumers have with each other (Cova, 1997), see figure 4:3.

Table 4:1 The one way Perspective on Corporate Branding versus The Communal Approach to Corporate Branding

The One Way Perspective on Corporate Branding	The Communal Approach to Corporate Branding
'Us' and our vision (the organization) versus 'them' (the consumers)	'We'ness' – the consumer is more than just a consumer. The consumer plays a central role in the organization's value creation process
The organization focuses on maximizing transactions	The organization is part of a social and cultural network
Employees are service providers	Employees are a connection
The consumer is a passive recipient of the organization's messages, products and services	The consumer co-creates the organization's messages, products and services
The organization alone defines the corporate brand	The consumer influences, negotiates and spreads awareness of the corporate brand, which in turn influences other consumers' perceptions of the brand

In relation to the Weight Watchers example, the corporate brand supports users by translating the vision and culture ('...that overweight people help other overweight people to lose weight') into products and services that support users in their common efforts to reach their individual goals. The Weight Watchers image of being an effective and sympathetic organization also supports users in their self perception of succeeding with their project.

These two questions will therefore be central to the future corporate brand: 'What issues are of *real* significance to the organization's users?' as Lafley, CEO of Procter & Gamble, highlights, and 'what can the corporate brand do to strengthen the bond users have with each other?'.

Figure 4:3 The Communal Approach to Corporate Branding Supports the Links Between Consumers

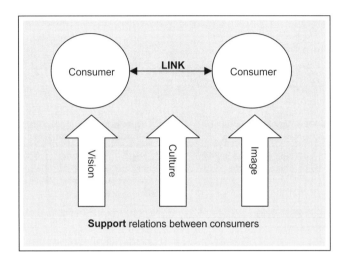

Conclusion

The perception of the consumer as a passive recipient of an organization's products and services is currently being replaced by a new perception of the consumer as creating, connected and empowered. At the same time, more than ever before, innovation has become central to an organization's competitiveness. 'Innovate or die' is the mantra of our time, and in contrast to earlier perceptions of the organization as being solely responsible for creating value, today the consumer is seen as being an important and central source of both knowledge and innovation. Consumers are better educated, better connected, and better informed than ever, and these facts are being felt – just ask the music and film industry. The communal approach to corporate branding aims to recognize and integrate the consumer into the organization's life and culture. The brand community phenomenon provides a possible 'space' in which the organization and consumer can meet, with a common interest in a given brand, product or service.

The possibilities the communal approach to corporate branding raises are numerous. Firstly, it motivates the organization to create and set new agendas. The communal approach invites the organization's stakeholders to take part in creating meaning in the corporate brand. This makes the organization more interactive and helps abolish the traditional distinctions between organization and consumer. With its focus on co-creation, the communal approach can also have a positive impact on an organization's R&D. Finally, the organization receives more direct feedback on the corporate brand identity, which can help sustain the relevance and competitive power of the brand.

The challenge associated with the communal approach is the risk of fragmenting the corporate brand, which particularly applies where the organization lacks integration and coordination mechanisms. The corporate brand can become fragmented if the organization, in its interaction with consumers, blindly follows the inputs it receives from its environment. Such a situation has been referred to as the 'headless chicken' syndrome, where the organization charges around with no direction or goals (Schultz, 2004). The communal approach requires that the process of managing the corporate brand be democratized, as discussed by Antorini and Schultz in chapter 3. The challenge is to open up and allow more of the organization's stakeholders to participate in the management and development of the corporate brand. As the Brimstone Butterfly and Ldraw examples show, inspiration can be drawn from the new voluntary networks as to how broad involvement and coordination of competencies can be achieved.

The communal approach is particularly relevant to enterprises that focus on consumer experiences, and which want consumers – both existing and potential – to experience many facets of the organization. The communal approach is basically about being out where the action is, utilizing consumer knowledge and ideas, and managing the organization according to the motto: He who integrates wins!

CHAPTER 5

LIVING THE BRAND

Esben Karmark

The employee factor is one of the most important to consider for a corporate brand strategy to be successful. This chapter investigates how employees engage in *living the brand* in theory and practice. Two perspectives are presented: the marketing and communications based perspective, and the norms and values based perspective. Examples from major Scandinavian companies provide the basis for a discussion of the implications of these perspectives for the employee's role as a living brand.

Within the branding field, the role of the employee has increasingly become an important focus of study. In marketing and product-oriented branding, service marketing in particular has been concerned with the connections between employees' commitment and performance and the consumers' perceptions of the (service) brand (e.g. O'Cass & Grace, 2003). In the corporate branding field, the role of the employee is accentuated further. Schultz (Chapter 2) for instance, argues that the employee becomes both a co-creator of the brand as well as a key actor in delivering the brand's content and promise. In the brand literature, the relationship between the brand and the employee is conceptualized as living the brand. The main premise behind the concept is that the brand becomes a central strategic factor for the organization, which links the internal organization, i.e. its culture and identity, to its external stakeholders i.e. its customers and other key stakeholders, through the corporate brand identity (Kapferer, 2004; Ind, 2001; Hatch & Schultz, 2001).

As is the case with many branding concepts, the living the brand construct is a seductive one (Klein, 2000). First, because it is linked to the values inherent in the brand and the organization. Living the brand suggests that the employee will internalize these values, thus enabling him or her to deliver the brand's promises to the consumer in a 'natural' way:

'If the values are deeply rooted and coherently interlinked, then the relevance of the brand's values and the connections staff make with the brand enable them to deliver the brand promise in a more natural manner, with passion and commitment. This, in effect, brings the brand to life and enhances the likelihood of a better performance'.
(de Chernatony, 2002:122).

Second, living the brand is usually presented as rooted in a more values-based approach to management. Accordingly, many living the brand models advocate employee empowerment, i.e. a shift from direct control to a more subtle normative control (Kunda, 1992) enabled by the employees' strong identification with the goals of the organization and the brand. Old-fashioned control mechanisms are replaced by modern and post-modern ones, in which the values and the symbols and stories inherent in the brand keep employees' behavior aligned with the brand values or 'on brand' (Olins, 2003; Ind, 2001; Jensen, 2002).

While the promise of the living the brand construct seems to be a win/win situation for employees and the (brand) organization, in practice the reality appears to be less than ideal. For instance, Ind (2001: 80) reports on a study of 700 business professionals by tompeterscompany! which revealed that 70% percent of employees do not support their company's branding initiatives and that 90% do not know how to represent the brand effectively. Similarly, Mitchell (2004), quoting E. Schein, points out that attempts to get employees to 'buy in' to their organization is nothing new. Mitchell, however, also points out that anecdotal evidence suggests that the effect of internal branding programs on employees is not convincing:

'A few people convert, but their effect is pretty much cancelled out by an equally small number of fanatical resisters. That leaves the vast majority with their heads firmly below the parapet, going through only those motions that that are necessary for them to survive until the storm has passed. So the net result of all those carefully crafted, expensive events, away-days, workshops, storytelling sessions, dramatisations, cascading programs, internal videos and newsletters? Once the initial excitement has died down, it's a big round number: zero.' (Mitchell, 2004:30).

Mitchell suggest that the problem with living the brand programs is that there is too much focus on changing employees' attitudes and behavior, and too little focus on translating brand values into real-life experiences - such as how to translate the value 'fun' into a specific job situation. While this is a valid criticism of the living the brand construct, and one which will also be addressed here, the goal of this chapter is to re-examine the construct in order to arrive at a more nuanced one. If we leave living the brand as it stands today, we face a real risk that it will be perceived by organizational members as empty rhetoric, the latest in a line of management fashions that come and go. This may very result in living the brand initiatives becoming a catalyst for cynicism and resignation in the organization rather than its intended source of commitment to the brand (Christensen & Cheney, 2000).

This chapter re-examines a number of assumptions related to the employees' role as living brands, such as: the assumption that the employee can become a living brand through following directions and guidelines as they are spelled out in a brand book; that he or she can be expected to represent the brand wholeheartedly (as in 'brand ambassador'); and that the employee is expected to become the co-creator of the brand, e.g. The chapter raises questions such as: what do all these roles entail? Can we expect every employee in the organization to take on such brand roles, or are these roles implicitly hierarchically contingent?

The chapter provides case-examples from LEGO Group, Novo Nordisk, Nordea, and Danisco, and concludes with a discussion of some of the implications that rethinking the living the brand construct may have for contemporary corporate brand models.

The Employee as a Living Brand

By considering the employee a living brand, it is assumed that the brand can undergo a process of anthropomorphizing or making an inanimate object like the brand into something humanized or personalized (Fournier, 1998). This process is, in many ways, at the heart of how we are generally looking at brands. One of the most common metaphors in the brand literature is that of 'brand as person,' which includes the idea that brands can have emotions and personalities (Aaker, 1996; Davis & Chun, 2003). This metaphor, however, has been extended to the notion that we can have relationships with brands, which requires the brand to have a human dimension. For instance, Fournier (1998) used terms such as 'flings,' 'courtships,' and 'committed partnerships,' to describe the relations between the consumer and the brand.

In the living the brand construct, however, the process of anthropomorphizing the brand is taken one step further. Here, the notion is that the employee, in fact, becomes the brand; the living brand. According to Ind (2001:26), the employees become living brands because it is through the relations between employees and customers that the brand is brought to life:

'The relationship between employees and consumers is (therefore) at the heart of the brand experience. Just as in any successful relationship, the employee/consumer relationship needs honesty, openness and a unity of interest. When the unity of interest is intuitive, with employees and consumers sharing the same passions, it is particularly powerful'

The starting point, in the brand literature, for employees to act as living brands is that they are sincerely committed to the brand:

'[...] Employees need to feel that it is their brand, that they understand it in their own terms and contribute to its development' (Ind, 2001: 125).

Related to the commitment that is required of employees to become living brands is the notion of loyalty. Loyalty is linked to the 'brand as person' metaphor. As pointed out by Davis and Chun (2003:52), loyalty implies the human trait of being exclusively and enduringly linked with another person, to be true and trustworthy in a relationship. At least implicitly, the underlying expectation is that the employee's sincere commitment' to the brand includes loyalty towards the brand. However, as is also pointed out by Davis and Chun, when the loyalty dimension is applied to the relationship between people and the brand in the literature, the exclusivity issue is often ignored: 'So we are unclear as to what we are expected to surmise about the consumer's loyalty and fidelity and how long the relationship should last' (2003: 52).

This is also the case with living the brand. In the literature, there is little discussion as to the limits of the employee's commitment and loyalty. What exactly are the expectations placed on the employee as a living brand? And how are the roles that the employee is expected to play defined in relation to the brand?

There are a number of roles that the employee can play as a living brand: Co-creator of the brand (Schultz, Chapter 2), delivering the brand (Kunde, 2000), brand champion (Ind, 2001), and brand ambassador (Gotsi & Wilson, 2001), to mention some of the most frequently mentioned ones. These roles, however, are often applied to the employee in a manner that is non-reflective and does not consider the deeper implications for the employees' relationship with the brand. For instance, the literature rarely considers whether it is viable that all employees should act as brand ambassador or what the role of brand ambassador really implies for the employee.

On a more conceptual level, we might say that there is little reflection as to how the connections between the company's culture, values, and brand expressions are merged in the employee as a living brand. Should the employee be infused with the culture and values in all types of brand-related behavior? Do we imagine a brand-cult, where the brand takes on religious overtones to the employees (Kunde, 2000)? And how can we prevent living the brand from becoming acts of self-seduction and self-absorption, in which employees' involvement in the brand is unrelated or simply unimportant to the demands of external stakeholders (Christensen & Cheney, 2000; Paustian, 2003)?

Living the Brand: A Marketing and Communications Based Perspective vs. a Norms and Values Based Perspective

The starting point for dealing with the questions raised above is that both the brand literature and practice in brand organizations operate within two approaches to, or perspectives on, living the brand. These two perspectives are somewhat similar to the two perspectives on identity in organizations: Corporate identity and organizational identity (cf. Antorini & Schultz, Chapter 3).

Whereas corporate identity is anchored in a strategic and visual perspective, with a focus on identity as positioning and corporate communication, organizational identity is anchored in a cultural perspective. Accordingly, organizational identity focuses on how organizational members make sense of issues relating to the question of 'who we are as an organization' in the context of the organizational culture and history (Albert & Whetten, 1985).

Approaches to living the brand can be seen from two similar perspectives. From the first perspective suggested here, the marketing and communications based perspective, the employee should first and foremost understand the brand values as they are defined by the brand organization. The primary means for attaining this understanding are internal communications, branding, training and development. Here the role of the employee is to deliver the brand's values to key stakeholders primarily by following brand guidelines. This implies that living the brand becomes, in effect, to take the form of living *by* the brand. The brand guidelines are often presented in the form of a brand book or other types of manuals that specify the meaning of the brand values to the employees.

The norms and values based perspective is more concerned with the employee's identification with the brand, and this identification is attained through the employees' socialization into the organization's cultural values (Schein, 1992). From this perspective, the role of the employee is to represent the brand, where the content and promise of the brand is expressed through the behavior and the attitude of the employee. It might actually go beyond representing the brand and imply a deeper personal connection and involvement. It is within perspective we might think of the employee as being the brand. The norms and values based perspective builds on the premise that the personal values of the employee become congruent with the brand values rather than relying on the brand values as guidelines for the employees to live by on the job. Consequently, the mechanisms involved in living the brand programs are, from this perspective, more linked to fostering employee identification through the use of cultural 'tools', such as storytelling or events, that might evoke emotional attachment. The two perspectives on living the brand are summarized in table 5:1.

Table 5:1 Perspectives on Living the Brand

	The marketing and communications based perspective	The norms and values based perspective
Management orientation	Communications and implementation	Values-based management
Role of the employee	Understanding the brand Delivering the brand (living by the brand)	Representing the brand Being the brand
Mechanisms and initiatives	Internal brand communication, training and development, brand books and manuals	Fostering brand identification through culture-embedding mechanisms, storytelling and events

Table 5:1 elaborates on the two perspectives on the living brand in relation to theory and practice in companies. The consequences for the employees' role in relation to the brand following from the two perspectives are also discussed.

The Marketing and Communications Based Perspective: Living by the Brand Values

In the marketing and communications based perspective, the employees are, to a large extent, seen as one of the target audiences for the company's brand communication. According to this philosophy, management's primary task is to formulate the brand values and to communicate them to the employees. According to Kunde (2000:166):

'If employees in the front-line are left to themselves to find the best way of doing things, the results will be highly variable. Some do

fantastically well, others less well. It's not so surprising – a brand's values contain many possibilities, like so many different facets around the brand itself. But for a brand to become a success, its values must be communicated identically.'

Ind (2001:146-147) elaborates on the role of internal communications in building employees' commitment to the brand:

'Internal communications are important in engaging employees in two respects. First, they can convey the benefits of the brand idea and encourage involvement (...) Second, external communication campaigns (assuming they are true to the brand) should be marketed internally (...) When it comes to the internal marketing of external campaigns, the degree of employee commitment varies. At its best, companies treat their employees as a key audience.'

Typically, internal brand communications occur through manuals and 'brand books'. For instance, McDonald's operates with a brand 'bible,' which specifies to employees how the brand values 'Quality', 'Service' and 'Cleanliness' is to be practiced in the day-to-day work situation. Kunde says of McDonald's approach to living the brand (2000:176):

'Education and systematization down to the last onion ring can create awesome commitment and action in an organization.'

Internal branding also puts emphasis on the issue of control. Leaving the brand values open to interpretation may be considered risky. According to Kunde (2000:171):

'Entrusting people with the brand is risky business – far more risky than running massive advertising campaigns, where the message – however well executed – is within your span of control. Carefully ensuring that people are committed, and understand and accept both the whys and the hows of brand delivery however, can turn a risk into a powerful asset.'

The following section provides an example from practice of the marketing and communications based approach to living the brand.

Living the Brand in Nordea: Brand Book and 'Cascade Process'

The Nordea group is the largest financial services company in the Nordic countries and has 37,000 employees. The group, as it looks today, is the result of a large cross-Nordic merger, in which a number of financial services companies in Denmark, Sweden, Norway, and Finland were merged during the 1990s. In January of 2001, the company simultaneously launched an internally- and externally-directed branding campaign.

As part of this campaign the Nordea name was introduced as well as the common values that were established for the merged companies. These values were called 'Nordic Ideas'. The primary goal of the campaign was to explain to all internal and external stakeholders that the new brand Nordea stood for 'Nordic Ideas.' Internally, the brand book and the 'Nordic Ideas' were communicated through the brand book, which was called 'Making it possible'. The brand book was to be part of a 'cascade process' called 'from words to action.' The goal was to implement the values in the organization through a process where the values would spread from the top of the organization and ultimately reached all organizational members in a cascade-like process.

The managers of the HR departments together with the managers of individual units were made responsible for planning the cascade process, and their task was to translate the Nordea corporate brand and values into concrete actions (Søderberg & Mathiesen, 2003).

The Nordea approach to 'living the brand' falls directly within the marketing and communications based perspective. The brand values are diffused throughout the organization in a top-down fashion by a simultaneously run internal and external branding campaign. The tools for implementing the brand values are communications-based: a brand-book with the purpose of making the employees understand the brand values. Through the cascade process, the values are supposed to reach the employees in the various units of the Nordea group where the 'Nordic Ideas' are translated into local meanings. The role of the employee in relation to living the brand becomes, to a large extent, a matter of living by the brand. The brand values are defined in the brand book and are ultimately translated into local meanings by the management for the employees to follow.

Søderberg and Mathiesen, who investigated the corporate branding process in Nordea, point to further issues that have relevance for the employee's potential for living the brand. One of these issues is related to the one-way communication inherent in the internal branding-based approach in Nordea, which does not support a deeper involvement with the brand on behalf of the employee. Søderberg and Mathiesen quote a HR employee (2003:28):

'Top management initiated the branding process and made a promise to the employees about a continued dialogue. But they did not redeem it, and that is fatal. The branding process was conducted as a top-down process, and top management did not show interest in getting any kind of feedback. The department 'Group Identity and Communications' made it into an issue about how Nordea gets a new profile and thus differentiates itself from other companies. But they totally underestimated the big challenge concerning how to further the employees' brand identification process.'

In their analysis, Søderberg and Mathiesen also point to another significant consequence of the marketing and communications based approach for the employee's role in livng the brand. In a discourse analysis of the Nordea brand book, the authors show that the story of Nordeas brand and values presented in the brand book is unrelated in many ways to the day-to-day experiences of the Nordea employees. Rather, the brand book resembles an external advertising campaign with aesthetic pictures of Nordic landscapes and young, blond and blue-eyed people. Søderberg & Mathiesen further suggest that the story told in the brand is actually not a story as defined by a storytelling perspective.

What is lacking in the Nordea brand story is both a sense of direction (where are we coming from and where are we going?) and an opponent (e.g. which challenges did we overcome in the merger process?).

Through these omissions, the marketing and communications based approach might, in fact, end up hindering the employee's involvement in the brand. When advertising 'language' is used to convey the brand values to employees, there is a risk, that the employee will not perceive the values as relevant to their everyday lives. When corporate branding as in this case also is used as 'sugar-coating' internally (Schultz, Antorini & Csaba, Chapter 1), there is a real risk that attempts to involve the employees in the brand will fail. In Nordea, accordingly, Søderberg & Mathiessen found that many copies of the brand book ended up in the waste paper basket.

In the following sections, the focus is turned to the norms and values based perspective on living the brand.

The Norms and Values Based Perspective: Being the Brand

The norms and values based perspective emphasizes the employee's identification with the company and brand values. This perspective builds on the relationship between organizational identity and employee's identification with and attitudes towards the company, as established in research such as that of Dutton, Dukerich & Harquail (1994). Gotsi & Wilson (2001:100) point out that:

'In order to encourage stronger commitment to the organization and its core values, employees need to internalize and adhere to the organization's values and norms in their attitudes and behavior. At the same time, organizations need to ensure that their actions reflect what at is distinctive, central and enduring about the organization's identity to strengthen employees' identification. Senior management are therefore increasingly faced with the challenge to clearly define and communicate the brand values internally, to encourage employee identification with the corporate identity and enhance commitment, enthusiasm and consistent staff behavior in delivering the core values and organizational objectives.'

Even if the norms and values based perspective also relies on internal brand communication, other 'tools' are often suggested in order to further the employee's identification with the brand. Ind in his book 'Living the brand' (2001), for instance, builds extensively on the case of the outdoor clothing company, Patagonia (2001:3):

'Patagonia is a standard bearer for an 'employee-centric' approach that stresses the value of engaging people with the organization they work for and stimulate them to live the brand.'

According to Ind, the 'stimulation' to live the Patagonia brand is based on the employees' identification with the company's identity and values, which are based on protecting the environment and acting in an ethical and responsible fashion. But this identification also builds on storytelling, as in when the employees tell about their experiences with the products as well about the customers' experiences. The underlying premise of the norms and values based perspective is that the company, by having clearly stated and strong values, can promote further aspects of living the brand, such as accountability and authenticity.

Other 'tools' for building employee's identification with brand values are events and sponsorships. For instance, Kunde (2000:89-90) suggests that the Nike company makes use of events to build 'brand religion' also among employees:

'Nike is to a large extent controlled by the big sports events where the stars present the products. All Nike's outlets are sports shops or in-store departments, where the shop assistants are young, sports oriented people who always wear the same shoes that the sports gods are currently wearing (...) It's crucial that the winner ideology is not only communicated externally as brand religion, but is also firmly rooted in the organization as a corporate religion. Philip Knight [the Nike CEO] has created a remarkable and robust business culture based on Nike as a winner religion. Connected to the stars via sponsorships, their commitment to being at the forefront of development is clearly understood (...) Sponsorships are therefore the external information carrier of brand religion, at the same time creating and communicating an internal corporate religion.'

In Kunde's example, norms and values sustain living the brand among employees in two ways. First, employee identification with the brand is supported by the strong corporate culture in the organization. This culture-based identification, is reinforced through events with and sponsorships of 'sports gods,' which serve both to build the brand's image among consumers and also foster identification among employees. Clearly, Nike steps out of the sphere of the company into a wider public sphere in order to build internal brand identification. It can be argued that this approach to fostering living the brand among employees also requires that their relationship with the brand become less private and more public. The 'corporate religion' in Nike and Patagonia demands that employees' attitudes and behavior at work as well as their entire lifestyle must be compatible with the brand values in order for them to 'be the brand' (Ind, 2001).

When it comes to the issue of control, it is clear that the norms and values based perspective is less concerned with direct control than the marketing and communication based perspective. Control, however, can also take the form of normative control, where management attempts to influence and direct employee's actions by controlling the underlying experiences, thoughts, and feelings that influence behavior (Kunda, 1992). It is fairly clear that a brand culture such as the one found in the Nike Company, creates a strong, normative pressure on employees to conform to the brand values.

The following section provides an example from practice of the norms and values based approach to living the brand.

Living the Brand in LEGO Group: Implementing Brand Values through a Brand Champion

LEGO as a company holds strong values that, in many ways, have been fairly constant since the company's founding in 1932. The LEGO name itself is derived from the words 'Leg Godt' which means 'good play' or 'play well' in Danish and reflects the founder Ole Kirk Kristiansen's focus on developing toys that were of good quality. Later, the LEGO name became synonymous with construction toys that stimulated learning and child development mainly because of the launch of the famous LEGO brick. Thus, the LEGO values developed from good play into creativity and learning (Gjøls-Andersen, 2001). Consequently, the LEGO Group's culture and organizational identity are closely linked to the values and LEGO product 'characteristics' by various generations of company owners.

When the LEGO Group set up the Strategic Business Unit LEGO Media International in 1996, it constituted something of a cultural revolution in the organization. The objective of LEGO Media was to develop and market computer games and other media products for children. As a result of this focus, LEGO Media was operating in a business area that was completely new to the LEGO Group. Furthermore, LEGO Media was also geographically separated from the LEGO Group headquarters in Billund, Denmark; instead, it was placed in London. Among the reasons for the London location was the availability of talent from the electronic media business. LEGO Media emerged as culturally different from headquarters in Denmark. First of all, the average age of employees was young (the managing director was 32 in 1997). Second, the electronic media business operates with much shorter product development cycles than the traditional toy market. In terms of investment, electronic video game-titles involve a high risk of market failure, and therefore offer much less certainty than the investments LEGO were used to from the construction toy business.

Nevertheless, LEGO Group management made it a priority that the LEGO values should guide the marketing and branding as well as the development of LEGO Media products. To transfer the brand values, LEGO appointed a brand champion. This was a manager who had been with the company for a number of years and who was considered to have internalized the LEGO brand values. The plan, however, turned out to be a less than easy task. First, LEGO faced the problem that the new employees already held strong views about the LEGO brand values – those formed through their own images of the company and the product. This meant that clashes arose between the 'official' (i.e. LEGO Group headquarters') interpretation of the brand values (e.g. creativity and learning) and the interpretations among LEGO Media employees. In fact, the LEGO Media employees perceived that their interpretations of the LEGO brand values were more in line with the original meanings and intentions behind those values. This perception was further strengthened by the fact that the LEGO Media employees felt that they held a more accurate perception of the LEGO image held by young consumers compared to the perceived image at LEGO headquarters (Karmark, 2002).

The LEGO Group has spent significant resources in specifying its values in different 'principles' that characterize the company and the products. The paradoxical aspect of the LEGO example is that the norms and values based approach to living the brand involves the risk that culturally rooted brand values may end up being understood exclusively by employees who are very close to the origin of the values (e.g. headquarters). This implies that new organizational members find themselves excluded from the commonly held values in the organization. What may be worse for the organization, however, is that this also implies that brand values, as they are held by organizational members, are cut off from the perceptions held by external stakeholders such as consumers. The organization runs the risk of building a brand culture that is closed off to external influences and internal criticism to the extent that it ends up in narcissism and self-seduction (Hatch & Schultz, 2002; Christensen & Cheney, 2000).

Another paradoxical aspect of the norms and values based perspective is that, from this perspective, the accountability towards the brand is taken to be a result of strong brand values (e.g. Ind, 2001). Adherence to these values, however, may also be demanded of top management by the organizational members. Whereas living the brand models almost always assume that this accountability replaces direct managerial control and thereby concerns the non-managerial members, the LEGO examples show how accountability demands can also emerge from the bottom-up.

Hybrid Models: Integrating Internal Branding and Norms and Values

The previous sections have discussed the premises of the marketing and communications based perspective and the norms and values based perspective on living the brand. Case-examples from Nordea and the LEGO Group demonstrated how these perspectives are applied in practice, and these examples also pointed out a number of limitations for the employees' role as living brands. Other companies, however, also use living the brand approaches that are hybrids between the two perspectives. In these hybrid-models, attempts to get employees to live the brand rely heavily on the cultural heritage and norms in the organization. This culturally based approach, however, is backed up by an equally strong communications and direct control based approach to implementing living the brand among employees.

The following sections discuss examples of the hybrid living the brand model.

Novo Nordisk: The 'Brand Police' Model

The pharmaceuticals company Novo Nordisk has defined its brand proposition as 'Defeating Diabetes.' The brand is also linked to a number of values contained in 'The Novo Nordisk Way of Life' (NNWOL). To ensure that the NNWOL is practiced by the various units of Novo Nordisk around the world, the company management has established a sort of travelling values-control corps called facilitators. These facilitators, operating within a predefined time schedule, pays visits to the departments and business units to monitor that the company and brand values are being implemented (Schultz, Hatch, Rubin & Andersen, 2004).

The Novo Nordisk values were communicated through a campaign called 'Being There', which was used in both an internal and external branding capacity. However, Novo Nordisk also went beyond a communications-based implementation and defined a number of actions that could translate into the 'Being there' values. For instance, the company introduced a policy whereby the employees are required

117

to spend at least one day a year with a diabetes patient. The goal of this policy is for employees to gain a first-hand understanding of what it means to be diabetic and get ideas about how to further improve the patients' lives.

The Novo Nordisk example suggests a hybrid-model approach to living the brand because even though the company has strong and well-defined values, the employees' potential for identifying with the brand is restricted by the management-driven definition of what the brand values entail, such as spending a day with a diabetic patient. This 'way of life' as sanctioned by management is not only communicated to employees through the charter, etc. but is also 'policed' by the facilitators who are assigned the task of ensuring that the employees live by the values. This approach might avoid an employee's uncertainty about the exact meaning of the brand values. On the other hand, the free and easy identification with the brand based on congruence between the employees' personal identity and organizational identity as foreseen by the norms and values based perspective may very likely be jeopardized by the direct-control approach Novo Nordisk uses through the facilitators.

Bang & Olufsen: Discovered Values vs. Invented Values

The audio-visuals company, Bang & Olufsen, is another example of a company that applied a hybrid-model to living the brand in connection with a corporate branding process. The starting point for defining Bang & Olufsen's brand values was the company's culture and historically-based identity as a producer of high quality products with a bauhaus-rooted design tradition. The idea was that the values were to be (re-)discovered in the company's culture and identity rather than 'invented' or thought up anew by identity consultants. Accordingly, a number of workshops were conducted among the company's employees. The purpose of these was to 'tap into' the collective definition of 'who we are as an organization' based on the company's culture, history, and product development (Ravassi & Schultz, 2005).

According to Christensen & Cheney (2000:257-258), however, in the end it was the company's management, with the help of consultants, who came up with the final definition of the values: Excellence, Synthesis, and Poetry:

'Using philosophers and artists to articulate and present the company's new values of excellence, synthesis, and poetry to staff members, Bang & Olufsen emphasizes that, whereas other organization's simply invent values, Bang & Olufsen has found these values in the organization's own culture (...) It is ironic that so many organizations still issue in a controlled and top-down manner messages that are expected to be 'owned' by all segments of the company's membership.'

In many ways Bang & Olufsen is an example of a company that, at least in the value-definition process, sought to formulate values that were close to the employees' perceptions of the company identity and the brand, and under these circumstances, the potential for the employees' to identify with the brand and to live the brand appears to have been present. However, the example also shows that the ideal norms- and values-based approach, with its emphasis on commonly held values, accountability, and total employee identification, is somewhat illusionary. As Christensen and Cheney point out, many companies simply consider their identity and brand to be too valuable to leave to the employees to interpret. This may be an overly critical perspective, but it is clear that living the brand as it is imagined in the literature, particularly under the norms and values based perspective, remains something of an ideal rather than a reality found in practice.

Based on the 'lessons learned' from the discussion of living the brand in the litterature and practice, the next sections raises three main issues. These issues should be considered if living the brand is to achieve its full potential of becoming a force for coherence and integration in the organization.

Issue # 1: Job Function & Hierarchy

First, it is clear that the marketing and communications based perspective and the norms and values based perspective place different types of demands on the employees in their roles as living brands. As a starting point, the marketing and communications perspective seems more suited to a more routine-based job. McDonald's is an example of a company where there is a fit between the living by the brand approach (as specified in manuals and brand books) and the more or less routine type job functions that the employees perform. This might reflect a realization that in the company that has given low-pay and high-turnover jobs its name i.e. McJobs, expectations that employees will 'live and breathe' the brand will go unrealized. McDonald's therefore can not rely either on employee identification with the brand or on accountability based on norms and values to turn employees into living brands. On the other hand, Klein (2000), pointing to a darker side of brand identification, mentions that other food retail-chains such as Starbucks have succeeded in convincing employees that their job is less a job and more of a lifestyle represented by the brand values. Klein also claims that this enables such brands to pay employees a minimum wage and offer less than optimal working conditions.

Conversely, it can be expected that a high level of brand identification is easier to achieve among employees in job functions where there is a greater autonomy in expressing the brand values. The design manager at Bang & Olufsen, for instance, will more easily identify with the values of Excellence, Synthesis, and Poetry because he or she has the potential to contribute decisions about how these values will be made tangible in the products. In contrast, manual workers at the production lines in Struer, Denmark (where Bang & Olufsen is located) will have little influence on how the brand values are expressed.

An additional and related point is that some types of organizations and companies are more culturally suited to a norms and values based approach to living the brand across most or all hierarchical levels. In companies that have a long history of being committed to certain values and which may still be owned by the founding family, there seems to be a higher degree of probability that norms and values can promote a sense among employee that they act as living brands. Shipping company AP Møller© and pharmaceuticals/personal products company Johnson & Johnson are examples of companies where the norms and brand values appear to permeate the whole company and support a sense of 'being the brand' among employees (Collins & Porras, 1994). The same may be true for start-up companies where a weak sense of hierarchy is built into the organizational culture. The point to be made here is that one of the reasons why many living the brand programs fail correlates with the 'one size fits all' approach that seems to be prevalent in the literature and in practice. For instance, a strongly norms-and values-based company such as Patagonia© is held up as an example where everyone from the receptionist to the managing director act as living brands. However, in many other companies, this would constitute a 'brand utopia' rather than reality. Most companies have to distinguish between those employees who hold positions and functions that will enable them to identify strongly with the brand (such as employees who are close to or part of the brand vision) and those employees who are less likely to be affected by the brand vision and values. With the latter employees, a manual-based approach may be a more effective way of spreading the brand message.

Issue # 2: Commitment & Loyalty

Most living the brand models, whether marketing and communications based or norms and values based, aim to achieve a deeply rooted commitment and loyalty to the brand among employees. However, we might ask if this is a realistic or even desirable outcome for companies and brands? For instance, Christensen & Cheney (2000) suggest that one of the reasons that living the brand campaigns do not have the desired effect in organizations is that employees are simply not as involved in the identity and brand values in the organization as top management likes to think. LEGO Group discovered this when an employee satisfaction survey was conducted in the late 1990s. Here top management was surprised to find that employees expressed a lack of awareness concerning the strategic direction and vision of the company. Top management, on its part, was certain that in the LEGO Group there was an 'intuitive' understanding of the 'LEGO spirit' that was the foundation for the LEGO brand values (Karmark, 2002). Christensen and Cheney take a more critical perspective. They suggest that employees are not as engaged in the brand values as management likes to think because the values are simply not as compelling or interesting to the employees as management imagines. In fact, because of a narcissistic involvement in their own identity and brand, companies are seducing themselves into believing that employees and other stakeholders are far more engaged in their organization than they actually are. At the very least, companies need to consider 'what's in it' for the employee to engage in the brand. There is a more or less theoretical notion that brand values are replacing declining religious and social values. Therefore companies imagine that brand values are fulfilling an essential need for employees (e.g. Ind, 2001). This is not, however, something that companies can automatically rely on if living the brand programs are to create coherence both within the organization and outwards toward external stakeholders.

Another point to be made is that deep engagement and loyalty to the brand may lead to over-identification with the brand and that kind of collective brand identification can lead to a collective blindness towards trends in the market or demands from stakeholders. In such situations, the brand values run the risk of becoming exclusive in the sense that signals from external stakeholders or internal criticism of the execution of the brand values are ignored or silenced by the organization's members. Again, this can lead to a lack of dynamics in the brand development and may create an 'arrogant bastard' culture in the organization, where brand values are decoupled from the demands and wants of external stakeholders (Hatch & Schultz, 2002). Another kind of problem can result from high intensity attempts of the organization to engage employees and other stakeholders in the brand. In this case, employees and other stakeholders will simply experience this intensity as 'brand claustrophobia,' feeling as though there is 'no escape' from the 'brand cocoon' (Klein, 2000).

Finally, there is a real risk that that employees will actively resist living the brand campaigns. In 1997, the food ingredients and sugar company Danisco ran a campaign to profile Danisco as an ethical company. Under the headline, 'I also have to be able to look my children in the eyes' the ad campaign featured Danisco employees who discussed how they represented the Danisco brand in an ethical way both on the job and in their lives in general. The campaign included employees' statements that they should be able to justify the way in which they and Danisco conducted themselves also to their children (Mandag Morgen, 1997). Such campaigns may effectively backfire as they suggest to the employees that living the brand involves the employees' entire existence including their personal (family) lives. In that sense, the employees are cast as brand ambassadors in a way which evokes the true meaning of the ambassador metaphor. While it can be expected that a real ambassador is required to represent his or her country 'brand' 24 hours a day, seven days a week, this cannot be realistically expected by most employees in a company such as Danisco. Many may simply consider it unethical for companies to appropriate employees' entire existence in their efforts to create coherent brand behavior (e.g. Klein, 2000). And such attempts to control the employees' personal identity can lead to active resistance from the employees[1] (Alvesson & Wilmott, 2003).

---

[1] In the Danisco example, however, while the company was criticized for the campaign, it did raise a discussion among Danisco employees on the limits for acceptable behavior on and off the job.

Issue # 3: Brand Life

As the final issue to be discussed in this chapter, we may (re-) raise the question of what it means to live a brand or claim that the brand has a life. One of the main purposes of this chapter has been to demonstrate that the terms and constructs relating to living the brand are often used in an unreflective manner, both in the literature and in practice. The brand is anthropomorphized and linked to the employee through dimensions such as commitment, involvement, passion, and 'living and breathing the brand' without any real attempts to relate it to what it means to be alive. For instance, as Paustian (2003) suggests, life is experience-based. In other words, life is linked to events and to the experiences that we as humans gain through these events. In contrast, living the brand models are often not linked to events in the organization. Rather, the models are based on communication of brand values or on the more normative implementation of brand values that are often formulated by top management and their advisors. Brands such as Virgin and Harley-Davidson, however, are examples of companies where the brand values are often experienced by the employees. In Harley-Davidson, employees go on bike runs with fan clubs and in Virgin, employees experience how the owner of the company stages large (media) events that express the brand's values (such as launching a hot air balloon with the inscription 'BA can't get it up' to express Virgin's brand position 'Up against the fat cats'). In such companies, brands are more likely to be considered alive by employees and therefore such brands are also more likely to get employees to 'live into' them.

Another aspect of experiences as a foundation for life is that experiences are not always good or positive. We use expressions such as 'what does not kill you makes you stronger' or 'live and learn' to say that bad or unpleasant experiences are part of life. In relation to brands, however, life-experiences are seen as singularly good or positive (passion, commitment, etc). In order for living the brand models and practice to go beyond this tendency, we must be open to including the negative or critical perspectives on the brand into the employees' life with the brand. In the LEGO Media example for instance, new employees held strong views that the LEGO brand held a vast and unrealized potential that required a different execution of the brand. In accordance with most living the brand models, this view was dismissed as irrelevant or even disloyal, which led to considerable friction between LEGO Media and the LEGO Group headquarters.

Instead, such internal disagreement can be used to bring the brand to life through the dynamics of different views on what the brand is and how it can evolve.

Implications for Corporate Branding

As a final point, we might ask about the consequences of the issues raised in this chapter for corporate branding of the living the brand. If we take as the starting point the corporate brand model introduced here by Schultz in Chapter 2, which views corporate branding as relations between the organization's vision, culture, and image, then the role of the employee falls within the culture dimension of the model. A living the brand approach to corporate branding, where the employee is seen as a 'co-creator' of the brand, therefore would take its starting point in the organizational culture. The question then becomes how to execute the corporate branding processes in such a way that the employees are given a real part in establishing the ways the brand is to be experienced and expressed in the organization. From the examples discussed in this chapter, it is clear that this is not an easy task for organizations. Some organizations, such as the LEGO Group, seem to think that their values are so embedded in the organization that they can be taken for granted. Furthermore, the VCI-model for corporate branding raises the diagnostic question of whether 'your vision informs all your subcultures' (Hatch & Schultz, 2001). This model, however, requires an acknowledgement that the vision may be understood differently by various groups in the organization, which again requires that the brand values are open for discussion and not seen as taken for granted. The Nordea and Bang & Olufsen examples showed that involving employees in the branding process requires a true commitment in the organization to taking the organizational culture as the foundation for the branding process. In both Nordea and Bang & Olufsen, the espoused intentions were to engage and involve the employees in the branding process, but in both cases the employee involvement was not realized. Consequently, from a living the brand perspective, we might turn around the question raised in the VCI-model and ask if all your subcultures inspire your vision?

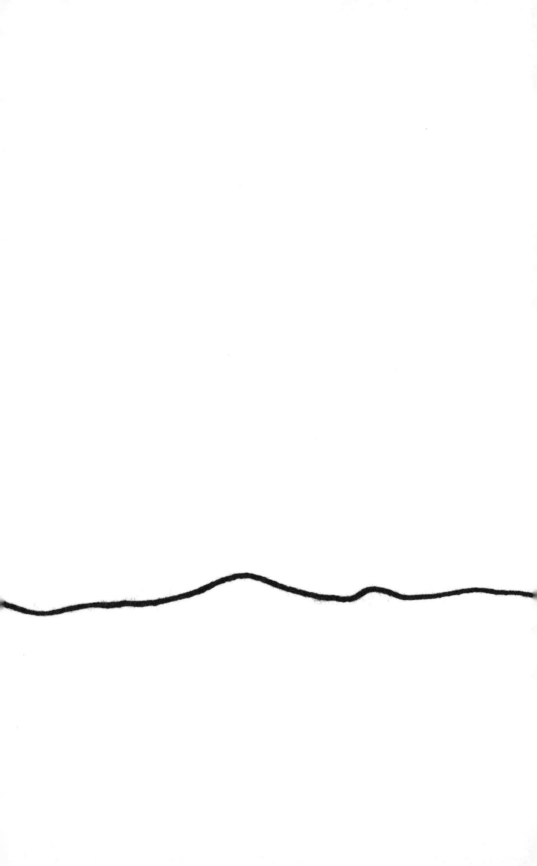

CHAPTER 6

THE LIMITS OF CORPORATE BRANDING:

The Application of Branding to Non-Profit Organizations and Places

Fabian F. Csaba

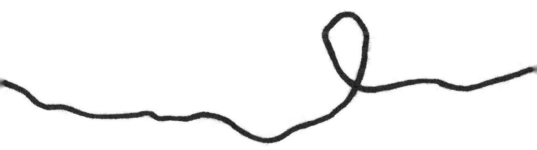

In principle, corporate branding applies to other types of organizations or phenomena than just corporations. Exploring work on the branding of nonprofit organizations and nations, regions and cities, this chapter assesses the influence of corporate branding outside the commercial realm. The chapter shows how and why branding principles and techniques have spread to other domains, and traces the ways in which corporate branding is appropriated and inevitably transformed once it is transplanted from its original domain.

Just a couple of decades ago, branding was a fairly insignificant topic in business studies and even a secondary concern in marketing, subsumed under product policy on par with labeling and packaging. Much has changed since then. Branding has been pronounced the cornerstone of marketing (Aaker, 1996) and has been addressed and embraced extensively across and beyond management studies (Van Ham, 2001; Balmer & Gray, 2003). Many business leaders have come to see brands as their company's primary asset, and to see brand management as a main priority. No longer bound by ties to tangible products, branding has been applied to entities ranging from individuals (Peters, 1997; Montoya, 2003) to nations (Papadopoulos & Heslop, 2002; Olins, 2002). As the discourse and practice of branding has proliferated, its virtues have been extolled and vices castigated widely in public debate around the world (Klein, 2000; Anholt, 2003).

Corporate branding represents an expansion and transformation of branding. It moves branding beyond products, beyond the marketing department and beyond the marketing discipline. So an inquiry into corporate branding raises questions about the limits and limitations of branding – about which organizations branding can be applied to. To date, corporate branding has dealt mainly with how branding should be transformed when it is applied to the organization rather than its products. But can branding principles be applied to all types of organizations? And when they are, do they follow the precepts of corporate branding?

The 'corporate' in corporate branding refers to an integrated, organization-wide scope, not the branding of business corporations. Balmer and Gray (2003) point out that corporate branding is not the same as 'company branding' – a term which in fact was used before corporate branding became the standard term. For, as they argue, managing branding at the corporate-level may involve dealing with other corporate entities than corporations as such. They cite as examples, subsidiaries, groups and networks of companies. But they also suggest that corporate branding may deal with countries, regions and cities. In practice, the ideas and techniques of branding and corporate branding have long found their way outside the traditional business context. Nonetheless, it is evident that the principles of branding and corporate branding originate from the analysis of the context and practices of commercial organizations. Are these methods and techniques readily applicable to organizations in the nonprofit sector? Do they lend themselves to complex entities such as cities and countries?

In exploring these questions, this chapter reconsiders the limits of corporate branding, and traces the ways in which corporate branding is appropriated and inevitably transformed once it is transplanted from its original domain. The aim is not only to investigate the uses of branding outside the corporate realm, but also to reconsider the principles and application of corporate branding in general. First, we will link the proliferation of branding to the expansionary ambitions of the marketing discipline.

The Broadening of the Branding Concept

Consideration of the expansion of branding echoes a long-standing debate within the marketing discipline known as 'the broadening of marketing'. A brief recapitulation of this debate will provide a backdrop for our consideration of branding's domain. From the late 60s, scholars started debating how widely marketing could be applied. The debates culminated in the early 1970s, but have remained important for the discipline's self-image. Most influential figures in the field supported the idea of a broad perspective, while only a few voices dissented. This meant that marketing, in the eyes of the discipline's main authorities, at least, had ceased being essentially a business subject dealing with market transactions. Other conceptions of marketing replaced the traditional view. In the moderate conception, marketing was seen as relevant for all organizations with customers, and for all types of organization-client transactions. But in a more radical formulation, marketing became a generic concept appropriate for all organizations and their relations, not only with customers, but with all their publics. Marketing, it was argued, applied to any social unit seeking to exchange values with other social units, not only economic and utilitarian values, but also symbolic—i.e. social and psychological values (Graham, 1993; Brown, 1995).

What were the motives behind the efforts to expand the scope and authority of the discipline? Brown (1995) likens the impulse to spread the marketing concept beyond the business realm to both evangelism and market development. 'Marketing evangelism' expresses a strong conviction about the virtues of the discipline, but also a sort of 'discursive imperialism' – a propensity to impose the marketing concept indiscriminately and frame the world in marketing terms. This is particularly evident in Kotler and Levy's famous pronouncement:

'The choice facing those who manage non-business organizations is not whether to market or not market, for no organization can avoid marketing. The choice is whether to do it well or poorly.' (Kotler & Levy, 1969:15).

Here we also sense that part of the driving force behind spreading the techniques and principles of marketing was to transfer professional standards and efficient, rational tools practiced successfully in business to struggling non-business enterprises. While this might have been motivated by market development – selling marketing in a new nonprofit market – it no doubt also represents a search for a higher purpose for the discipline. Harnessing commercial principles for the advancement of human welfare, rather than (solely) for economic gain, was a noble cause that could satisfy the discipline's desire for moral and social legitimacy. Critics of marketing, however, are deeply suspicious of the expansion of the discipline's commercial principles to cultural, religious, charitable and government organizations. Conservative critics see the influx of marketing into the nonprofit realm as an erosion of its higher values and public ideals by a crass, debasing, calculative commercialism. In a Marxist analysis, the spread of managerial principles represents commodification and illustrates a further advancement of the capitalist logic and the weakening of civil society and democracy.

But despite the general enthusiasm for its expansion, doubts about the broadening of the marketing concept were also expressed within the field (Graham, 1993). It was argued that when a discipline extends its scope to cover a range of diverse organizations, contexts and social processes, it will almost inevitably lose focus, precision and explanatory force. It will tend to apply broad, general concepts to whatever subject matter is under consideration, and ignore particularities of the situations and organizations it seeks to analyze. In spreading itself too thin, it risks losing its identity as a theoretical field.

Corporate branding departs from the marketing approach and its conception of branding in important ways. As Schultz argues in Chapter 2, corporate branding draws on principles and ideas from multiple fields, not only marketing. Hence, a more complete analysis of applications of the principles of corporate branding to nonprofit organizations and places would also have to trace the influence of strategic management, visual identity, organizational design, or corporate communications outside the corporate realm. This is beyond the scope of the present chapter. However, the debates over the 'broadening of the marketing concept' are interesting as they foreshadow issues faced in corporate branding.

This chapter will examine the application of branding in two fields, nonprofit organizations (and non-government organizations) and places. The nonprofit sector is defined in opposition to the private, for-profit sector. This raises questions about whether managerial principles developed to assist in generating profits are suitable for organizations driven by other motives. Does the adoption of brand management, corporate or not, go against the values or identity of being a nonprofit organization, or is there congruity between management and 'non-profitness'? Peter Drucker (1989) has argued that nonprofit organizations – lacking the discipline of the bottom-line – need management even more than business organizations do. Our inquiry includes non-government organizations, a category that at least nominally is defined against the public sector, not the private. We will not analyze in detail the influx of branding in the public sector. However, public or quasi-public agencies are usually key players in the associations of interests behind initiatives to brand places, which almost always rely on substantial public funding. Non-profit and business interests also are involved in the branding of places, making it a showcase of how organizations in different sectors meet and collaborate on branding projects. It also raises questions about the authority to represent territory and the links between (corporate) brand identity and national and regional identity. My investigation of branding non-profits and places in no way claims to be a comprehensive survey. The aim is to explore broader structural and conceptual issues, rather than detail specific practices. The inquiry seeks to answer the question of why branding has expanded beyond the corporate realm and how it is applied, first in the nonprofit (NPO) and non-government (NGO) realm, and then in the branding of places.

The Branding of Nonprofit Organizations

Interest in the branding of nonprofit organizations has surged in recent years (Wootliff & Deri, 2001; Hankinson, 2004). As their number and forms have proliferated, nonprofit organizations have become subject to growing attention and debate in academia and society over the past decades. Just like brands! And many nonprofit organizations have been exploring brand management as a tool for meeting the challenges of securing funding and advancing their causes. While the use of promotional techniques and visual identity programs is not new to the sector, there is evidence that nonprofits have started to embrace branding more fully, seeing themselves as brands and adopting more formal and comprehensive approaches to branding (Hankinson 2004; Mikkelsen & Schwartenbach 2004).

As DiMaggio and Anheiner (1990) point out, nonprofit organizations cannot be treated as a well-defined and homogeneous category. It is, in fact, difficult to establish any clear-cut generic differences between for profit and nonprofits, not least because of the wide variety of nonprofit organizations. 'Nonprofitness', they suggest, 'has no single transhistorical or transnational meaning; non-profit sector functions, origins, and behavior reflect specific legal definitions, cultural inheritances and state policies in different national societies' (1990, p.137). The penetration, uses and influence of branding in the nonprofit sector must be investigated with this caution in mind.

To explain the influx of branding into the nonprofit sector, we must first look at the changing relationships between the government, nonprofit organizations and the private, for-profit sector. These sectors are nominally defined against each other, which suggests difference, rivalry and competition. But the relationships may as well reflect collaboration, co-dependence, complementarity, mutual influence and blurred boundaries. Over time, the division of labor between the sectors has altered, and the power, size and influence of each sector has changed. In recent decades, neo-liberal political ideals, the demise of communism and effects of globalization have put pressure on the public sector and advanced market principles and for-profit enterprises. This 'marketization' has affected nonprofits in contradictory ways. Many nonprofits have suffered from declining government support and faced growing demands for accountability and efficiency in their performance. To compensate for the decline in government funding, many nonprofits have been forced to rely more on private and corporate support. But the task for nonprofits of promoting themselves and their causes has been complicated by the growing competition for public attention. They have had to compete not only against a growing number of other nonprofits, but also against professional commercial enterprises and public authorities, in an evermore overcrowded and fragmented media landscape. On the other hand, some nonprofits have found new opportunities in filling the role of declining public institutions, sometimes in competition against for-profit enterprises. Other nonprofits have been feeding off the growing resentment towards the perceived excessive corporate power or distrust of government, and have gained attention and support as champions of civic ideals.

Summing up, the restructuring of relations between the three sectors has put pressure on nonprofits to become more visible, efficient and accountable. Generally, government support has declined and now comes with more strings attached. Nonprofits increasingly need to recruit members, raise their public profile and document high standards, even to simply retain government subsidies. To do this they need to attract media coverage and public attention in competition with a growing number of other nonprofits and highly professional, commercial enterprises. Being in the public eye, in turn, makes nonprofits subject to media and public scrutiny, which places heavy demands on the ability of the organization to justify its causes and deliver on its promises. The capability of organizations to account for their raison d'être and performance is also vital in attracting, retaining, and meeting the expectations of members, volunteers and donors. Rather than relying solely on traditional sources of support, many nonprofits have courted support from corporations. Corporate partnerships can bring funds, awareness, professional expertise, and sometimes credibility to nonprofits, but these advantages come at the risk of alienating members, donors or other stakeholders, and involve meeting a new set of demands.

Branding as a management technique is arguably particularly appealing for the nonprofit sector. In 1998, Interbrand, one of the world's premier brand consultancies, established an arm to assist nonprofits in branding themselves. On this occasion, the chairman of the Interbrand Foundation, Alvin Schlecter, argued that branding is more critical for nonprofits than for corporate clients:

'They're competing for the attention of the public; they need to have their missions understood, to attract volunteers, to motivate staff, to get contributions. Sometimes it is hard to focus and remember who they are. [Branding] will portray their reason for being in an arresting way'. (Beardi, 1999:120).

As we discussed earlier, marketing thought entered the nonprofit realm long ago. Marketing practices are now widely accepted in the sector, and nonprofits have developed considerable skills in analyzing and targeting donors, employing fundraising tactics and communicating about their causes (Hyojin, 2002). Consequently, branding does not represent an entirely new approach for most nonprofits. In fact, it can be difficult to tell where marketing ends and branding begins – and much discourse on the branding of nonprofits looks like marketing under a different label. A survey in the mid-1990s suggested that NGOs tended to subsume brand development under direct marketing and cause-related publicity. However, indications are that branding is now being embraced more wholeheartedly (Hankinson, 2004:84). Whether fully distinct from marketing or not, brand management in the nonprofit sector is associated with certain key principles and objectives. Branding first and foremost implies a greater emphasis on differentiating the organization from other nonprofits and establishing a unique position in the minds of donors and other stakeholders. Under conditions where most nonprofits are using marketing, competition intensifies and imitation of successful promotional tactics increases. The development of a distinct brand position promises a way to stand out and attract more support and loyalty. Branding nonprofits usually involves a change of focus from individual campaigns and fundraising drives, to a concerted effort to establish what the organization stands for. As Interbrand's Schlecter suggested, this involves a clear articulation of the mission and values of the organization. It also means conveying the responsibility and capabilities of the organization, and doing so consistently over time and across media and stakeholder audiences. While campaigns and drives remain important in mobilizing public attention and support for causes, building a nonprofit brand is instrumental in moving from transactional donations to relationship building. The brand plays a role in the formation of bonds between nonprofit organizations and donors, volunteers and members.

Once established, the brand can become an asset for the nonprofit which can be leveraged to generate income or benefit the organization in other ways. There are different ways to leverage the brand. Nonprofits may sell branded merchandise or use the brand to support their own for-profit units that support them. They may also license their brand symbols or properties to commercial enterprises and collect licensing fees. Collaboration between nonprofits and companies can take on a variety of forms. Corporate sponsorships can bring the nonprofit funds, media exposure or company expertise (for instance in branding). Collaborating with for-profit companies offering pro-bono work, professional services or funding is one option for nonprofits. The relationships are not necessarily asymmetric and philanthropic. In fact nonprofits possess assets that can be of value to corporate partners. Millar, Choi and Chen (2004) discuss how multinational corporations can benefit from the knowledge of local customs, social capital and knowledge network of NGOs. In a survey of thought leaders in Europe, USA and Australia, Woodliff and Deri (2001) found that NGOs were significantly more trusted overall than business, government and media on issues relating to the environment, health and social policy. The picture was more in favor of business and less of government in the US, but even here NGOs wield significant influence. So while nonprofits lack economic muscle, they often have moral force and social legitimacy in society. Corporations can benefit from forming alliances with NGOs, which might take the form co-branding arrangements in which the nonprofit and company form partnerships for mutual branding.

Nonprofits also seem to have acknowledged that branding has internal implications for their organizations. In a recent study, Hankinson (2004) showed that senior managers in UK charities were becoming more acceptant towards internal branding, although many had reservations regarding the use of branding terminology (which they associated with the for-profit context and external communications). Branding or re-branding enabled nonprofits to clarify the values and sense of purpose of the organization and to communicate its message in simple terms. Clear articulation of the brand was seen to provide transparency, which in turn fostered a strong sense of loyalty and identification with the organization's values among members. Managers also found that the branding process could bring people together behind a common purpose, motivate them and serve as a catalyst for change. Finally, managers saw branding as part of an inevitable and welcome modernization and professionalization of the nonprofit sector.

Looking at the explanations and arguments for branding, we might regard the adoption of brand management techniques in the nonprofit sector as not only a necessary adjustment to environmental change, but also an approach with great potential for the sector. However, there are also limitations and problems in the application of branding to nonprofit organizations. The first reservation about branding is that it is seen as 'too commercial' in the eyes of external as well as internal stakeholders. We noted with DiMaggio and Anheiner that it is difficult to pin down exactly what 'nonprofitness' represents. But if the nonprofit category has any meaning, the denial of profit motives and commercial exchange must be part of what defines nonprofit organizations. Since the concept of branding is associated with commercial exchange and values, tensions exist between brand management and the ideals of altruism, voluntarism, democracy, and citizen and grass root action that are strong elements in the heritage, identity and culture of most nonprofit organizations. Most studies of the application of branding in the nonprofit sector address the various manifestations of these tensions (Ritchie, Swami & Weinberg 1999, Hankinson, 2002; Mikkelsen & Schwartenbach, 2004). Internally, prejudices against branding can lead to resistance to branding initiatives and processes. This means that branding projects, especially if they extend beyond fundraising and external communications, require concerted internal justification to win support. Arguments over branding may in some cases be fruitful and constructive, in other cases divisive and debilitating for the organization. Hankinson (2004:92) discusses a phenomenon she refers to as 'we do not call it the brand but it is there'. This phenomenon suggests unwillingness among senior managers in less brand-oriented organizations to apply the term 'brand', especially to issues regarding internal management of the organization. Hankinson argues that these organizations still practice internal branding, but conceptualize it in terms such as mission, values and ethos, rather than branding. In other organizations, reservations about branding are overcome by an ends-justify-the-means attitude, or the idea of harnessing commercial techniques for higher purposes. But the issue is not only about the image of branding as 'too commercial'. Reorienting nonprofits towards branding and brand management will often involve shifts in power and priorities. When a nonprofit embarks on implementing a formal branding strategy, it means giving more authority to branding experts inside or outside the organization. The process of articulating and aligning the organization behind brand values, while leading to clarity, consistency and a sense of purpose, may also centralize power and disenfranchise and alienate members. Reliance on the professional resources of branding agencies and funds from corporate partners can lead to a significant loss of control and autonomy and put the organization's reputation and relationships with other stakeholder at risk.

For nonprofits, especially charitable organizations, branding implies a strategy of investment in communication and public awareness. The aim is, of course, to attract further support and generate additional donations, enabling the organization to help its cause or beneficiaries more. However, brand building requires resources, and in the short run this will mean the diversion of scarce resources from beneficiaries to branding. If the branding effort succeeds, the investment will have been justified for the individual organization. If the collective branding efforts of nonprofits succeed in generating higher net donations and draw more public attention to charitable causes, we might argue that branding has a positive impact overall. However, if branding turns nonprofit organizations into aggressive rivals, competing on branding skills and resources, and inflating media and communication costs, the adoption of branding in the sector may not prove beneficial for the causes, beneficiaries and general legitimacy of nonprofits in the long run. Another risk, well known to large corporations, is that high visibility and exposure can lead to intense scrutiny and make the brand vulnerable to criticism. If the nonprofit has problems living up to the standards and performance expectations created by branding, or forms alliances with corporate partners that come under fire, the reputation of the organization can suffer great damage.

Finally, evidence suggests that branding is not equally effective in managing all of a nonprofit's stakeholder relationships. In a survey of the brand orientation of the UK's 500 top charities, Hankinson (2001) found that fundraising managers believed branding to be especially beneficial in fundraising, raising awareness of the organization, educating the public in the charity's aims and values, and attracting corporate sponsorships or funding. However, few believed branding to be effective in influencing the political process, securing government funding or changing public opinion. Perhaps more importantly, branding was not believed to be effective in promoting charities as moral leaders in society.

Despite the problems involved in applying branding in the nonprofit sector, it is difficult to see how nonprofits can avoid branding, or at least the ideas and techniques we associate with branding. Consequently, the question is not *whether* nonprofits should apply branding but *how*. While NGOs can and arguably must engage in active brand management, they clearly need to observe and play by different rules than most for-profit companies do. Certain branding concepts and tools do not apply to nonprofits in the same way as they do in the for-profit sector. Brand valuation, for instance, would be very difficult to extend to nonprofits. It is conceivable that nonprofits could estimate the value of their brand (leverage in generating funds through licensing, co-branding, and selling for-profit departments), but the very act of calculating the economic value of their brand could undermine the organization's nonprofit status, practically and morally, if not legally.

Nonprofits face different challenges in branding to commercial enterprises. In some ways, they are at a disadvantage, but in others they can draw on resources or pursue tactics which are not available to their for-profit counterparts. In terms of resources, nonprofits usually have far less funds available for investing in large scale branding programs or hiring professional brand management expertise. This is illustrated by the approach of the Interbrand Foundation. Realizing that many, especially smaller, nonprofits are unable to pay for Interbrand's services, the company donates it services and seeks corporate sponsors to cover the costs of implementing branding programs. As noted above, NGOs' lack of financial resources is partly compensated by their moral authority. But in order to maintain their legitimacy and integrity – both externally and internally – nonprofits need to manage their relationships with government and, especially, corporate partners with care. Of course, the same applies to companies which collaborate with NGOs. They need to avoid alienating stakeholders by making what they might see as irresponsible concessions to activists. Rather than seeking co-operative relationships, NGOs also have the strategic option of positioning themselves in opposition to corporations. By tapping into anti-corporate and anti-brand sentiments, they might attract public attention and the support of progressive citizens, media and political groups.

Simon Heap (2000) offers a typology of different approaches NGOs might take vis-à-vis companies. In Heap's scheme, Sharks and Killer Whales are polarizers, who do not hesitate to engage in attacks on companies. Sharks attack indiscriminately, while Killer Whales scrutinize the performance of companies and only attack those with a poor record, who are considered legitimate targets. Alternatively, Sea Lions and Dolphins are integrators, who seek cooperative relationships with corporate partners. Sea Lions collaborate with anyone, while Dolphins scrutinize the relative performance of companies and only form partnerships with those deemed appropriate. Each strategy has its strengths and challenges.

The limits of the integrative approach are still being explored and pushed. Nonprofits today offer private companies a range of opportunities for collaboration. Nonprofits still invite corporations to make the customary philanthropic investments and donations, but have moved to offering more 'quid pro quo' in terms of licensing, sponsorship, product promotion, co-branding, and employee involvement relationships. An example illustrating the development of NGO-company brand partnerships is a product promotion and co-branding collaboration between the Danish Red Cross and Danish mineral water company, Aqua d'Or (http://www.vandtilvand.dk;

http://www.aquador.dk; http://www1.drk.dk. Downloaded March 10 2005). The two organizations were brought together by a Red Cross fundraising team in a campaign to raise money to provide clean drinking water in the Third World. Aqua d'Or agreed to donate DKK 0.50 ($ 0.09, € 0.07) for each bottle of mineral water it sold during the 10-week campaign period. The fundraising campaign was supported by a daring, highly visible, advertising campaign. Appealing to a younger audience, it showed sensual images of two scantily clad, top Danish models (a man and a woman). In the TV version, the voiceover starts out by declaring that everybody knows that sex sells, and explains that this is why the models, Louise and Christian, have shed their clothes. Conceding that, 'maybe this a cheap trick', the speaker declares that if it can help more than a billion people without clean drinking water, '…it's OK with us!'. The voiceover, recorded by Danish-American actress, Connie Nielsen, concludes by explaining that viewers can help by drinking more water from Aqua d'Or. Members of the fundraising team, consisting of prominent figures from Danish business and the cultural scene, used their positions and connections to produce a campaign with a high level of professionalism and massive media exposure through pro bono work and substantial rebates (in buying advertising time/space etc.). Aqua d'Or had jumped at the opportunity offered by the Red Cross fundraiser. As an organization committed to corporate social responsibility, it has also donated its products to international aid agencies. In only a few years, the company gained a 50 per cent share of the Danish retail market for bottled water through aggressive, penetration pricing. However, in order to become profitable, the company had initiated an up-market repositioning of its brand. The strategy involved TV advertising and a higher price point to move closer to international brands like Nestlé and Evian. The Aqua d'Or/Red Cross campaign, with its reflexive argument and self-conscious commercial style, challenges conventions of how NGO's can communicate and engage in branding with corporate partners. The advertising campaign implies that humanitarian objectives justify the use of sex, celebrities, humor, sleek professionalism and sales appeals. The International Red Cross has a private sector strategy which includes ethical criteria and guiding principles for the organization's collaboration with business. These guidelines and ethical criteria stress that partnership should strengthen, but more importantly, in no way undermine, the capacity of the organization to carry out its activities worldwide in accordance with its mandate and principles. The collaboration with Aqua d'Or in Denmark complies with these principles, but highlights the practical difficulties of maintaining independence when engaging in branding collaborations. The Red Cross does not grant 'exclusivity' in partnerships, but to the extent that co-branding contributes to developing the brand of the corporate partner, ideals of impartiality and neutrality are difficult to maintain.

Polarizers exploit established brands in the opposite way. US-based animal rights organization, People for the Ethical Treatment of Animals (PETA), have not hesitated in targeting brands in their efforts to gain public attention for their campaigns and organization (http://www.peta.org; http://www.savethesheep.com. Downloaded on March 11, 2005). In a recent campaign to end perceived abuses in the Australian sheep industry, PETA turned its attention to Benetton to try to convince the company to stop using Australian wool. After unsuccessfully lobbying the company to change it practices, PETA engaged in an anti-branding campaign to put pressure on the company. This of course won PETA fame for its controversial use of social and political imagery and issues in building its brand. PETA used a full range of brand-based tactics in its campaign, attracting negative publicity by picketing at Benetton stores, encouraging a consumer boycott, enlisting celebrities (such as rock singer Chryssie Hynde), producing anti-Benetton advertisements (associating cruel practices with the brand), and establishing an anti-Benetton website (www.unitedcrueltyofbenetton.com), which imitated the brand imagery and slogan of the Italian company. Benetton responded by accusing the PETA activists of exploiting the prominence of the Benetton brand in an improper, self-serving and speculative manner (http://www.benetton.com. Downloaded on March 11, 2005.)

A collaborative approach requires the nonprofit to 'groom' itself as a branding partner for potential corporate collaborators, which involves playing the branding game by professional, corporate rules. Conversely, an adversary approach involves challenging and sometimes breaking the rules of the branding game, seeking to undermine corporate reputations through anti-branding tactics. Pursuing adversary approaches does not mean not engaging in branding, but it does imply breaking with orthodox brand managerial principles when necessary and exploiting whatever symbolic resources are available to the nonprofit organization.

The Branding of Places

'A national brand mightn't be necessary, but those who opt not to have one aren't going to get properly recognized. Countries now compete in a global economy against each other, and the unbranded may find themselves lost in all the clutter because those they try to influence don't know what they stand for.' Communications expert, Jack Yan (Cited in www.logolounge.com. Downloaded on January 6, 2005)

Over the past decades, branding has played a greater and greater role in the way places are perceived and shaped. This development can be taken as evidence of the dissemination of branding, but just as much as an effect of globalization. In the face of the widening, deepening and accelerating of global interconnectedness, the settled coherence and distinctiveness of places are being undermined. As places become integrated in a global economy, they compete against distant places to attract and retain businesses, jobs, capital, human capital and tourists. At the same time, places are becoming more alike as the same consumer products, technologies, business concepts and cultural styles become available everywhere. In this situation, places look for ways of justifying themselves, asserting a place in the world by claiming their distinctiveness, identity and uniqueness. Some have done so within the framework provided by branding.

Contemporary work on the branding of places appears under an array of headings, including nation branding (Anholt 2002), country branding (Papadopoulos & Heslop, 2002), city branding (Synghel, Speaks & Berci, 2002), place branding (Hankinson, 2004; placebrands.com), destination branding (Morgan, Pritchard & Pride 2002), and location branding (Hankinson, 2001). This conceptual sprawl suggests that we are dealing with a field characterized by inconsistent terminology and few common references, with multiple branding objectives and agendas, and different scopes. We might even question whether the diverse bodies of work on the branding of places forms a coherent field of inquiry. Much of the work addresses the branding of place from the perspective of a particular research tradition or professional field, and focuses on specific aspects and issues pertaining to that given field. So work in tourism management, for instance, deals with branding places as tourist destinations (e.g. Morgan, Pritchard & Pride, 2004) and contributions from urban planning address the redevelopment, gentrification and rebranding of city neighborhoods (e.g. Bennett & Savani, 2003). However, there are still good reasons to consider the branding of places as a whole. The different contributions all draw on and seek to apply concepts and models from branding. So although the branding principles applied and their applications differ, they all illustrate the extension of the branding concept. Another argument for treating work on branding of places as a more or less coherent field of inquiry is that an increasing number of theoretical contributions and branding projects deal with more than one perspective on the branding of places – some even develop general, interdisciplinary place-branding models (e.g. Anholt, 2002) and seek to build single umbrella place brands that cover and connect multiple aspects of branding particular places.

To understand the challenges of applying branding and corporate branding to places, it is necessary to outline the key dimensions and aspects of such branding. We might distinguish between two major dimensions, the geographical scope of place branding, which defines the branded entity, and the place branding perspective, which reflects the approach to branding and its objective and agenda.

Place branding can be applied to a whole range of spatial entities: Nations, transnational territories, regions, cities, urban districts, residential areas, industrial zones, theme parks or shopping areas. Specific issues exist at each level and we cannot assume that the challenges of place branding are the same for all types of spaces. Another matter is the relationship between branding efforts at different levels. Formal place branding initiatives have popped up at different levels at different times and usually without much coordination. This means that place branding programs might clash both with programs at the same level as well at with branding efforts at a higher and lower level. A city branding program, in other words, might compete against those of neighboring cities as well as those of the region and country it is located in. While the parties might see advantages in coordinating their efforts and joining forces, it is very difficult to enforce what one would call a clear overall brand architecture in brand management. The picture only gets more complicated when one considers the various perspectives on branding places and the different interests, aims and sectors they represent. We might distinguish between six perspectives or approaches to place branding:

- Promoting tourism
- Promoting exports and enhancing product place image
- Attracting investment, business and development

- Attracting people (as residents, workforce, students, citizens)
- Mobilizing internal support, building common identity
- Promoting external recognition and political influence

The most common and best established approach to the branding of places is the promotion of nations, regions and cities as tourist destinations. Travel and tourism are playing a greater economic role than ever, and now account for almost 12 per cent of the global GDP (Kotler & Gertner, 2004:47). According to the World Tourism Organization, tourism destinations are becoming expressive devices, communicating messages about identity, lifestyle and group membership (Morgan, Pritchard & Pride 2004). In this regard, they resemble lifestyle brands, and the tourist industry and authorities are increasingly constructing their destinations as brands and adopting brand management principles. The approach to branding has largely been promotion and marketing-driven, emphasizing external communication. But because of the need to build 'internal' support among highly diverse stakeholders (Ooi, 2003), encourage 'brand delivery', and handle the sensitive issue of representing collective values and self images, internal branding processes almost inevitably become important parts of destination brand management.

While the tourism perspective is a case of making the place a brand in its own right, the export or product place image perspective is about leveraging the place-of-origin for the benefit of organizations located in the city, region or country. The identification and certification of place-of-origin has been essential in the differentiation of products from the earliest days of commerce. While the identification of the producer or organization behind products has played a greater role in the formation of modern brands, the communication of provenance and use of product country image remains a vital element in many contemporary brand strategies. Papadopoulos and Heslop (2002) argue that product country image-based marketing is increasing in parallel with growth in global competition and market complexity. They believe that this reflects the fact that marketers are turning to country associations for differentiation in a market where products can be made almost anywhere and have standardized core features. Consumers, they imply, use origin images in dealing with 'information overload', reducing perceived risk and assessing the social acceptability of their purchases. Local companies and industries have, over time, built reputations for product standards and sought to use place images to their advantage in their branding efforts. Government agencies and policies, as well as local communities, have often supported these efforts. With the expansion of branding, countries, cities and regions are establishing agencies and formal strategies to manage place images and equity. From being elements in the branding of products and companies, places are becoming brands in their own right, managed to support local brands and businesses.

Place branding schemes are also being initiated by regional planning and economic development agencies to attract (foreign) investment and promote activity and job creation. In a global economy with increased mobility, places around the world are being forced to compete to attract and retain business and capital. Brand management techniques are becoming important elements in such efforts at many levels, from national economic development programs to schemes to redevelop struggling urban neighborhoods. The success of Costa Rica and Ireland in attracting high tech industries have been cited as exemplary cases of branding for economic development (Papadopoulos & Heslop, 2002), while schemes to lure Western companies abroad to developing countries with low labor costs and poor employment standards have received critical attention (e.g. Klein, 2000).

Another perspective is directed at attracting people to an area or retaining them. The aims and methods of this approach perhaps lie somewhere between tourism-driven and investment-oriented place branding. It aims to attract people more permanently than destination branding - migrants, immigrants - to fill jobs, study, pay tax, buy property, and stimulate growth and business, but also to retain existing citizens, enhance civic pride, and sometimes build and reinforce common identity. All projects to brand places imply a certain element of politics. When the aim is to attract investment or tourism, or enhance country-of-origin effects, the primary motive is economical. But sometimes the motives behind the branding of places are highly political. In fact, Olins (2002) argues that nation-building projects and revolutions are essentially manifestations of branding and rebranding. While Kemal Atatürk or Napoleon Bonaparte, both cited by Olins as champions of nation (re)branding projects, did not have access to modern brand management theory, leaders of newly independent nations of today do. Countries such as Croatia/Hrvatska (Martinovic, 2002) and Latvia (Frasher et. al, 2003) have formal branding programs which are as much about defining a national identity as promoting economic growth. Branding has also entered the international political scene. According to Van Ham (2001), nation branding has become an important component in international relations. 'Smart states', he argues, 'are building their brands around reputations and attitudes, much in the same way smart companies do' and the branding of countries now has considerable political and strategic implications, affecting even the dynamics of NATO and EU enlargement (Van Ham, 2001:4).

A core challenge of branding places is dealing with complexities arising from the multiple approaches to, and hence interests at stake in, the branding process. Place branding usually has to deal with the existence of multiple identities and conflicting interests among different stakeholder groups. And the organizations behind place branding projects tend to lack the unity of purpose and decision-making authority necessary to build a strong brand (Papadopoulos & Heslop, 2002). Even arriving at a clear, common vision, which is seen as prerequisite and key requirement for a successful branding process, can be a difficult challenge. When we look at different assessments of place branding projects we find other common difficulties. First, place branding projects are often met with resistance. The need for (re)branding, the process of branding, the cost of branding, and even the very idea of branding a place are questioned. Olins (2002) argues that prejudice against branding countries is widespread, but dismisses the criticism, pointing to the historical processes whereby nations have been invented and national identities have been constructed. What Olins perhaps fails to address fully is the tension between the sacred and profane in the meeting between nationhood, and other placed-based identities, and branding. The sacred is expressed in the sense of the moral grandeur of dying for one's country, or in the communal experience of singing national anthems. Even as their force is waning, nations are still capable of inspiring sentiments of attachment, love and self-sacrifice that are beyond comparison with what people would ever feel for commercial brands or organizations (Anderson, 1991). So the very idea of applying brand management to nations can be experienced, at best, as a vain attempt to manage a historically embedded collective identity, at worst, something bordering on sacrilege. The fact that the branding of cities can also provoke strong reactions is evident in this excerpt from a letter to the editor of a Norwegian newspaper complaining about the branding of the city of Larvik:

'My most important objection to 'city-branding' is thinking of the space of our everyday spiritual and physical activities as a commodity.

Fabian F. Csaba

This represents a distasteful degradation of democratic and spiritual values. In 'branding' one adds fabricated, marketing-tactical, emotional and experiential values to a commodity. I find this as a disrespectful rejection of the area's real values, which generation after generation have helped build' (Cited on www.city-branding.no. Downloaded on March 21, 2005).

Place branding projects usually receive substantial public funding and also raise questions about whether a place really needs (re)branding, who will benefit from branding, and whether resources for branding would be better spent on social welfare, health care or educational programs (Langer, 2002). Bennett and Savani (2004) suggest that the public ought to be suspicious. In their research on city rebranding projects, they observed that:

'To secure on-going funding for a project, local politicians and government officials had to be convinced that the area really needed rejuvenation. This meant transmitting messages and circulating promotional material that depicted the district as unattractive, dangerous and generally run down' (Bennett and Savani, 2004:82).

Apparently, the first step in realizing a branding project is to 'brand' the area (negatively) and the project itself (as urgently needed).

Another set of problems concern the process of branding places. Bennett and Savani (2004) found that new brand identities were determined in a top-down manner by local government authorities. Decisions were reached through extensive, systematic, and formal consultation with business interests and owners of property in the area, while consultations with existing residents were irregular and usually ad hoc. They also noted that rebranding processes depend heavily on PR and marketing to involve and communicate with internal stakeholders. Furthermore, projects lacked evaluation and measurement of effectiveness.

As noted with Ooi (2003), politics inevitably play a major part in the branding of places. Sometimes the democratic process is detrimental to brand development. When politicians are ousted in elections, the coalitions behind branding projects can fall apart and the continuity and funding required to build a strong brand are lost. Even between elections, power struggles and concessions to stakeholders with different interests can lead to ambiguity and capriciousness. As one urban planner explains in Bennett and Savani (2004:81): 'There is a perpetual conflict between business and local community and the politicians are constantly changing sides'. So clearly, diversity and lack of common identity among constituents can be a great obstacle to place branding. On the other hand, as Naomi Klein suggests, when governments strive for brand consistency they look distinctly authoritarian. Therefore, she argues, we should be wary of mixing the logic of branding with the practice of governance, 'Unlike strong brands, which are predictable and disciplined, democracy is messy and fractious, if not outright rebellious' (Klein, 2002:M1). The branding project of Latvia (Frasher et. al., 2003), illustrates how place branding in defining a common, national identity. The project is not only one of integration, but also implicitly one of disidentification, exclusion and devaluation (of the Russian minority, influences and identity).

Convergence, Difference and the Appropriation of Corporate Branding

The adoption of branding by nonprofits and places suggests that organizations across domains are converging in the way they organize and represent their difference, distinctiveness and identity. But are nonprofits and places in the process losing the part of their identity, distinctiveness and raison d'être?

In considering this question, we can relate DiMaggio and Powell's (1983) analysis of institutional isomorphism to the diffusion of branding outside the corporate realm. DiMaggio and Powell suggest that organizations become more homogeneous through mechanisms of coercion, imitation or normative pressure. We have seen evidence that nonprofits and organizations representing places are following the lead of for-profit organizations and embracing branding. They are adopting branding techniques because they must gain attention and communicate efficiently to attract or maintain support under competitive conditions (coercive). In the face of uncertainty about how to manage under new conditions, they are looking to successful companies such as Coca-cola and Nike as models, or learning from corporate partners (mimetic). And in their efforts to legitimize their decisions and strategies, they are adopting the professional standards of branding from the commercial realm, and employing or collaborating with communication and branding professionals (normative pressures).

However, the application of branding outside the corporate realm cannot be seen as a simple matter of nonprofits and places aligning themselves with for-profit organizations. First of all, it is not a one-way street. Branding and corporate identity owe much to the heritage of symbolism and identity strategies pioneered by national and other place-based institutions. And is it not corporate branding that is moving into territory normally associated with places, governments and civic institutions when it deals with culture, identity and social responsibility? Second, while nonprofit organizations and places can learn from for-profits, our investigations suggest, branding works differently in their contexts. Table 6:1 - summarizing some of the findings of our analysis - compares branding in the three domains, commercial corporations, nonprofits organizations and places. While many branding considerations of commercial corporations apply to any organization, it is clear that nonprofits and places face constraints or circumstances that force them to apply branding principles in different ways to the commercial realm, most notably the lack of resources and the politicization of branding. However, nonprofits also enjoy certain advantages over for-profits in building brands. They tend to receive comparatively more public attention, sympathy and trust than for-profits. This opens the door for favorable media relationships and co-branding partnerships with for-profits. Arguably, nonprofits are driven by a strong sense of mission and member identification than commercial organizations. Successful branding can tap into and strengthen such sentiments. Places face other challenges when engaging in branding. They must find ways of reconciling democratic principles with branding processes, and employ branding in ways which can represent diversity and pluralism, rather than enforcing integration and consistency. In doing so, adhering too rigidly to the conventions, concepts and principles of branding might be a mistake. One of the contradictions inherent in using branding as a tool for organizational development is that the application of branding, while defining difference, also restricts it. Effective branding does not necessarily mean emulating established professional standards, but rather creatively appropriating the principles and concepts of branding, or in other words, playing the game differently. This applies to for-profits as well as nonprofit organizations and places.

Table 6:1 Comparison of (Corporate) Branding in Three Domains

	Commercial corporations	Non-profit organizations	Places (cities, regions, countries)
Why corporate branding?	• Product branding is difficult and expensive to sustain. • Corporations must enhance efficiency of their branding activities. • Corporate branding allows companies to leverage corporate activities and programs. • Branding provides direction, purpose and meaning to internal and external stakeholders.	• Cuts in government support have increased the need to attract support from citizens and corporations. • Increased competition for public attention makes fundraising difficult. • Donors demand visibility and professionalism. • Branding represents opportunity to revive sense of mission.	• Globalization forces cities, regions and countries to compete against distant places to attract and retain businesses, jobs, capital, human capital and tourists. • Branding signals the renewal of places and public institutions. • The growing mobility of people for work and play expands the tourist market.
Barriers to successful corporate branding	• Lack of internal commitment to brand vision, promise and delivery. • Gaps between internal (culture) and external (image) perceptions of brand. • Lack of distinctiveness and trustworthy identity.	• Lack of competencies and economic resources for branding. • Internal and external resistance to branding the organization. • Failure to attract adequate commercial partners or sufficient branding expertise. • Branding is reduced to marketing tool for fundraising.	• Lack of unity of purpose and decision-making authority. • Clash with historically embedded collective identity. • Ambiguity and capriciousness prevents brand development. • Internal branding becomes branding of branding. • Problems with brand delivery.
Key challenges for brand management	• To balance vision and responsiveness to stakeholders. • To balance continuity and current relevance. • Making sure control and consistency does not discourage involvement and identification. • Delivering on brand promises.	• To preserve integrity and legitimacy vis-à-vis stakeholders. • To overcome resistance against 'brandspeak' or 'We do not call it the brand but it is there'-phenomenon. • Choosing between integrative and adversary approaches vis-à-vis corporate brands.	• To revitalize heritage in ways that are relevant to stakeholders without losing identity. • Acknowledging the political nature of branding places. • To involve local citizens and represent diversity of interests and identities.

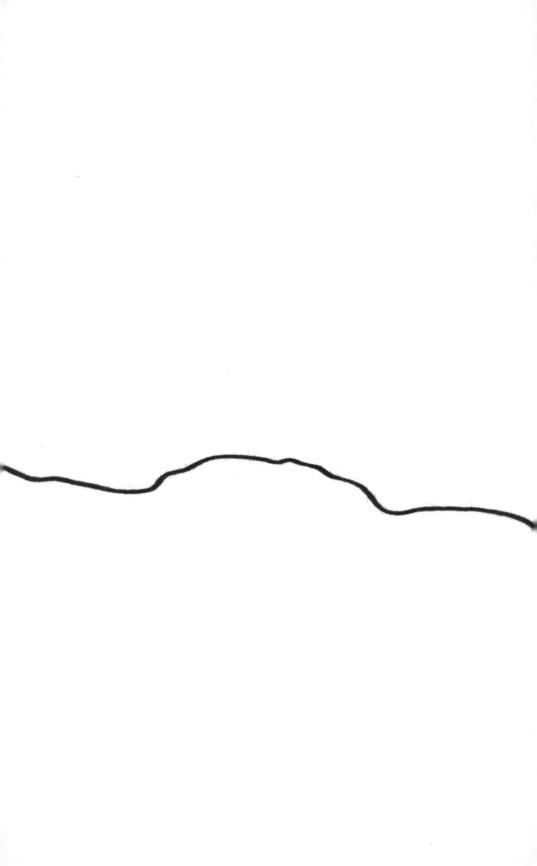

CHAPTER 7

CORPORATE BRAND STRETCH

– *Brand Extension in a Corporate Branding Perspective*

Pernille Gjøls-Andersen & Esben Karmark

Companies are increasingly taking their corporate brand into new and unrelated business areas in order to capitalize on their brand equity. This chapter analyzes the implications of such a 'Corporate Brand Stretch' strategy. Particular focus is given to the roles of culture and identity in relation to the success of a corporate brand stretch strategy. The 'Corporate Brand Stretch' model is introduced, and application of the model is illustrated using a case-example from LEGO Group contrasted with Walt Disney Company.

Pernille Gjøls-Andersen & Esben Karmark

'Many great brands are like amoebae or plasticine. They can be shaped twisted and turned in all sorts of ways and still remain recognizable. That's why so many brands can be divorced from the products/services with which they were originally associated' (Olins, 2003:18).

The above quotation by the grand old man of corporate identity, Wally Olins, points to one of the most essential strategic issues concerning corporate branding strategy: Brand extension. With the increasing focus on optimization of brand value, one of the main strategic brand issues for companies to consider is how the brand (equity) can create value across more activities, markets, and product categories (Balmer & Grey, 2003; Aaker, 2004). Many companies therefore work at stretching or extending their brand into business areas that are not related to the business in which the brand originated. These companies are wrestling with the question: How *far* can the brand stretch? What we propose in this chapter, however, is that we still know little about why some brands, such as Virgin, seem to be able to be stretched across a wide range of business from music to airlines, trains and bridal wear. And why other brands, such as BIC© and Levi's©, are less successful in their brand extension efforts.

We focus in this chapter on brand extensions in organizations with a Branded House strategy, implying that the Corporate Brand dominates all organizational as well as product levels. In other words, the phenomenon of interest here is when an organization is pursuing the Branded House corporate brand strategy, by moving the corporate brand into new and unrelated business areas. In the following we call this phenomenon 'Corporate Brand Stretch'.

Our main assumption is that one significant explanation for the relative success or failure of Corporate Brand Stretch is to be found in the role played by the culture and identity of the organization in the brand stretch process. Brands and organizational culture and identity are becoming more closely interlinked. This is due to the fact that brands are increasingly perceived to be powerful symbols of the organizational identity, i.e. organizational members' perceptions of 'who they are as an organization', (cf. Albert & Whetten, 1985; Hatch & Schultz, 2000; Karmark, 2002). A Corporate Brand Stretch strategy and the organizational culture and identity will therefore mutually influence each other in at least two ways: 1) Since a Corporate Brand Stretch strategy often involves the creation of new business units staffed by people with professional backgrounds new to the company culture, new subcultures will emerge in the organization. 2) Because the corporate brand is linked to organizational members' perceptions of 'who we are', a change in corporate brand strategy, such as stretching the brand, will have an impact on the organizational identity. Organizational identity is rooted in the strategic and cultural history of the organization. The point we are making in this chapter is that both these issues raise the need for organizations to involve the organizational members in the brand stretch process in a dynamic way. We suggest that, otherwise, the strategy will not obtain the necessary 'buy in' from the organizational culture and identity required for it to succeed.

In this chapter we will demonstrate that, in theory as well as practice, there is often a lack of focus on the culture and identity dimensions when it comes to the specific corporate brand strategy, here defined as Corporate Brand Stretch. Much has been said in the corporate branding literature about the characteristics of a corporate brand and how it differs from a product brand (Hatch & Schultz, 2001; de Chernatony, 2002; Balmer & Grey, 2003; Schultz, Chapter 2). As pointed out by Schultz (in Chapter 2), the key strategic issues for 'classical' branding strategy here are brand architecture, brand positioning and product identity. Corporate branding, for its part, takes a broader, call it holistic, approach and is concerned with branding as a strategic force; relationships between strategic vision, organizational culture, and stakeholder images; and brand alignment. We suggest, however, that the literature on a corporate branding strategy, such as Corporate Brand Stretch, remains concerned with the 'classical' strategic issues rather than applying the holistic corporate brand perspective. This implies that corporate branding is still largely concerned with the question of how to express the brand visually to the external audiences.

Similarly, in corporate branding practice, we see that resources are still widely allocated to customer research and external communication about a new strategy, while the internal organization is often left alone with a 'kick off' meeting and core values printed on a mouse pad or a plastic card.

This chapter is structured as follows: First, we review the literature on corporate branding and discuss the shift in the construct from a focus on the visual and semantic (brand architecture) to integration of strategic vision, organizational culture and identity and external images. We then move on to discussing the literature on brand extension. We demonstrate that this literature is exclusively concerned with the effects of a brand extension strategy on the external brand image, while the internal organization is more or less ignored. However, the literature points to the redefinition of brand identity, which is essential in the multidisciplinary process. We propose a Corporate Brand Stretch Model in which we seek to link the dimensions of organizational culture, identity and employee involvement to Corporate Brand Stretch and the traditional external dimensions. We apply the Corporate Brand Stretch Model to the brand development in LEGO Group, and demonstrate that the LEGO Group in this process did not pay sufficient attention to the effects on the internal organization. We contrast this LEGO case, with the corporate branding strategy in the Walt Disney Company, and finally we conclude and discuss the scope of the model.

Corporate Branding Strategy:
From Structure to Process

In line with the recent, more multidisciplinary, approach, the notion of corporate branding is regarded as processes that involves more than the use of name and logo. Corporate branding is not just about form, but about the substance of the relationship between the company, its business units, products and its stakeholders. From this perspective, corporate branding is defined as all processes that are intended to enhance the value of the corporate brand, externally as well as internally (Fombrun & van Riel, 1997; van Riel & Balmer, 1997; Hatch, Schultz & Olins, 1998; Hatch & Schultz, 2001; de Chernatony, 2002)

From being a structural concept based on visual and nominal identification, the corporate brand has become an integrated concept based on communication and coherence in content – however until recently with a strictly external focus. Today, due to the multidisciplinary approach to branding, this integration is pointing inside the organization, acknowledging the importance of communicating to internal stakeholders.

Corporate branding strategy, however, is still primarily described in terms of a brand hierarchy (Keller, 2000). The brand hierarchy determines how closely the company relates its products to the corporate brand. One influential example of a brand hierarchy was proposed by Olins (1989, 2003). This approach is rooted in the design school, with a focus on logo, visual style and symbols, and links the brand structure to the company's corporate identity structure. Olin's classification levels relate the identity structure and the corporate brand in a broad sense, separating structures in three different categories; *monolithic identity, endorsed identity* and *branded identity*. Although Olin's framework is very focused on the use of visual symbols, it reflects the company strategy in degrees of centralization or decentralization, divisions and subsidiaries:

'The identity structure is not superficial; it is built deep into the management system. It is more than just a way of naming things; it's a deep commitment to a particular way of doing business.' (Olins, 1989:78)

Using Olins' frameworks, we can see, for instance, that BMW employs a monolithic hierarchy and brand on all its cars, using the BMW label and a modifier (e.g. 116i, 320i, 530i, 760i) to designate its various models (Keller, 2000). The Accor hotel chain pursues an endorsed strategy, endorsing the Sofitel, Mercure sub-brands with the Accor name, whereas Proctor & Gamble© follows a strictly branded strategy where the Procter & Gamble name is not related to the company's brands (e.g. Ariel/Tide©, Vicks©, Pringle© and Pantene©).

Van Riel (1995) describes the same spectrum from a communication strategy point of view by introducing a continuum of parent visibility with various degrees of endorsement of the corporate name on all communication activities. Various authors in the field of classical brand building and brand management have elaborated upon the different brand structure hierarchies with a recent high priority on the use of the corporate brand at different levels (e.g. Kapferer, 1992; Upshaw, 1995; Aaker, 1996, 2004; Keller, 2000). Figure 7:1 illustrates Aaker's and Olin's way of describing the phenomenon.

The weakness of these well described different categorizations is that they are very complex, and yet fail to capture the whole complexity of the relationships between the different levels. The reason is simply that for many organizations it is difficult to place their strategy in one 'box', and furthermore, the underlying reasons for certain brand portfolio structures are often random and illogical. Research, as well as the authors' personal experience with brand consultancy, shows that the reason for choosing a certain brand strategy is a mix between consumer needs and habits, and also dependent on corporate history, company structure, management, resources etc.

Figure 7:1 Relating Aaker's Brand Relationship Spectrum to Olins' Identity Structures

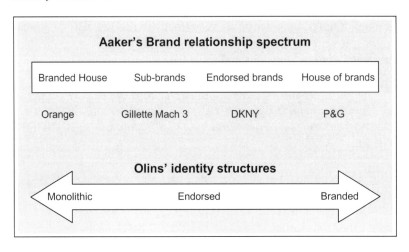

Recently, we have seen contributions in the literature with the emerging holistic understanding of corporate branding applied to strategy. Balmer & Grey (2003) suggest an extended corporate branding architecture with a framework that includes six corporate brand categories: *Familial* (the sharing/adoption of the same corporate brand by two entities, e.g. Shell UK – Shell the Netherlands); *Shared* (like familial, but sometimes operating in distinct markets, e.g. Rolls Royce airplane engines and cars); *Surrogate* (a franchise arrangement, whereby one organization's products/services are branded as those of another, e.g. British Regional Airways use of the British Airways brand); *Supra* (an arch brand used to supra endorse company brands, e.g. One World and Star airline alliances); *Multiplex* (multiple uses of a corporate brand among a variety of entities in a variety of industry sectors, e.g. Virgin, Virgin Atlantic, Virgin Trains); *Federal* (the creation of a new corporate brand by separate companies who pool their resources to create a new identity/company, e.g. Airbus). Even though Balmer & Grey's framework is more complex than Olins' and covers more of the corporate brand structures we see today, like Olins', it is still closely linked to the corporate identity framework (how the brand is presented to external stakeholders).

Similarly, Aaker (2004) developed *his* Brand Identity System to relate to corporate brands. According to his system, what we might call the Corporate Brand Identity System, a corporate brand will be characterized by: Heritage, Assets and Capabilities, People, Values and Priorities, a Local or Global Frame of Reference, Citizen Programs and a Performance Record. Aaker's Corporate Brand Identity System comes somewhat further towards including the dimensions of culture and identity that we are advocating in this chapter. However, when it comes to involving employees, Aaker is still firmly rooted in a corporate identity/marketing framework (2004:11):

'The translation of the corporate brand internally to employees must be supported by the mission, values, and culture of the organization. It is important for employees to buy into organizational values and programs. The corporate brand serves as a link between the organization and the customer. Thus, it can play a role in articulating these elements to employees, retailers, and others who must buy into the goals and values of the corporate brand and represent them to customers.'

Aaker thus considers employees to be recipients of the brand identity communication on par with others (retailers and customers). However, what we suggest is that a Corporate Brand Stretch strategy should involve employees as part of a dynamic corporate branding strategy, rather than a passive audience for the communication (Karmark, Chapter 5). In practice, we see many examples of changes in corporate brand strategy that have a strong one-sided external implementation focus, spending large amounts of resources on informing the world outside about, for example, a new acquisition, a new product launch, or a new market, and not doing more than merely informing the employees.

Brand Extension:
Strong Focus on the External Perspective

From a product brand perspective, what we call a Corporate Brand Stretch is the phenomenon called *brand extension*. Brand extension is basically when any brand, not necessarily a corporate brand, is used to enter and create advantage in other product categories. In the literature, brand extension is discussed primarily in terms of vertical and horizontal brand extension[2] (e.g. Quelch and Kenny, 1994; Aaker,

---

[2] Kotler (2003) suggests five types of brand development: 1) *Line extensions* (existing brand names extended to new sizes or flavors in the existing product

1997). Vertical extension implies that the company takes the brand into markets that are above or below the brand's current position. Armani is an example of a brand that exists in virtually every segment of the apparel market, ranging from the Giorgio Armani© label in the ultra high-end segment, to the Armani Exchange label in the midrange segment. Horizontal extension means that the brand is extended, either within the product category (known as line extension), or across product categories (through sub-brands). The Kraft Foods Inc.® company, for instance, has extended into a number of different food categories, from beverages, to coffee, to cheese and sauces, through sub-brands such as Kool-Aid®, Maxwell House® and Philadelphia®, all of which are endorsed (Olins, 2003) by the Kraft brand.

A potential new brand extension must be judged by how effectively it leverages existing brand equity from the 'parent brand' (the brand of the original product or service) to the new product, service or business. Accordingly, consideration must be given to how the introduction of a brand extension affects the brand as a whole. In other words, the effects must be considered both ways – on both the original and the new product/service, and a clear understanding of the brand identity is essential (Kapferer, 1992; Aaker, 1996).

These strategic arguments and potential implications of brand extension decisions have received extensive focus both in business practice and academic research. Particular attention and research has been devoted to identifying when such decisions will lead to favourable consumer evaluation of the extended brand (e.g. Aaker & Keller, 1990; Boush & Loken, 1991; Broniarczyk & Alba, 1994; Dacin & Smith, 1994) and whether extensions result in negative feedback for the 'parent brand' (Loken & John, 1993; Park, McCarthy & Milberg, 1993).

An influential study by Aaker & Keller (1990) shows that consumer acceptance of a proposed brand extension is dependant upon the perceived quality of the brand, a perceived fit between the two product categories, transferability of the skills and complementarity of the two

---

category; 2) *Brand extensions* (brand names extended to new-product categories); 3) *Multibrands* (new brand names introduced in the same product category – also known as *sub-brands* (Aaker, 1997); 4) *New brands* (new brand name for a new-product category); and 5) *Co-branding* (combining two or more well-known brand names). In this chapter we are concerned with brand extensions – the strategic process of taking the brand into new product categories and business areas.

products, and the characteristics of the category that is entered. Their findings also showed that possible negative associations can be neutralized more effectively by focusing on the attributes of the brand extension, rather than reminding consumers of the positive associations with the 'parent brand'.

Extensions always carry the risk of diluting what the original brand name means to consumers, especially in the case of extensions that are inconsistent with the brand's existing image. This dilution has also been investigated through empirical research and there are results showing that under certain conditions, a brand extension can diminish consumer feelings and beliefs about a brand name. The risk of diluting the 'parent brand' also called flagship product, defined as the product consumers most closely associate with the brand name, is also a concern (Keller, 2000). The flagship product is often regarded as synonymous with the brand name, and is the most tangible expression of everything important that the particular brand stands for. However, a study by John, Loken & Joiner (1998) shows that beliefs about the flagship product are most immune to dilution, showing a greater resistance to change than other products bearing the brand name.

The conclusion in most research on brand extensions is that the brand needs to be a strong brand with a very precise meaning - a solid brand identity - in order to cover a broad range of unrelated products.

'The more a brand covers different categories, the more it stretches and weakens, losing its force like an elastic band.' (Kapferer, 1992:161).

An example of a well known brand that has been stretched too far is the Pringle® brand, known for its colorful high quality knitwear for men and sponsorship of top golfers. In 1993, the company rolled out a diversification strategy, and suddenly the Pringle brand appeared on everything from jeans to cotton dresses, blazers, luggage, belts and silk. Pringle even moved into retailing, launched a chain of Pringle shops selling their own apparel, and soon discovered the logistic nightmare which this rapid expansion entailed. All new product lines, apart from knitwear, were outsourced and were found to be difficult to coordinate. They became too diversified too fast, in areas that the consumers did not expect them to be in, e.g. cotton dresses that seemed out of step with the masculine Pringle brand. From a theoretical perspective, it can be argued that Pringle extended its brand in directions that, in the minds of consumers, did not fit with the original masculine, high class image closely connected to knitwear. The core identity was compromised, and the organization also seemed to lack the necessary competencies for the expansion, so the launch failed and the cotton dresses were pulled off the market again.

But in relative terms, one must concede that the distance between a Pringle male knit sweater and a Pringle cotton dress seems less than between a Virgin record store and Virgin bridal wear. So why did Pringle fail, and why has it been possible for a brand like Virgin to stretch beyond what would be considered reasonable by any standard (airline, record company, bridal wear, financial services, beverages, condoms, etc. etc.)? The answer lies in Virgin's well defined brand identity based on attributes and four solid values that work for a large set of products and services – serving as the glue that holds the Virgin business empire together. And furthermore, an identity dominated by the type of attributes that permit stretching, as expressed by the following quote from Aaker:

'When a brand's identity moves beyond product associations to organizational associations, brand personality, and (in general) more abstract associations, it will travel farther. Some bases for identity – such as prestige (Rolex), fashion (Vuarnet), and health (Healthy Choice), are not associated with specific product classes and will be capable of casting a wider shadow than an attribute that is tied to a specific product.' (Aaker, 1996:297)

This argument corresponds to one of Aaker's identity traps that Aaker calls the product-attribute-fixation-trap, where overly strong product attributes linked to a brand limit the potential for extensions. In order to maximize future extendability, a brand should try to enhance the value to consumers of characteristics associated with its brand name which are not product-specific. The Virgin underdog image, the strong Branson personality, and the values of quality, innovation, fun/entertainment & value have made it possible to stretch the Virgin brand very far (although even the Virgin brand has experienced limitations to brand extensions, as shown in the Virgin Vodka example discussed in the introduction).

To conclude on the challenges involved in extending a brand, it is vital that the brand identity and how it is perceived externally is understood in order to decide the scope of the extension. Thus, identifying and agreeing upon core competencies and the core essence of a brand, are what many brand experts and researchers alike agree to be the basis for stretching a brand to new businesses. There are numerous contributions to the literature concerned with the consequences and pitfalls involved in extending brands which focus on the implications for consumer perceptions, brand image and flagship products. However, these contributions do not take into consideration the effects that brand extension might have on the internal organization. That is, we are left with little knowledge or discussion of how employees will react to brand extensions, or how they will effect the culture and identity of the organization. We will now discuss the connections between organizational culture and identity and brand extensions, before examining the consequences of brand extension in the LEGO Group.

Corporate Brand Stretch and Organizational Identity and Culture

Even if corporate branding as a multidisciplinary construct has been recognized in both the academic literature and at the management level of all organizations, as described above, the links between Corporate Brand Stretch and culture and identity have only been considered to a very limited extent.

The construct of identity in organizations has traditionally been seen from two perspectives or schools: The Corporate Identity School and the Organizational Identity School. The corporate identity perspective has roots in graphic design and is, in many ways, synonymous with the company name, logo, house style, architecture, etc. It emphasizes the way in which the company (i.e. top management) expresses its *central idea* to external stakeholders (see the discussion of Olins above.) Organizational identity, on the other hand, is more internally directed and is concerned with the way in which organizational members perceive the 'core, distinct and enduring' aspects of their organization as expressed in the question: 'Who are we as an organization?' (Albert & Whetten, 1985). More recently, Hatch & Schultz (2000) proposed a more holistic perspective on identity in organizations which includes both corporate and organizational identity elements. According to this perspective, identity in organizations involves both the symbols which top management decides to express visually to the external world, and the way in which these symbols are interpreted by organizational members in the context of their organizational culture.

The construct of organizational culture is usually seen to be relevant to identity in organizations in that it provides a context for organizational members to interpret 'who they are as an organization' based on the organization's history and values, and the day-to-day practices of organizational members. In that sense, culture is usually seen as operating on a less conscious and reflexive level than identity (which involves the conscious choice of symbols and the self-reflexive question of 'who we are') (Schein, 1992; Hatch & Schultz, 1997). Culture, however, is a complex construct, and is usually seen as not necessarily encompassing all organizational members homogenously. Rather, cultural complexity includes subcultures, which may be functional/occupational, driven by geographical decentralization or divisional separation, or differentiated by product, market or technology (Schein, 1992). The presence of subcultures in the organization suggest that the questions of 'who we are as an organization' and 'what core symbols such as the corporate brand mean to us' can be interpreted in different cultural contexts in the organization. For example, organizational members at corporate headquarters are likely to interpret the corporate brand in terms of its overall strategic implications for the organization, whereas a subsidiary is more likely to interpret the meaning of the corporate brand in the context of the implications for the specific day-to-day operations of the subsidiary, as well as the conditions on the local market (Karmark, 2002). Subcultures may exist in relative harmony with the dominant culture of the organization, or they may be in conflict, even to the extent of constituting a 'counterculture' (Van Maanen & Barney, 1985; Martin, 2004).

Some effort has gone into discussing the links between organizational identity and diversification – a construct related to Corporate Brand Stretch. For instance, Barney & Stuart (2000) suggested that companies engaging in diversification, i.e. taking the company into new business areas, will also have to reformulate their organizational identity to reflect the stretch beyond the core competencies that the company originally built on. Barney & Stewart suggested that organizational identity and core competencies are linked because both constructs constitute schemas for top management and organizational members in the organization. Organizational identity acts as a values-based schema that reflects what is central, distinctive and enduring about the organization, and which provides direction in relation to what events in the competitive or operating environment must be attended to. Core competencies, for their part, are schemas and belief-systems about how to attend to these events. When companies diversify (and thus when the brand is stretched into new business areas) it becomes more difficult for them to define their core organizational competencies in terms of a single product market. Barney & Stewart suggest that companies can 'get around' this problem by defining their organizational identity at a higher level of abstraction.

We suggest that a factor that is almost completely overlooked in the literature is the fact that stretching a brand into a new business area, in many cases also involves setting up a new organizational division. And such new organizational divisions are likely to develop subcultures, which may or may not be strongly differentiated from, or even in opposition to, the main (dominant) culture. Extending a brand therefore often involves the question of how to involve new organizational members in a common perception of the organizational identity. And this identity may be closely linked to a core product and brand in the organization (Gjøls-Andersen, 2001; Karmark, 2002). We will argue that such a reformulation of the organizational identity is a long and difficult process in many companies, unless the collective understanding of 'who we are as an organization' and 'what are our core competencies' are taken sufficiently into consideration in the process.

The Corporate Brand Stretch Model

In figure 7:2 below, we have depicted the factors which we suggest influence a company's Corporate Brand Stretch process. Firstly, in the centre, we illustrate the importance of a well-defined, focused brand identity, which determines the scope of the extension. Secondly, we suggest that the potential for extending a corporate brand is linked to the alignment of four factors: two internal and two external. Our main claim is that even if the concept of corporate branding, in academia as well as in practice, involves internal organizational dimensions, the focus is still external in a Corporate Brand Stretch process. In existing literature on classical product brand extension, the focus is entirely on external dimensions such as image, associations, market situation etc. We are therefore left with little knowledge of how employees are involved in brand extensions and how they will affect the culture and the identity of the organization. We therefore present a model that takes external as well as internal dimensions into account when both planning and implementing a Corporate Brand Stretch. The model is divided in two by a vertical axis, illustrating the internal and external dimensions of Corporate Brand Stretch elements. There is no horizontal axis, but merely a line dividing the elements

Brand Identity. The first challenge when preparing for stretching a brand into new businesses is to understand the brand identity and to therefore identify and agree upon core competencies and the core essence of the brand. In defining the brand identity, the four surrounding dimensions in the model serve as sources for exploring the brand identity. One rule of thumb is that a brand identity which focuses too strongly on product attributes linked to the brand will limit the potential for extensions. In order to maximize future extendability, the re-definition of the brand identity should therefore enhance the value of characteristics associated with the brand that are not product-specific.

Internal Dimensions. The internal element in the upper left hand corner is the *identity* of the organization, and in the lower left hand corner, the *company's culture*. The identity of the organization is here defined as the organizational identity concept discussed above. The culture is defined as embedded practices and heritage. We suggest that a company's brand heritage, linked to certain product characteristics and core competencies, influences the culture and in turn has an effect on how employees perceive what the company stands for - the identity. We claim and illustrate in the model that organizations which are extending their brand beyond the core product must therefore make a sustained effort to get employees to understand, accept and 'live' the organization's 'new identity' – a 'new identity' covering a broader range of unrelated product-categories. At the same time, the organization needs to understand that new divisions and competency areas established as a result of new product areas create new subcultures.

External Dimensions. The element in the upper right hand corner is the *corporate image*, meaning the perceptions of the company among external stakeholders. In order to succeed with a brand extension, it is vital that the consumers accept the new scope of the brand and the new products/services which together will have an effect on the overall brand image. Image and associations with flagship products versus new products, etc., have received much focus in the classical marketing and branding literature, and in practice, image is one of the important measures of the success of a brand extension. And this element is very important both in the redefinition of the 'new' brand identity and when communicating the result. If the consumer's image of the brand initially seems to limit the potential for stretch, it is necessary to consider whether it is at all possible within a reasonable time frame and resources.

The dimension in the lower right hand corner, *competitive environment and consumer trends,* is a different kind of construct than the other three (which are all interlinked in corporate branding theory). However, this second external dimension represents an important criterion for succeeding with a brand extension strategy. The position the brand is able to establish on a new market is dependent on the strengths and nature of the competitors. Success is obviously also very dependent on consumer needs and behavior – you should not consider moving a brand into the market without knowing and monitoring consumers' needs and behavior.

The four factors related to Corporate Brand Stretch processes will be discussed shortly in relation to the LEGO case. At the end of the chapter we will return to how this model can be used in practice.

Figure 7:2 The Corporate Brand Stretch Model

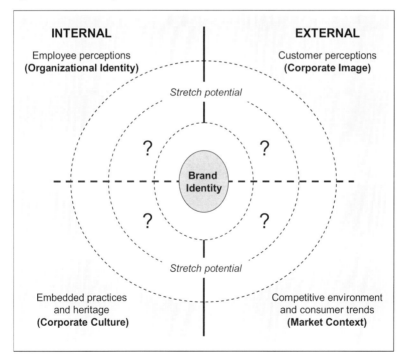

Corporate Brand Stretch in the LEGO Group[3]

In the mid-1990s, the company launched a brand extension strategy that took the LEGO brand into LEGOLAND® theme parks, electronic games and children's media, lifestyle products (watches and accessories) and clothing. Following disastrous financial results early in the new milenium, LEGO Group has now closed down or divested itself all of its non-core (non-brick-related) activities. As the latest example of this, the company is now preparing to sell off its LEGOLAND theme parks (Politiken, March 11th 2005).

The LEGO case example demonstrates the interplay between the dimensions in the model in a Corporate Brand Stretch strategy process. We will begin by providing an overview of the brand strategy development in LEGO Group, and then move on to discuss the internal and external dimensions of the Corporate Brand Stretch Model in a LEGO Group context.

The LEGO Brand Strategy History. LEGO began as a small carpenter's shop in 1916, and was converted into a wooden toy manufacturer when demand for housing construction collapsed during the Great Depression in the 1930's. The founder, Ole Kirk Christiansen, commissioned an employee contest to come up with a brand name. The suggestion chosen – LEGO – is a contraction of the Danish words, 'leg godt'. Directly translated, 'leg godt' means 'play well'. An 'amplified' version that has been used in the company is: 'Have a good time playing but mind your manners and improve yourself in the process'. By sheer coincidence, in Latin 'lego' means to 'put together or assemble', an activity which has been characteristic for the LEGO brand throughout the twentieth century. In 1958, the LEGO brick was invented, with its unique plastic stud-and-tubes connection system, and LEGO decided to build its future on plastic toys, with the LEGO brick soon becoming a popular global children's toy brand. The development of the brand has been in the hands of three generations of the Kirk Christiansen family, although just recently the latest CEO, Keld Kirk Kristiansen, turned over the management to a non-family member.

The LEGO brand strategy was for many decades a monolithic identity strategy, with a uniform visual style throughout their

---

[3] The data from LEGO Group used in this case example have been published prevsiously in two Ph.D. dissertations (Gjøls-Andersen, 2001; Karmark, 2002).

communication and using the LEGO brand at both the corporate and product level (although with periods where strong sub-brands were closely linked to the LEGO brand). Developments in the LEGO brand strategy have been strongly linked to the company's history, trends in society and general market trends. Between 1932-1964 the company had a very product-oriented strategy, focusing on the superior quality of the brick and its unique attributes. During this period, the brand was leveraged through line extensions within the existing product category, with a focus on refinement and the development of new construction themes and ideas to increase loyalty within the existing, broad target group – children.

In 1965, LEGO changed its brand strategy focus and put children at the centre of all extensions. The fact that there were different needs and different ways of playing with LEGO depending on age and gender became obvious, and children and their playing habits were researched thoroughly. The first sub-brand was launched – LEGO Duplo – for younger children, and was soon followed by LEGO Technic, for the more advanced older boys.

This strategy was changed to an endorsed strategy in 1979, when each product category was given its own, more independent, identity. E.g. the DUPLO® brand had LEGO as an endorser, but it had own visual style and identity. The reason for this change in strategy was to emphasize the vision of the LEGO Group – to manufacture and develop creative and high-quality toys for children of all ages. This strategy lasted for more than a decade, before LEGO reverted in 1992 to using the LEGO brand as the main driver on all products.

The reason was a need to refocus on strengthening the LEGO brand and the new diversification strategy that was under serious planning. The organization was researching and preparing for expansion of the scope of the LEGO brand, by stretching it across different categories in the children's universe. The company's LEGO brand had dominated the construction toy market for decades, but in 1993 they faced the need for a major change in brand strategy. Interest in playing with construction toys had been declining, and the company was also faced with the phenomenon known as KGOY (kids growing older younger), which meant that children were leaving traditional toys earlier, moving into the world of lifestyle products as early as at the age of seven. The pace of technological development was also creating new and exciting areas for children to explore, and boxes of LEGO building bricks were beginning to be seen as boring and old fashioned. LEGO therefore decided to extend their brand into new areas of the children's universe.

After having been synonymous with their epoch-making plastic brick for much of the century, in the mid-90s, LEGO started to launch products in three new areas: 1) clothes & accessories, 2) media products and interactive multimedia robots, and 3) LEGOLAND family parks, all under the LEGO brand.

External Influences on the LEGO Brand Identity. The first step towards stretching the LEGO brand and expanding the Branded House strategy was an analysis of the status of the brand image among children. Not only were LEGO not present where children were focusing their attention, LEGO was also faced with children who valued new trends and instant gratification over the 'serious play' that was perceived to be the essence of the LEGO brand. In image studies conducted by LEGO, the company found that the image was increasingly described as less desirable, and somewhat dull and old-fashioned. At the same time, the brand image was dominated by product attributes – attributes linked to the famous, unique but obviously outdated building brick. The challenge was expressed by a LEGO middle manager as follows:

'If you use an umbrella as a metaphor for our brand, we have a situation today where we want to unfold the umbrella in order to embrace a larger part of the children's universe – but the umbrella 'point' has to stay the same. We want that umbrella point to cover all the new products. Today this point is too close to a brick and the question is if the LEGO logo is able to cover more. We are many skeptics with regard to LEGO being more than a brick.' (Middle Manager, LEGO, 1997)

In other words, even though the LEGO brand had a solid and focused brand identity, this identity was dominated by a type of attributes – product attributes - that are very limiting for a brand's ability to stretch across unrelated business areas. This phenomenon is what Aaker (1996) calls the product-attribute-fixation-trap, and LEGO was therefore advised by an external brand consultant to reinterpret the powerful core of the brand. The nature of the core of a brand is that it is timeless, and it is this consistency in the core essence that builds a strong brand. The challenge was therefore not to change the construction element at the centre of the LEGO brand, but to re-interpret it in the way it was brought to life. Figure 7:3 shows the

Corporate Brand Stretch

reinterpretation of the construction element from assembly to creativity.

The success of such a reinterpretation lies in the way this 'new identity' is expressed and communicated in everything from products and advertising to behavior. *'Stimulate creativity'* was chosen as the brand essence from which all brand actions should derive, with the purpose of creating brand associations with creativity in consumers' minds, instead of with the brick, and to thus allow the brand to cover a broader range of products. In the company's strategic intent, the ambition was expressed as follows:

'As a dependable partner for parents, it is our mission to stimulate children's imagination and creativity and to encourage children to explore, experience and express their own world, a world without limits.' (LEGO Strategic Intent, 1998)

Figure 7:3 Reinterpretation of the LEGO Brand Identity

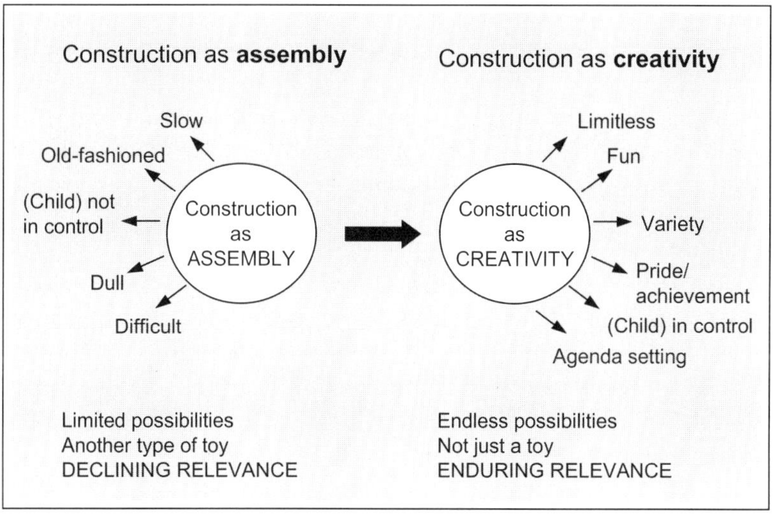

```
Construction as assembly              Construction as creativity

        Slow                                  Limitless
Old-fashioned                                        Fun
(Child) not    ┌──────────┐           ┌──────────┐
in control ←── │Construction│         │Construction│ → Variety
               │    as     │    ⟹    │    as     │
               │ ASSEMBLY  │          │ CREATIVITY│ → Pride/
        Dull   └──────────┘           └──────────┘   achievement
                                              (Child) in control
     Difficult                              Agenda setting

Limited possibilities                 Endless possibilities
Another type of toy                   Not just a toy
DECLINING RELEVANCE                   ENDURING RELEVANCE
```

One could therefore claim that LEGO prepared for their brand extension 'by the book', by working on and clarifying the brand identity, and agreeing upon core competencies and the core essence of the brand. However, we suggest that this was done strictly with an external communication purpose in mind. An advertising campaign was developed with a new tag-line – 'Just imagine…', and the new set of brand values and essence was implemented in and began to guide all new product development activities. The positioning of LEGO as a strong brand among families with children, rather than a construction toy brand, was also considered. In this respect, Disney was a brand that LEGO saw both as a role model, but definitely also as one of their main competitors.

'If we just said imagination in our tag-line we would have competed with Disney. The difference between us and Disney is expression. Who expresses in Disney? It is the art directors. They sell fast food and we sell raw material. That is the difference. It is a prefabricated feeling and it does not teach you anything - at least not substantial. But please do not write anything bad about Disney as I have great respect for Walt Disney and it would be a loss to the world if he did not exist. But we are very different from them when it comes to brand values.' (Top Manager, LEGO, 1998)

Despite the intention of delivering raw materials from which creativity could flourish, LEGO launched products for which the creativity stimulating element was compromised, and consumer expectations of the LEGO brand were still strongly linked to the brick. For example, the clothes that were launched were not that different from competing colorful clothes brands, and customers expected them to have 'brick' features such as lasting colors and construction features (Gjøls-Andersen, 2001).

Internal Influences on the LEGO Brand Identity. From 1996 – 2000, LEGO was going through a major change process, not only in strategy but also in terms of identity. Parallel to the external efforts to re-invent the LEGO identity, the internal organization struggled to do the same, although driven by a less focused strategy, as expressed by a LEGO Group manager:

'Our identity has developed over time. In 1970, we had an identity crisis – there was a feeling that there were no more possibilities to pursue, and that, you know, where should we go as a company? Now, with the new business areas, there are some new possibilities to develop.'

Through an analysis of LEGO's organizational identity, we found that this identity was characterized by three main dimensions: *The LEGO*

Corporate Brand Stretch

history and family, the concern for and knowledge about children and as the central and most dominant: *Tthe unique product idea.* Furthermore, the LEGO identity was perceived by LEGO Group managers to be very closely linked to the personal values of the three generations of the owners of LEGO, the Kirk Kristiansen family, and, by extension, local Danish values. We believe this product and regionally based culture meant that the organizational members found it difficult to accept the new brand identity which was supposed to include the new product areas. For example, a LEGO Group manager said:

'There is a tendency towards different perceptions of LEGO in the [new] business areas. For one thing, they're treated like step-children in LEGO. Some of it has to do with geographic distance. For instance, take the 'ponytails' in London [LEGO Media]. The subculture there is different than here on 'Mount Parnassus', and I think in general the culture in the business areas is perceived very differently.'

The brand stretch strategy also led to an extension beyond the former core competences into the new business areas. The LEGO Media subsidiary or strategic business unit provides an example of the interplay between the Corporate Brand Stretch strategy and the internal dimensions (competencies, culture and identity). LEGO Media was established in London, and new product development centers were set up in San Francisco and Milan. The LEGO organization, as it looked in around 1998, is shown in Figure 7:4, below.

Figure 7:4 The LEGO Organization

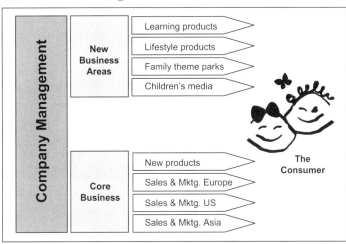

LEGO Media International opened in London in 1996 with the aim of developing competencies within the children's media market. These new competencies also drove a new subculture and new ways of interpreting the LEGO identity. This began to cause problems as these new ways of perceiving the LEGO identity clashed with the old ways that dominated perceptions at LEGO Group headquarters in Denmark. The attitude at headquarters, viewing the new business areas as stepchildren, caused a strong subculture to emerge in LEGO Media. We found that this subculture even took on the characteristics of a counter-culture, in which organizational members defined themselves in opposition to the *dominant* culture at LEGO headquarters in Billund. For example, as expressed by a member of the LEGO Media organization in London:

'My image of LEGO Billund is that it is a rather cold place. They are a bunch of engineers, and they have an intellectual mindset towards the product [...].'

For LEGO Group, these cultural differences (which were left to go unresolved) led to mutual distrust over the management of the LEGO brand. In terms of expressing the LEGO identity to external audiences, the LEGO Media organization attempted to be loyal to the brand (which the new company was, of course, highly dependent on):

'The LEGO Media vision originates in the [LEGO Group's] Idea, Exuberance and Values vision. LEGO Media's vision has to do with offering something to parents – they can trust in the high quality of LEGO Media software. And also that Media is striving for continuous improvement – trying to be better than anybody else. An analogy between the LEGO brick and LEGO software is that software is never finished – there is a similarity between designing LEGO System toys and designing software.'

Internally, however, the mutual distrust was expressed openly. For instance, managers at LEGO headquarters were not convinced that the LEGO Media members acted according to the 'proper' LEGO values. This was, in part, a result of the cultural perception that both the identity of LEGO Gorup and the brand were tightly linked to the brick. Furthermore, the managers perceived the interpretations of the company values at headquarters as the 'correct' interpretations. For example, one manager at LEGO Group headquarters said:

'How do you ensure that the 'child' has the same value as you do and is still his own person – like with a teenager? This has caused greater problems than we expected. Our advantage has been that we are a little more value-focused and not as marketing focused. The people at LEGO Media are business people for good reasons, but not as closely connected to the LEGO values and identity. They try, and they are working with it, but it is hard. I mean what is 'caring' in software?'

Paradoxically, the LEGO Media members felt strongly connected to the LEGO Group values and brand, but this was partly from the external image of these dimensions, rather than from what they perceived as a very different cultural reality. LEGO Media members felt that the perceptions of the LEGO brand among managers in headquarters were out of touch with consumer demands, and that this was preventing the LEGO brand from fulfilling its true potential. As expressed by a LEGO Media manager:

'The way the brand is interpreted in Billund is restrictive and traditional, and it keeps them from seeing opportunities – we try to follow the guidelines that make sense, but we would like the brand to be vibrant rather than boring, conservative and uncreative. LEGO Media really adds dynamism to the brand'.

To sum up on the role of the internal dimensions on the new, extended LEGO brand, we can say that the LEGO culture and identity were unprepared for the organizational consequences of extending the brand into new business areas, and the resulting need to include new competencies and subcultures. The new areas were treated as 'stepchildren' and not properly integrated into either the LEGO organization or the brick and heritage-based LEGO culture. The dominant identity perceptions at LEGO remained close to the core identity built on the LEGO heritage and the unique product idea: The LEGO brick.

Regarding the Corporate Brand Stretch strategy at LEGO, it became obvious during interviews with managers involved in the strategy that all new product development was benchmarked in relation to LEGO as a brick, rather than the more inclusive dimension of *stimulation creativity*. The transfer of LEGO values to the computer universe proved to be easier in theory than in practice. New questions popped up like; 'How does a LEGO person move in a virtual environment?' and 'what is the sound of the 'click' when two virtual LEGO bricks are being put together?' In relation to the lifestyle products such as clothes and accessories, the LEGO employees spent time considering whether LEGO clothes could be pink and not just the classical LEGO signal colours and whether they had to have 'construction features' like zip-on hoods, pockets etc. – all compared to the basic brick look and functions. While having all the right external intentions, the extension efforts were slowed down by an organizational identity very closely related to the brick.

The Walt Disney Company: A Comparison

The Walt Disney Company seems to be a company in which the potential for extending the brand is almost intrinsic to its culture and identity. This is, we suggest, closely connected to the brand heritage of the company. One of the driving forces of the Disney brand is that all business units of the Walt Disney Company are grouped around one core value – entertainment. Entertainment and the Disney brand's supporting values of quality, variety and fun have been successfully diversified into different areas. (Disney Case, 2003; Balmer & Grey, 2003).

Today, the Disney brand is probably the world's strongest brand measured over time in the children's universe, and a very strong brand in general. From beginning more or less as a mouse and moving to animated film, Disney's brand is today to be found on four business segments: Media Networks, Studio Entertainment, Parks and Resorts and Consumer Products – which include children's electronic items, magazines, the Disney-branded Bank One credit card, breakfast foods and personal care products.

'Disney broadly diversified into television, commercials, music, comic strips and amusement parks at a time when other studios could think of little but celluloid.' (America's sorcerer, Economist, 1998)

How has this been possible? Even within the core business – film animation – Disney has introduced an incredibly large number of different stories and characters to the world over the years, and yet we still recognize 'The Disney Way' so clearly! And how is it possible to succeed with something like a Disney credit card? The first place to seek an explanation is in the philosophy of Walt Disney himself – a philosophy that is still the foundation of the Disney brand today. He was very creative, combined with extraordinary management skills and an admirable persistence in everything he did. He was the pioneer of animation, and challenged technology by making cartoons in around 1920. He and his organization has since won 48 Academy Awards for their exemplary work in this field. He broke the rules for family entertainment when creating his Disneyland, deeply disliking the traditional carnival and circus style. And one could even claim that he pioneered a whole new way of thinking marketing and branding. He was the first film producer to have a complete merchandising program, and the concept that all brand managers focuses on today - brand experience - was successfully implemented when Disney brought Mickey, Donald and Goofy to life in Disneyland. Furthermore, it could be claimed that Disney invented or set the standards for brand stretching by moving his brand gradually and successfully into new areas (Olins, 2003).

The core competencies of the Disney brand have been identified over the years in various analyses as a combination of *'globally recognized products'*, *'excellent human resource management practices'* and *'superior narrative powers in creating the 'Happiest Place on Earth'* (Brannen, 2004). In other words, the Disney brand today has its core competencies in three categories; products, practice and ideology, and all three can be traced back to the core philosophy and personality of the founder, Walt Disney.

The Walt Disney personality has been implemented and perpetuated in continual 'reinvention' of the firm, and has been successfully managed by Michael Eisner since 1984. Articles describing Eisner's management philosophy and style focus on his efforts of 'regrouping' through creativity and innovative idea generating processes. The Walt Disney Company is known for encouraging their people to have their say, and diversity of opinion, even friction, is seen as central to creating ideas and stimulating creative processes (Wetlaufer, 2000). This focus on employee involvement and creativity was formalized in 1993 in a concept called 'performance excellence', whereby all employees, from top to bottom, are involved, given responsibility and put in the centre of creative solutions. For example, three times a year, executives at the Walt Disney Company host a 'Gong Show' in which everyone in the company - including secretaries, janitors and mailroom staff - get to pitch movie ideas to the top executives (Chatman & Cha, 2004). Such cultural rituals at least suggest that the Walt Disney Company is open to new ideas that originate inside the company.

This management philosophy and heritage has fostered a culture in the Walt Disney Company that appears to be able to encompass a wide range of business areas and a diverse work force, ranging from the movie industry to the retail sector. One exception to this rule is the problems that Disney has encountered with its Euro-Disney theme park near Paris. The Disney culture appeared to clash with French/European culture, as employees refused to follow the strict rules for personal appearance demanded by Disney, and adult European customers refused to 'enjoy Coca-Cola' with their meals. As a whole, however, Disney appears to have an innovative and inclusive culture. And in contrast to the LEGO Group, brand extension has very much been an intrinsic part of the Disney Corporation's cultural heritage.

Conclusion:
Brand Extention in a Corporate Branding Perspective

In this chapter we have analyzed the LEGO Corporate Brand Stretch process in the context of the Corporate Brand Stretch Model. We have also given a brief account of the brand extension history in the Walt Disney Company for the purpose of comparison. In table 7:1 below, we summarize the comparison between the LEGO Group and the Walt Disney Company on the basis of key dimensions in the Corporate Brand Stretch Model.

Table 7:1 Comparison Between Corporate Brand Stretch in the LEGO Group and the Walt Disney Company

Dimension	LEGO Group	Walt Disney Company
Brand Identity	Reinterpretation of core from 'brick' to 'creativity' after over 60 years	Gradual development in scope, but a strong focus on the same core – entertainment
Organizational Identity	'Who we are' related to unique product idea (the LEGO brick)	'Who we are' related to value; entertainment (quality, variety and fun)
Corporate culture	Product-based culture	Brand stretch culture
Corporate Image	Linked to LEGO brick	Linked to variety of products and emotional attributes
Market Context	Construction toys under pressure from market (KGOY, electronic games, etc.)	Film, media and story consumption is steadily growing among children and adults

Corporate Brand Stretch

We opened this chapter with Wally Olins and will listen to him again here at the end. In one sentence, Olins once explained the difference between the scope of the LEGO and Disney brands:

'Disney is a badly drawn mouse with a lot of emotions – LEGO is a genius building brick without any emotions' (Wally Olins)

The statement by Wally Olins above highlights one of the main reasons for Disney's successful Corporate Brand Stretch strategy and the barriers the LEGO Group has been facing. Disney's brand identity, as mentioned earlier, is centered on the core brand essence – *entertainment* – backed up by values such as quality, variety and fun. In many ways, this is a very broad and rather generic essence. But the way it has been managed and expressed over time, from telling stories to movies, parks and books, always with a touch of magic and imagination, has given the brand a distinct Disney 'feel'. Disney is a brand 'born' with associations linked to a founder-personality and philosophy, rather than a product idea, which allowed the extendability from cartoons to credit cards.

From the perspective of the Corporate Brand Stretch model, we can say that LEGO got caught in the product-attribute-fixation-trap, with a brand identity dominated by product attributes. For the LEGO brand, it proved to be a trap in more ways than one. Even if LEGO redefined the core of the brand to a single-minded brand identity with an emotional focus, consumers would not quickly let go of the associations linked to the building brick. And neither would the organization and the employees. Changing a brand strategy that has been equal to a product – and a unique one at that – for a lifetime, requires much more than just communicating this new strategy to employees. It is a matter of cultural change, and changing the deeply rooted understanding of what the company and brand *is*. The time factor also plays an important role, as a gradual diversification strategy over several years would have made this process smoother, both internally and externally.

Furthermore, a brand image that has been built and reinforced for decades and generations does not change overnight, and one major reason for LEGO's difficulties is this time aspect. Consumers were not ready – and might never be – to regard LEGO as anything but colorful plastic bricks. We believe that the transition from being a brick to a broader perceived brand – *stimulating creativity* – should have happened gradually, with greater investment in communicating this to the consumers, backed up with proof, which in this case would mean successful products.

In contrast to the LEGO Group, the Walt Disney Company seems to have been able to align both the internal and the external demands of brand extension. We can see on various measurements of strong brands (such as Young & Rubicam Brand Asset Valuator and Interbrand's top 100) that Disney is a consistently strong brand. We have not researched the culture and identity of the Walt Disney Company as we have in the LEGO Group. However, the fact that Disney has not abandoned its brand extension strategy (although it has scaled down, for example, on its retail operations) suggests that the company is still able to support this strategy, also in terms of culture and identity. Furthermore, the Disney brand was 'born' with an emotional core and hence the scope of the extensions did not call for radical cultural changes, while LEGO has had to redefine this core and make larger changes, both in internal self perception and external associations.

We believe a Corporate Brand Stretch needs to be regarded as being as strategic and holistic as all other corporate branding issues. There is a tendency both in practice and academia to fully acknowledge the fact that corporate branding has internal as well as external stakeholders, and that corporate branding is a management matter. But when it comes to actual strategic changes, such as brand extension, the focus is still external and the perspective tends to be classical marketing.

The Corporate Brand Stretch model can serve as a strategic perspective on brand extension at two levels:

1) As an *analytical framework* for analyzing the potential of a Corporate Brand Stretch, where the two internal and two external

elements are the areas that need analysis and research in order to gather input on competencies, organizational identity, current external image and brand associations, as well as the competitive environment and consumer trends in the potential new markets. This information should serve as a basis for determining the potential and scope of the brand, as well as for understanding and agreeing upon the core essence of the brand – defining a precise brand identity (the centre of the model) for the future strategy.

2) As an *implementation framework*, illustrating the areas that need to be addressed in relation to the prior analysis of the four elements. In practice and in the literature, the traditional marketing perspective focuses on and allocates resources to communicating the changes to the external audiences and positioning the activities according to the competitive environment. Our focus and the contribution of the model is thus the implementation of the brand strategy change among the internal audiences, with a focus on organizational identity and culture. The alignment of the four factors in the implementation process implies that in order to succeed at brand extension, the internal focus is crucial.

The answer to the question we posed at the beginning of this chapter – why some brands such as Virgin are successful in their brand extension efforts while others are less successful – should be found not by only looking at external issues, but also by considering the way in which the internal factors support the brand extension strategy. We see that while the corporate branding literature is generally paying increasing attention to internal factors, this is not acknowledged in the 'extension' literature. Furthermore, practice is still lagging behind in terms of allocating the necessary resources for examining the cultural readiness and support in the organization for any brand strategy issue. We recognize that it is possible to align organizational identity and culture to a new market position or organization containing several new product areas and brands (cf., for example, Morsing, 1999). However, as we have shown, this is a risky strategy and cannot be done overnight. Trying to do so may ultimately force a company to give up the Corporate Brand Stretch strategy (as the LEGO Group has done). We therefore close this chapter by suggesting that a Corporate Brand Stretch should begin with the question: Do our organizational identity and culture support the strategy? And if not, what will it take, in terms of time and resources, to make the necessary changes?

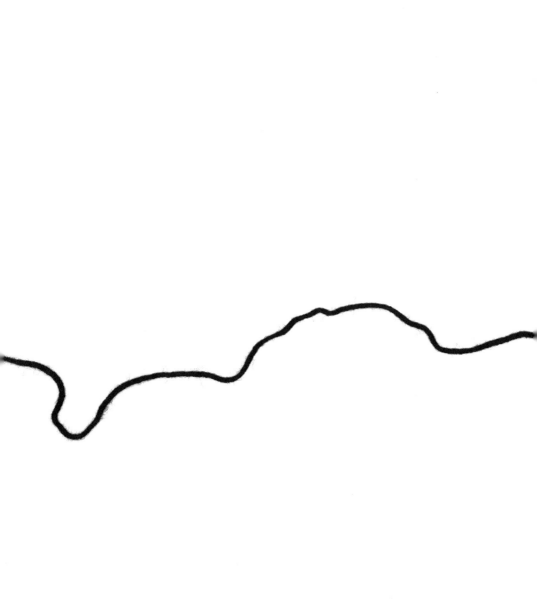

CHAPTER 8

CORPORATE BRANDING AS ORGANIZATIONAL CHANGE

Majken Schultz

Chapter 8 offers an analytical framework for how to understand and manage the implementation of corporate brands and argues that corporate brand implementation can best be conceived as processes of organizational change. Similar to change management, the implementation of corporate branding involves a series of cycles with different managerial and organizational challenges. These cycles are defined as 1) Stating; 2) Organizing; 3) Involving; 4) Integrating; and 5) Monitoring. The chapter advances a dynamic model for creating and implementing corporate brands and points at the risks comprised in the transformation between the change cycles.

One of the most profound implications of the shift from classic branding to corporate branding is that corporate branding becomes a strategic process. This is because the implementation of a corporate brand requires an organization-wide change involving multiple internal and external stakeholders. The most significant difference between classic branding and corporate branding concerns the involvement of managers and employees from different functions and subcultures in realizing the vision of the corporate brand. Clearly, the depth and scope of a corporate brand change process depends on the specific strategic context. However, it is the overall argument of this chapter that the implementation of corporate brands poses different managerial and organizational challenges than the implementation of product brands or sub-brands. The chapter further suggests that organizational change serves as a relevant lens for understanding the particular challenges of second wave corporate branding. Thus, I argue that concepts and experiences from change management and organizational development are able to contribute to the analysis and management of the corporate brand implementation processes (e.g. Quinn & Cameron, 1988; Beer et al., 1990; French & Bell, 1990; Kanter et al. 1992; Tichy & Sherman, 1993; French et al., 1994).

All too often, the implementation of a corporate brand is viewed as a more comprehensive version of product branding. This entails a strong focus on the aspired brand position and communication of the desired brand identity, particularly in relation to consumers. As a result, corporate branding programs are often restricted to the definition of the brand essence (identity and position); the elaboration of brand design and architecture (from logos to brand manuals), and the launch of the new brand ideas in marketing campaigns and media-driven brand building programs. Although brand scholars, such as Keller (1998), Aaker & Joachimsthaler (2000) and Aaker (2004), have stressed the implications of brand strategy for organizational structure and processes, they focus on issues related to brand portfolio management and rarely address the managerial and organizational challenges involved in the execution of corporate brands.

The analysis and suggestions for corporate brand implementation in this chapter are based on my work with Mary Jo Hatch. Together we have developed a process model for how corporate brand implementation can proceed - The Cycles of Corporate Branding (Schultz & Hatch, 2003, 2005). It is a further development of the

Corporate Branding Tool-Kit (Schultz, Chapter 2; Hatch & Schultz, 2001, 2003). The Cycles model suggests a sequence of the stages – or cycles – that companies ideally go through as they implement corporate brands. However, based on our collective and individual work with a number of companies, we have found that in practice, branding processes tend to involve more challenges, complexity and conflict than suggested by the earlier versions of the Cycles Model.

As part of our research activities, we invited corporate brand management executives to join us in a mutual learning network called the Corporate Branding Initiative (see www.brandstudies.com). The companies involved included LEGO Group, ING Group, Johnson & Johnson, Boeing, Nissan, Novo Nordisk, SONY, and Telefonica. Change expert, Phil Mirvis, has also been essential to this process. From these companies, we learned that corporate branding is a highly dynamic undertaking, where managers change their own theories of action as they engage in the corporate brand implementation process. We also learnt that there are many reasons why corporate branding poses special challenges to the implementation process.

Firstly, the *scale* of corporate branding is different from that of product branding. Corporate branding involves the entire organization and cannot be realized without strong support from the CEO. It almost inevitably requires a reallocation of central corporate resources, as different business practices are being revisited with the corporate brand in mind. Furthermore, corporate brands often span different business areas and markets. This makes building, revitalizing or redirecting corporate brands a very comprehensive and time-consuming effort for all C-level executives.

Secondly, the *scope* of corporate branding is more comprehensive than product branding, as corporate branding involves myriads of internal and external stakeholders. In order for corporate brands to express their central idea as a company, the implementation process includes everyone from top managers to the front line sales force. As a result a host of different interests and voices among internal stakeholders form opinions about the corporate brand. Also, the exposure and transparency of corporate brands mean that a range of different external stakeholders, besides consumers, build relationships with a corporate brand.

Finally, the *tensions* embedded in corporate brand implementation exceed those for other kinds of brand implementation. In particular, the cross-disciplinary and cross-functional nature of corporate branding makes the implementation process vulnerable to turf-issues, corporate power struggles and status conflicts. These factors make corporate brand building more time consuming and conflict-ridden than other types of brand management (for an overview of brand strategies see Aaker & Joachimsthaler, 2000; Kapferer, 2004).

In combination, these issues often leave corporate brand implementation processes more messy and non-linear than suggested by normative frameworks. This brings the implementation of corporate brands closer to the processes often described by organizational change scholars. As mentioned above, this chapter is founded on the cycles of corporate branding, as developed by Schultz and Hatch (2003, 2004). The chapter expands the cycles using concepts and insights from organizational change and transformational leadership. It also elaborates the tensions and challenges which corporate brand implementation poses to companies and managers alike. Furthermore, it suggests some levers from change management that may guide organizations through the change processes.

The Cycles of Corporate Branding

Parallel to much thinking on organizational change processes, a corporate brand building process can be conceived as a sequence of several stages or cycles (Schultz & Hatch, 2003; Schultz & Hatch, 2005). The five cycles can be summarized as:

- Cycle 1. *Stating* who you are and who you want to become
- Cycle 2. *Organizing* behind your identity
- Cycle 3. *Involving* all relevant stakeholders
- Cycle 4. *Integrating* all expressions of your brand
- Cycle 5. *Monitoring* results through performance measurements

In their most orchestrated version, these cycles represent different stages in the formation or renewal of a corporate brand. As such they serve as a normative framework for the strategic management of corporate brands. They are initiated by top management, but involve the whole organization. The suggested sequence of cycles is based on studies from several corporations and conceptualizes the intentions and direction often found in corporate brand implementation. But organizations may well experience branding processes which are less straightforward. For example, organizations with a strong tradition for employee involvement such as universities and professional service companies may start with an involvement cycle, as employee commitment is intrinsic to the statement of the brand. By the same token, companies with a strong global outlook may originate from an integrating cycle defining the scope of a possible future brand identity in relation to its global presence and local stakeholder involvement. Thus, based on how corporate branding occurs in practice, the cycles can also be conceived as a conceptual framing of the emergent processes of corporate branding. These processes sometimes co-exist and unfold in less predictable ways than suggested in the above sequence.

In the remainder of this chapter, the definitions and sequence of the cycles will serve as the overall analytical framework for a deeper discussion of the actual tensions, challenges and levers within each cycle. The conceptualization of the cycles is based on the Corporate Branding Tool-Kit in the sense that each cycle addresses all elements of the corporate brand: Organization culture, strategic vision and stakeholder images all related to organizational identity. The brand elements of the Tool-Kit will most likely form different constellations in each cycle. The different cycles are illustrated in relation to the Corporate Branding Tool-Kit in figure 8:1

Figure 8:1 Cycles of Corporate Branding

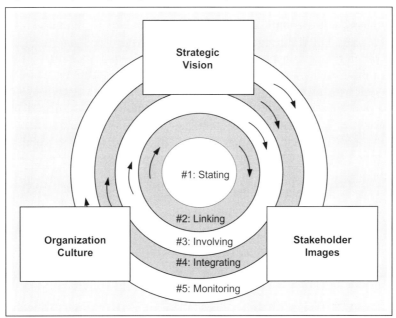

Looking across the five cycles of corporate branding, there are a number of concerns that are particularly emphasized when corporate branding is conceived as a process of organizational change. Inspired by the work on life-cycles and the shifting challenges to change management suggested by Greiner and others (Greiner, 1972; French & Bell, 1990; Schein, 1992; Greiner & Malernee, 2005), the cycles of corporate branding also pose shifting requirements to managers and open up a changing array of potential tensions and crisis. However, change management also inspires a range of action opportunities for corporate brand implementation (Quinn & Cameron, 1988; Beer et al., 1990; Kanter et al., 1992; Tichy & Sherman, 1993; French et al., 1994).

As argued by Schultz and Hatch (2003), the dominant change mode shifts between decentralization and centralization, which is mirrored in the ways organizational structure and processes are adapted to support the corporate brand. Obviously, the specific change organization depends on contingencies such as company size, organization culture, management style, etc., but all other things being equal, the organizational requirements to support the corporate branding process also change with the cycles. The key processes and activities of each cycle are summarized in table 8:1.

As argued in the life-cycle model (Greiner, 1972; Greiner & Malernee, 2005) the transition phases between the different stages in a company's life comprise a special set of risks or requirements that need to be fulfilled in order for the organization to be able to move on to the next stage. Inspired by this stream of thinking, it can be argued that there are certain conditions that need to be met within each cycle in order for the cycle to be fully completed. A lack of completion of the activities critical to the completion of the cycle may distort the further development of the corporate brand. In contrast to the determined sequence of stages suggested by the life-cycle models, Schultz & Hatch (2003) have argued that the sequence of corporate branding cycles vary in practice, just as branding cycles sometimes overlap or are executed simultaneously.

Table 8:1 The Challenges of Corporate Brand Implementation

Cycles of corporate branding	Cycle 1: Stating	Cycle 2: Organizing	Cycle 3: Involving	Cycle 4: Integrating	Cycle 5: Monitoring
Key Problems	Fragmented company-wide brand expression.	Lack of coherent brand organization and execution.	Generate shared mindset among employees and customer involvement.	Make full move from product to corporate brand behavior.	Ensure full operation ownership to all business units: the brand is everywhere.
Key Process: Corporate Branding Tool-Kit	Stating the identity and vision of the corporate brand: Who are we as an organization and who do we want to become?	Linking vision to culture and image practices: How can we reorganize behind the brand?	Involving stakeholders through culture and image: How can we involve internal and external stakeholders in the brand?	Integrating vision, culture and image around a new identity: How can we align the organization behind the brand?	Tracking corporate branding gaps and brand performance: What are the critical factors in our internal and external brand performance?
Challenges of Change: Key Tension	Brand narcissism embedded in culture and identity vs. brand hyper adaptation driven by image.	Brand policing directed by programs and manual vs. brand turfs generated by functions and markets.	Brand commitment and identification vs. brand overload and process exhaustion.	Brand isolated in headquarters vs. brand fragmented by local subsidiaries.	Brand obsession with quantitative measurement vs. intuitive follow up on brand performance.
Change crisis	Needed to create vision among top managers.	Need to conduct full organization wide execution.	Need to involve all internal subcultures.	Need to generate local brand owner ship and involvement.	Need to insist on cross-functional knowledge.
Levers Key Activity:	(Re)articulate core values and define identity behind brand.	Reshape organization managerial structure and processes.	Engage employees in execution and involve consumer images.	Create brand balance between global coherence and local buy in.	Set up relevant monitoring systems.
Change Organization	Top management guidance. Internal task force. External visual identity.	Top management execution of cross-functional structure and process changes.	Internal organizational development process. Consumer reactions (focus groups, communities).	Organization wide execution of structure and local process. Local stakeholder involvement.	Monitor unit including internal and external knowledge. Organization wide distribution of knowledge.

Elaborated from Schultz, M. & Hatch, M.J. (2003): The Cycles of Corporate Branding: The Case of LEGO Company, *California Management Review*

Similar to the life-cycle argument, I believe there are certain needs that are likely to generate a crisis in the corporate branding process, if they are not being met within each individual cycle – independent of the sequence of cycles. These needs are illustrated within the life-cycle framework in figure 8:2 using the different cycles as a parallel to the growth stages in the life-cycle work (see Greiner & Malernee, 2005: 274). The model illustrates that the cycles develop over time, just as the implementation, all other things being equal, becomes more and more comprehensive within the organization.

Figure 8:2 Potential Crises in Corporate Brand Implementation

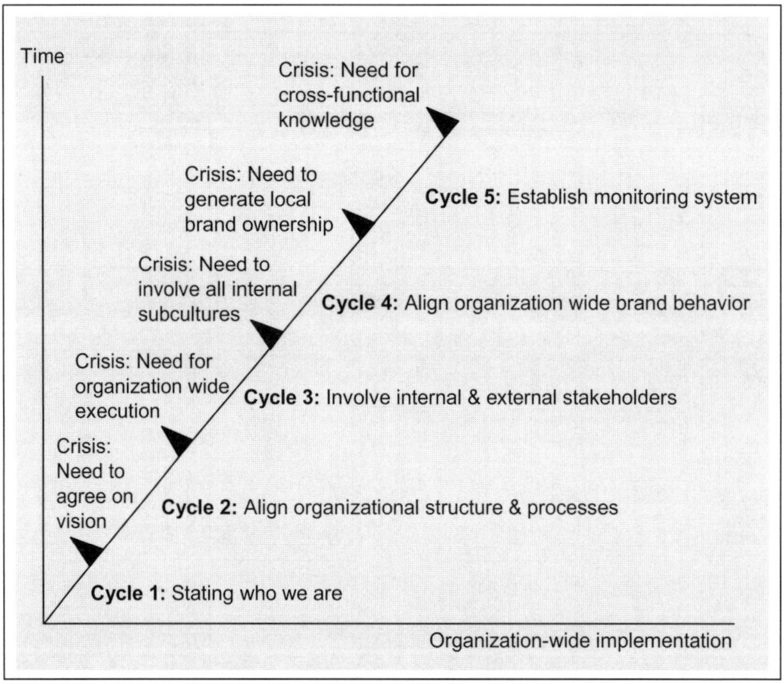

```
Time
                                Crisis: Need for
                                cross-functional
                                knowledge

                Crisis: Need to
                generate local         Cycle 5: Establish monitoring system
                brand ownership

            Crisis: Need to
            involve all internal
            subcultures              Cycle 4: Align organization wide brand behavior

        Crisis: Need for
        organization wide     Cycle 3: Involve internal & external stakeholders
        execution

    Crisis:
    Need to
    agree on
    vision           Cycle 2: Align organizational structure & processes

        Cycle 1: Stating who we are

                                            Organization-wide implementation
```

Stating the Corporate Brand

The first cycle focuses on *stating* who we are as an organization (identity) and who we want to become (strategic vision). The impulse for a Stating Cycle can, of course, be the need to build a new corporate brand. However, most often the key concern behind the Stating Cycle is the fragmented brand expressions that develop over time in most companies. They typically derive from mergers, acquisitions or expansions into new business areas. In its most obvious form, such fragmentation can be observed by incoherence in the claimed brand identity (e.g. different logos, taglines, web-sites). But for corporate brands, fragmentation includes all manifestations defined by the Corporate Branding Tool-Kit (Schultz, Chapter 2; Hatch & Schultz 2001, 2003).

Key Change Process. The Tool-Kit can be applied by managers to analyze the various brand elements and diagnose the depth of gaps between them. This is useful in order to motivate the organization to acknowledge problems in the current expression of the brand and move towards a restatement of the brand. In assessing and restating the vision for a corporate brand, managers need to consider both the *organization culture* (e.g. past identity claims and their embedment in the organization culture) and *stakeholder images* (e.g. past and current stakeholder perceptions of the company, its products and people). Such analysis requires a combination of cross-functional knowledge. This is because knowledge about organization identity and culture is typically located within human resources units, while knowledge about image and reputation most often reside within marketing and corporate communication functions.

When organizations go through a Stating Cycle, cross-functional knowledge can be brought forward as part of the organizational process. This involves managers and employees from different business functions meeting and exchanging knowledge about perceptions and performances of the brand. In my experience, such exchanges of cross-functional knowledge rarely happen in most companies, but generate huge surprises and valuable company-wide insights when they do occur. The Corporate Branding Tool-Kit can serve as a foundation for restating the brand. For example, awareness of branding gaps enable companies to distinguish between *constructive gaps,* such as when vision and identity challenge existing culture and images and are able to mobilize employees in moving towards the aspired vision; and *destructive gaps,* such as when a vision is completely detached from the organizational culture and seen as untrustworthy by external stakeholders.

The Stating Cycle can be initiated by top management in many different strategic contexts. It can be the beginning of a new brand, as when Amazon.com© or Virgin was founded with a unique identity. More often, it emerges from the need to renew the corporate brand because the company is facing a new strategic situation. Such a situation can result from mergers, take-overs or expansion into new areas or markets. Or the need to renew can simply derive from the fact that the brand has lost its competitiveness, attraction and ability to engage stakeholders. Many companies regularly revisit their corporate brand and restate the expressions of their brand identity. For example, Danish audiovisual technology producer, Bang & Olufsen, has regularly redefined the balance between their cultural heritage and adaptation to shifting trends in design and lifestyles in the global marketplace. This is seen, for example, in the development of their company logo (e.g. Ravasi & Schultz, 2005, and illustrated in figure 8:3).

Figure 8:3 Bang & Olufsen's Changing Visual Identity

Another example is the historical development of the Volkswagen brand through a series of transformations, as told by Olins (2004). Here, significant symbolic expressions of the Volkswagen heritage have been combined with reinventions of the brand that have enabled the company to innovate and yet preserve its brand identity for decades.

Challenges of Change. From the beginning of the implementation, managers are confronted with tensions and contradictory developments. They need to be balanced and orchestrated carefully in order for the corporate branding process not to get side-tracked or disrupted. The activities within the Stating Cycle are typically decentralized in the sense that stating a credible vision for the corporate brand requires managers to combine multiple types of knowledge generated by different business functions and articulated by different stakeholders. Internally, this knowledge covers an understanding of the company's cultural heritage and of how organizational members perceive identity claims and strategic vision. Externally, managers need to obtain knowledge about (global) consumer images and what the brand means to different stakeholders. As a consequence, when stating the vision and identity for the brand, top managers are often confronted with internal forces arguing to express the brand vision and identity grounded in the cultural heritage, as this heritage represents the most unique, non-imitable resource of the brand. Other organizational members, belonging to different business functions, are more inclined to suggest that the identity of the brand should reflect current needs and perceptions among consumers. Otherwise, the brand will lose its relevance and emotional attraction to consumers.

As argued by Hatch and Schultz (2002) these tensions can lead to either narcissism (brand defined by internal cultural expressions only) or hyper-adaptation (brand defined by external image adaptations only). In both cases, this tension derives from a disconnection between organizational culture and stakeholder images, and may cause either a neglect of stakeholder images or a loss of organizational culture. Balancing the insights generated from both culture and images when stating the corporate brand is therefore one of the key tensions facing top managers (see also Schultz & Hatch, 2003; Ravasi & Schultz, 2005). It becomes further complicated by the fact that in most companies, these two perspectives on how to state the corporate brand are nested by different business functions.

In the companies I have worked with, I have observed this paradoxical tension manifest itself as misunderstandings, power conflicts and the deliberate creation of obstacles to managers and employees representing the opposite point of view. For this reason, one of the most crucial top managerial tasks in corporate brand implementation is to foresee and address such key paradoxes, as they re-emerge in all stages of the brand implementation process. Following the advice of proponents of paradox management (Quinn, 1988; Poole & Van de Ven, 1989) the managerial goal should not be to eliminate such tensions, as they represent valuable contributions to the brand implementation. Rather they should be acknowledged and kept alive as part of the corporate brand – while also being confronted and carefully balanced. Due to these tensions, the most pertinent crisis occurs when top managers (the C-level) are not in agreement about the vision and identity for the brand. The subsequent cycles of organizing and involving will suffer extensively from the power struggles, politics and in-fighting that accompany a lack of top-management buy-in. This is not an unusual crisis in many larger companies, and the CEO often underestimates the need for a full cross-functional buy-in to a corporate brand strategy. The need for managerial commitment across business areas is also stressed in transformational leadership in the importance of sharing the awakening and envisioning act among top managers.

Levers for Change. It is my argument that managers involved in corporate branding can learn from change management when coping with the challenges of brand implementation. Building on change management, the first steps towards corporate branding include the need to explain to employees and other close stakeholders *why* the company has chosen a corporate brand strategy. This calls for leaders to be explicit about the competitive and/or political pressures on the company and 'mobilize commitment to change through joint diagnosis of business problems' (Beer et al, 1990: 161). Regardless of the specific circumstances, a (re)stating of the corporate brand will demand a change in everyday practices from many employees, as a revised brand identity most often requires new ways of enacting the brand towards external stakeholder (i.e. renewing culture-image relationships). Thus, a redefinition of strategic vision demands that employees are able to re-conceptualize the future direction of the organization and link it to their current practices. Together these activities entail a substantial change effort at many levels in the organization. According to change management, creating a sense of urgency is an important foundation for motivating employees to open themselves to a change process (Kotter, 1995). Experts in transformational change have called this the 'awakening' act, which supports employees' motivation to disengage from the past by feeling the need for profound organizational change (Tichy & Sherman, 1993).

A starting point in many companies is an audit of current brand expressions showing the fragmented ways in which the company has expressed its identity when interacting and communicating with various stakeholders (culture and image). The data audited depends on the nature of the business. It may include everything from observations of employee and consumer interaction, crucial in service industries, to a critical scrutiny of packaging, corporate advertising and marketing material, central in many consumer brands (Olins, 1989; 2004). A company wide audit sometimes uses external consultants with expertise in visual identity. Furthermore, branding 'creatives' are often involved in making the new identity and vision comprehensive and evocative through the design of symbols and other tangible brand expressions. This interaction with external consultants poses huge challenges to top managers. One challenge includes avoiding internal business functions, such as marketing or corporate communication, identifying more with the aspirations of the consultants than with the requirements of the company. Another temptation is for top management to delegate the stating of the brand entirely to external consultants, at the risk that the brand does not get sufficiently grounded in the organizational culture. As a result it becomes difficult or impossible for employees subsequently to deliver the promises of the brand to external stakeholders.

To create the organizational support for the Stating Cycle, top managers may set up temporary, cross-functional teams to provide the substantial input to the brand vision and identity claims, for example, by collecting and analyzing various sources of knowledge (past tracking, culture and image insights). However, the actual decisions about vision and future identity are most often made in a strategic setting (workshops, board seminars) orchestrated by top management. In such a setting, the development and communication of a strategic vision for the brand is a source of shared direction that offers a reduction in the uncertainty and anxiety provoked by the awareness of the need to change (Beer et al, 1990; Kanter et.al, 1992; Kotter, 1995). Thus, the Stating Cycle constitutes the beginning of the envisioning act, which continues through the subsequent cycles (Tichy & Forman, 1993). Finally, the mobilization of political support in the organization by forming a powerful coalition, or other forms of organizational buy-in (e.g. line up political sponsorship as expressed by Kanter et al, 1992), is stressed as a necessary condition for successful change (French et al., 1994; Borum, 1995). The cross-functional nature of corporate branding makes a political buy-in process more complicated, but also more essential, as a corporate branding effort cannot be implemented by top management or any marketing or communication function alone. Compared with classic change management, the Stating Cycle collapses the first of several change phases, such as establishing a sense of urgency, the development of a shared vision and the first steps in building a powerful coalition among key internal stakeholders.

Organizing for the Corporate Brand

The second cycle, *organizing,* aims to reshape organizational structures and processes to support the restated vision and identity of the brand. While still heavily involved in communicating the brand vision to stakeholders, top management has to concentrate on reorganizing the company to support the implementation of the brand strategy developed in Cycle 1.

Key Change Process. The goal of the Organizing Cycle is to link the aspirations of the brand (vision and identity) with the practices of the brand in relation to internal (culture) and external (image) stakeholders. In other words, the Organizing Cycle seeks to facilitate a stronger alignment between Brand Talk and Brand Action. In most cases, such alignment entails a reorganizing effort in order to enable employees to 'walk the talk'. A company wide assessment of the need to organize and follow up action is typically a top-down process - in contrast to the Involvement Cycle, which has a much stronger bottom-up character. When the strategic vision and brand identity have been restated, top management must ensure that organizational systems and processes enable organizational members to work in the desired direction. Top management can actively initiate a redesign process aimed at reconfiguring structures and processes in ways that support the brand strategy. Based in the vision and identity statement, managers should consider how they can enable the various subcultures in the organization to deliver a credible 'brand promise'. As shown in chapter 2, the shift from product branding to corporate branding creates opportunities to develop more comprehensive relationships between consumers and the brand. In classic branding, consumers' brand experiences are created through individual products and services only. This is different in corporate branding, where a much more complete brand experience is created through all business processes relating to the consumer, as all processes are intended to express the brand identity. This means, for example, that distribution, communication and innovation processes should be reorganized in the light of the brand identity and their contribution to the strategic vision. This organization of business processes as brand expressions is illustrated in figure 8:4.

Corporate Branding as Organizational Change

Figure 8:4 The Shift from Classic Branding to Corporate Branding

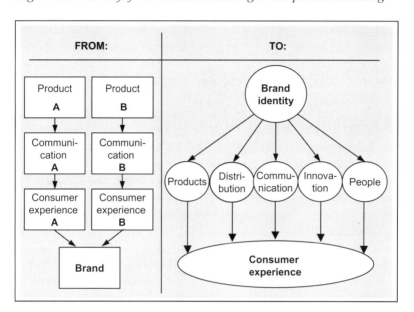

For example, when restating their identity in the mid-nineties, the top management of Bang & Olufsen concluded that their distribution also had to convey a strong experience of the brand along with their products. This led the company to reorganize its distribution and communication processes. They decided to establish their own Bang & Olufsen brand stores and abandon a large number of their previous multi-brand dealers, from the local radio store to the large discounters. This had huge implications for their stakeholder relations, as the dedicated Bang & Olufsen dealers became much more affiliated with the company and part of the organizational culture. Similarly, when Dutch financial services ING Group launched their consumer friendly bank, ING Direct, in the United States, their web-based services were accompanied by a series of small ING Direct Cafés in central city districts, where customers could access their on-line financial services, while enjoying a café latte.

Challenges of Change. The consequences of revisiting business processes are often changes in organization structure and performance systems. For example, some companies aim at a more coherent brand organization by designing a new corporate branding unit, as pharmaceutical company, Novo Nordisk, and LEGO Group have done

(Schultz & Hatch, 2003). Others develop liaison roles or ensure buy-in processes among managers of the involved functions. Companies are increasingly rethinking the definition of roles and responsibilities for managing the brand in order to create stronger linkages between the different business functions and their contribution to the corporate brand. For example, some companies support a stronger integration between corporate communication and marketing by creating one large communication unit, such as Danish financial services company, Danske Bank. Others, such as Novo Nordisk, have enhanced the relationships between corporate communication, human resources and their corporate social responsibility activities through recent reorganization. New structures and roles are often accompanied by brand driven performance measures facilitating a stronger alignment between employee behavior (organizational culture) and the central identity claims (brand values).

As one would expect, such significant redistributions of power and status often cause clashes between subcultures and/or resistance towards the inclusion of new cultures with competencies required to fill in the new brand organization. This is illustrated by Gjøls-Andersen and Karmark (Chapter 7), in their discussion of how a new business unit - LEGO Media, aimed at supporting the restated corporate brand - required the inclusion of a completely new professional culture (programmers and software experts). These new professionals soon became a subculture in the company. Thus, the reorganizing cycle often poses managerial challenges that emerge from the interrelatedness between organizational structure and organizational culture (see Martin, 2002, and her inclusion of structural practices in the culture concept; Schein, 2004).

In relation to stakeholder images, the Organizing Cycle often results in a new or revised brand architecture and portfolio management system following from the brand identity (Aaker & Joachimsthaler, 2000; Aaker, 2004). A typical ambition is to design a more consistent, clear and accessible organization of brand experiences, which explains the scope and levels of the brand to external stakeholders. For example, through a series of acquisitions, SONY has gradually, but systematically, brought the various companies from different industries closer to the SONY brand by changing the balance between the SONY name and that of the acquired company. Another example is the way that Apple has used their iconic 'I' in their brand extension into music (i-pod, i-tunes etc.). As mentioned in chapter 2, there is a close relationship between brand architecture and organization structure, to

Corporate Branding as Organizational Change

the extent that many business units are defined according to their overall brand architecture. For example, the brand architecture of large corporations such as FedEx and Virgin reflects the range of business units, as both companies use a combination of their corporate brand and descriptors stating the nature of the business unit. This is demonstrated by some of the Virgin brands shown in figure 8:5.

Figure 8:5 Examples of the Virgin Corporate Brand

A core tension of the Organizing Cycle concerns how the reorganization of the brand is manifested in the full range of brand expressions. The classic tension is between a centralized top-down policing of the brand to ensure that all brand manifestations are expressed according to the identity guidelines (e.g. brand manual, design principles) and the brand architecture, versus a decentralized insistence on the value of expressions emerging from individual business units, historically based sub-brands, specialized customizations etc. This debate on the equity of decentralized brand expressions typically becomes an argument between managers from headquarters and managers from local markets, business units or functions with a more arms-length relationship to headquarters. Top management is confronted with the need to balance these brand tensions, acknowledging the risk that managers from corporate headquarters are most inclined to argue in favor of brand policing and may have little appreciation for the more decentralized arguments. Symbols, artifacts and other brand tangibles often serve as magnets of emotional involvement and personalized adaptations in local subcultures, such as when the logo is given an individual twist or local business units develop their own ways of expressing and communication the brand (Pratt & Rafaeli, 2005). Depending on the importance of organization-wide, global brand coherence to the company versus the equity of local adaptations, top management must balance between a complete turn-around of the brand identity and a more incremental, step-wise execution of the brand identity.

Levers for Change. Referring to classic change management, top management needs to 'empower others to act on the vision' as the foundation for the Organizing Cycle (Kotter, 1995). Leaders must also ensure that the organizational setting allows people to start working towards the vision for the brand by developing 'enabling structures' (Kanter et al., 1992; French & Bell, 1994). Other change experts stress the development of the organizational competencies needed to act on the new vision (Beer et al, 1990). This is often supported by a strong focus on short term wins, where employees early in the implementation process experience the satisfaction of accomplishment and learn that top management is dedicated to allowing them to 'walk the branding talk'. A profound top management commitment is needed to sustain employee motivation during these periods of reorganizing, often followed by a comprehensive communication to employees of the achievements and short term wins in the process (Kanter et. al, 1992; Ind, 2001).

We know from change management that reorganization is bound to cause anxiety and speculation among employees about the implications for their personal position within the company. The need for employee communication along with reorganization has often been underestimated by top managers, as classic branding has been dominated by an external focus and the expectation that market communication will reach employees through auto-communicative processes (Christensen & Cheney, 2000). If top managers acknowledge the potential resistance to reorganization behind the corporate brand, they are better equipped to state the business case for corporate branding and communicate it to the various subunits in ways that seem relevant. For example, on the path to corporate branding, the central branding units of Telefonica were confronted with severe skepticism from different business units (Mobile area) and markets (Latin America) about the relevance of the corporate brand to their business area. In this situation, it became necessary to be very specific about the benefits of corporate branding to the overall company. For example, Telefonica would gain substantial cost savings from corporate branding by reducing the number of agencies involved. Corporate branding would enable subunits to take advantage of the high profile corporate initiatives in areas of corporate social responsibility and social reporting. The corporate brand would also allow the company to expand more easily and quickly in new markets, as it reaped synergies between its different business areas.

In general, the need to reorganize has a more limited role in change management than is normally found in corporate brand implementation. A fundamental reason for this is that the move to corporate branding implies a cross-functional alignment and a critical scrutiny of the interfaces between marketing, corporate communication, sales, human resources and innovation. Furthermore, corporate branding typically requires a reorganization of the global organizational set-up, both internally and in relation to external agencies etc.

Involving Internal and External Stakeholders

The third cycle, *involving,* is dedicated to the involvement of all relevant stakeholders in the further realization of the corporate brand.

Key Change Process. The Involving Cycle seeks to align culture and image to vision through bottom-up processes. The brand identity and vision are further interpreted and applied by various key stakeholders through their active contributions. The core processes concern the facilitation of organizational culture change through involving employees. In my mind, a corporate brand implementation process opens up special ways of involving stakeholders that contributes to corporate branding as organizational change.

Firstly, corporate branding has a much stronger awareness of symbols, artifacts and other kinds of brand expressions than classic change management. Symbols evoke strong emotions and invite involvement due to their embedded, ambiguous nature (see Pratt & Rafaeli, 2005; Schultz et al., 2005). For example, LEGO Group developed a brand school where the deliberate use of core symbols and artifacts became part of the learning process (as cited in Schultz & Hatch, 2005; see also Schultz & Hatch, 2003). The goal was to introduce the vision for the LEGO Corporate brand to employees and create opportunities for them to make the new LEGO brand identity relevant to their various roles and responsibilities. The Brand School was founded in 2002 and consisted of 1-3 day workshops facilitated by a team of internal coaches supported by top management talks. The first round of Brand Schools focused on generating increased awareness of company values and brand strategy by communicating and debating the identity claims of the LEGO brand (e.g. value statements and brand personality). As it turned out, people had difficulty making these values relevant to their ongoing work and connecting them to the LEGO everyday behavior. These experiences influenced the second round of the Brand School, which was more concerned with 'living the brand' by creating role models among LEGO managers for how the LEGO brand values could be enacted on an everyday basis. This ambition inspired the construction of new brand expressions with strong symbolic meanings, such as exercises and working methods, in which abstract brand values were turned into tangible symbols by the Brand School participants. In this process, the use of the brick as the core artifact rooted in the LEGO organizational culture was particularly important. It led to several creative applications of the brick, as participants were invited to create their own expressions of the brand, e.g. playing with giant bricks made of soft material and engaging in self-expressive building exercises, such as building company values and discussing their symbolic meanings with others afterwards. The Brand School deliberately used the strength of the LEGO brand image to generate enthusiasm and creativity among employees. The Brand School also constructed new cultural forms, which took on new symbolic meanings; e.g. a 'value gallery', which is a game where pictures are used to help the participants articulate their associations with company values. In total, close to 2000 employees participated in the LEGO Brand School.

Secondly, corporate branding is more concerned with external stakeholders than change management. This may encourage managers to use insights, ironies and diversity from stakeholder images to question existing internal assumptions. But external stakeholders also create opportunities for direct interaction between employees and customers. Organizations can use the energy and surprises often found in such encounters to stimulate the elaboration and relevance of the brand. Many companies make substantial efforts to create dialogue between top management and employees in everything from global road shows to more intimate culture oriented programs. However, a branding perspective highlights the direct involvement of external stakeholders in these internal conversations. They can motivate employees to commit to the promises of the brand and bring new knowledge to the brand.

For example, in the launch of their 'I wish' branding campaign in 2000 (seeking to bring the lives and hopes of people suffering from diabetes center stage), Novo Nordisk encouraged each employee to spend a day with a diabetic, utilizing the connections between culture and image. According to the company, this initiative had profound influence on employee involvement in the brand. Likewise, when recruiting new employees to support their strong service brand, US carrier, Southwest Airlines©, always invites customers to sit on the recruitment panel, as they say 'Who knows more about the service that they want than the customers' (cited from Harvard Business School video). Others create value workshops and other kinds of process initiatives, where employees are engaged in the further interpretation of the brand identity and in translating its implications for their everyday behavior. External stakeholders can also be directly involved in these.

Thirdly, although general market and reputation research are included in Cycle 1 when assessing stakeholder perceptions of the brand, it is during Cycle 3 that direct stakeholder involvement starts to influence the branding process itself. Depending on the type of company and the depth of its relations with consumers and other stakeholders, companies can encourage more or less proactive consumer involvement. For example, a new brand architecture developed through Cycle 1 and 2 was consumer tested on a global scale in LEGO Group, including a series of focus groups made up of mothers and children in different countries. The ambition was to test the fit between consumers associations with the LEGO brand and the new architecture, to ensure that it covered the complete LEGO play universe in the minds of consumers. The test was based on a qualitative semiotic framework that delved deeply into an understanding of consumer associations and perceptions. Companies, such as Nissan, have developed extensive psychological profiles of their core customers based on a close interaction with customers dedicated to the Nissan brand.

Other kinds of stakeholder involvement are facilitated by sponsoring and brand events, where stakeholders are invited to participate in the orchestration of the brand experience. This is the case, for example, in the international ING Group, where a global program to sponsor significant global marathon races, the ING Globerunners Program, grew out of their ambition to build their corporate brand attributes, www.ing.com). After considering a range of different sponsoring alternatives, long-distance running was chosen, as it offered extensive opportunities to involve stakeholders, employees and potential customers directly in the brand experience by active participation in the growing number of global marathons, e.g. the ING Amsterdam Marathon, the ING New York Marathon etc. When they launched their sponsorship of the ING Amsterdam Marathon it was manifested through the use of another significant symbol of the ING Group, namely their famous corporate headquarter office close to Schiphol airport in Amsterdam. The whole building was dressed up as a gigantic running shoe, see figure 8:6.

Figure 8:6 ING Headquarters Dressed up as a Running Shoe

Finally, the accelerating growth in the co-creation of brand experiences through involvement of brand communities will facilitate an earlier and more dialogue-based adaptation and translation of the brand to specific consumer cultures, markets or individual needs (see Antorini & Andersen, Chapter 4; Muniz & O'Guinn, 2001).

Challenges of Change. From a top management perspective, Cycle 3 is the most challenging of the cycles, as leaders are required to switch from a top-down mode, using organizational structure design and management communication, to a bottom-up mode, facilitating and coaching the engagement of both internal and external stakeholders.

In relation to brand implementation, managers need to find the balance between constructive involvement and irrelevant brand overload. On the one hand, top management has to make a strong effort to involve employees in the branding process by offering all kinds of engaging opportunities inspired by organizational development, values-based management etc. On the other hand, managers need to acknowledge the risk of overloading and wearing out key employees with branding issues, which to some of them can be perceived as distant from their everyday activities. This may become even more the case when change processes in practice often consist of multiple, sometimes disconnected, change initiatives. As argued by Kanter et al. (1992), it becomes important for top management to consider how corporate branding activities interact with other ongoing changes taking place in the organization. This is particularly important, since many changes relevant to branding are not necessarily planned, but emerge from a shifting business context (e.g. new customers, shifting stakeholder relations, reinterpretation of identity in the marketplace).

The difficulties associated with cultural change have been emphasized by many scholars, just as the boundaries of legitimate normative control have been debated (Kunda, 1992; Martin 2002). There is no reason to believe that corporate branding processes will avoid the political and managerial tensions associated with cultural change. Thus, it becomes even more challenging for managers in organizations consisting of strong subcultures (functional, business areas, markets, etc.) to orchestrate the involvement of stakeholders. The dialogue between top and middle management will often have to balance the local perception of the brand within different subcultures with the concern for an overall company-wide direction. For this reason, the Involvement Cycle should allow a confrontation of sub-cultural conflicts and debate the implications of the brand for everyday employee behavior.

A classic mistake is to restrict corporate branding to employees working in marketing and communication units only, and to underestimate the need for the full organization to be involved. The need for top management to involve all subcultures is not only relevant to the understanding of the brand vision, but also the enactment of the corporate brand in the relationships with different stakeholders. Otherwise, a corporate brand risks creating further misalignment between organizational culture and stakeholder images, or exacerbating internal cultural fragmentation, for example between marketing, human resources and business development. In order to avoid change crises, it is crucial that top management is able to find ways to engage the different subcultures. This often entails the willingness to offer enough flexibility to create a meaningful dialogue between top management and the rest of the organization. In one of the companies I have been working with, the difficulty top management had in engaging in dialogue was expressed by a middle manager as follows: 'The keyword for the top manager is dialogue, but only as long as we all agree with him'.

Levers for Change. As argued by Beer et al., it is not sufficient for top management to try to push programmatic change processes through from the top. Employees need to be engaged in the revitalization of the brand and find their own connections with the new strategy (Beer et al., 1990). Thus, through employee involvement and additional market research, organizational culture and images are given a more proactive and decentralized role than in previous cycles. The importance of engaging employees has been stressed extensively by change management, both in the design of organizational processes and in the managerial honesty and integrity required in situations of change (Kanter et al., 1992; Tichy & Sherman, 1993). Furthermore, the continuous and immediate execution of short-term wins is central to change management, as it demonstrates the willingness of managers to 'walk the talk' and generates organization-wide confidence in the vision for change (Kotter, 1995). Finally, short-term wins are often executed by employees, giving them a more contributing role than just learning to 'talk the talk'. In this respect, the Involvement Cycle builds on the efforts initiated during the Organizing Cycle.

The involvement of employees will benefit from process insights and methods from organization change and development. The aim is to enhance employee commitment to the vision and identity for the brand and plant the seeds for cultural change. For example, the Involvement Cycle can include initiatives to strengthen cross-functional conversations and overcome myths, prejudices and stereotypes that exist among marketing, corporate communication and human resources. The development of a culture of collaboration and shared enthusiasm is an important foundation for realizing the aspirations of the brand. The change organization is very different in the Involving Cycle, than the in previous cycles. The internal ambition is to create an organizational process that invites employees to get involved in the brand and explore its implications for their everyday practices. Companies often combine opportunities for employees to interact with top management with cascading efforts, where employees in small groups or within their unit jointly conceive and elaborate the brand implications, as often suggested by organizational development programs (French et. al., 1994; French & Bell, 1990; French et. al., 1994).

When seeking to involve employees, top managers can take advantage of the uniqueness of the brand identity and use the evocativeness of brand symbols and imagery. In the notorious events at Scandinavian Airlines, former top manager, Jan Carlsson, deliberately used the airport hangars and air-captain mythology to engage front-line employees in his extensive rebranding effort (i.e. the Businessman's Airline). At the LEGO Group, top management playfully exploited the 'Pit-stop' image from the car racing world to stage their global road-shows. Very often, large global organizations also create on-line events encouraging global dialogue between managers and employees. Likewise, direct interactions and personal encounters between employees and consumers are facilitated by large-scale change programs. Sometimes these may turn into comprehensive, joint learning projects, as when Unilever created a program for transformational change encouraging a new cultural mindset. They combined new ambitions of leadership with a radical change of their business and brand (Mirvis et al., 2003). This change took the Unilever managers on a personal journey many places in the world, including the Sinai desert, stretching the boundaries of managerial involvement in brand transformation.

Integrating Behind the Brand

The fourth cycle, *integration,* has as the ambition to move forward in the organization-wide alignment by further reducing the gaps between the vision, culture and stakeholder images and their relations to the brand identity.

Key Change Process. Although it is never possible (or ideal) in a fast changing multi-cultural world to reach a fully integrated corporate brand, the integration cycle returns to a centralization mode by giving the company-wide brand alignment full attention. Particularly in large and global companies this may entail a substantial managerial effort in considering how the corporate brand should be implemented in local marketplaces, which will each have their specific organizational cultures and stakeholder images. Local employees and external stakeholders must get involved in the further translation of the brand, repeating the processes of the Involvement Cycle at the local level. As a result, the Integration Cycle often leads to new local cycles of brand involvement that facilitate the reshaping of the brand identity to the requirements of local cultures and images – all within the defined boundaries of the brand vision. As a consequence, the local business processes are scrutinized according to the new brand strategy. Most often, both the headquarters and subsidiaries need to redefine their ways of interacting with respect to both attitude and behavior.

Obviously, companies differ in the extent they will stress a global 'one-company-culture' or encourage a diverse set of local cultures. However, a corporate brand strategy sets much higher aspirations for the global development of a more shared internal brand culture than product driven brands, as the mindset and behavior of employees are a crucial foundation for the brand. Particularly in many international service companies, such as airlines and professional and financial services organizations, aligning attitudes and behavior across national cultures is a condition for a credible corporate brand. By the same token, many brands serve global customers or are faced with the same customers in different geographic settings.

Integration activities may also take place in periods outside big new launches or redefined statements of the brand. New business opportunities and ongoing brand extensions will challenge the boundaries of the brand identity and force managers to rethink the stretch and scope of the corporate brand. For example, when FedEx bought US-based Kinko's in 2004, the new FedEx corporate brand architecture was in place and the company had to decide how to integrate the rapidly expanding Kinko's into the FedEx corporate brand. The company was linked to the FedEx brand idea by being conceived as the 'office for the road' for traveling business professionals and remote workers, and was soon rebranded as 'FedEx Kinko's Office and Print Services'. This maintained loyalty to Kinko's while at the same time including it in the FedEx brand (see www.fedex.com). Time will tell whether the new Kinko's can deliver on this brand promise, or remain within its previous image, closer to the poor student's office hang out. As shown by Gjøls-Andersen and Karmark (Chapter 7), corporate brands have used different strategies for brand extensions and corporate brand integration.

Challenges of Change. Since a corporate brand partly originates from claims about who we are as an organization, there will most likely be a strong bias towards headquarter perceptions and experiences. Creating brand alignment at the local level and striking a balance between the classic dilemma of global integration and local adaptation is therefore a key challenge of the Integration Cycle, particularly to international companies and organizations. For most brands, striking such a balance between global and local elements has profound managerial and organizational implications.

For example, in their massive expansion into Latin America, Spanish-based telecom company, Telefonica, was faced with huge integration challenges when they wanted to enable local phone companies to provide the services, attitudes and social responsibility defined as the central foundation for the Telefonica corporate brand. In each market, this took substantial local involvement in order to translate the aspirations of the brand into the local society, business context and human competencies. This integration was further complicated by the fact that many Latin American stakeholders perceived a strong Spanish market presence as a modern form of suppression (i.e. a kind of perceived neo-colonialism). This reminds us that corporate brand integration at times also has to confront cultural resistance and hostility in local market places. This cultural resistance has particularly confronted many US-based brands in recent years and shown the limitations of the classic assumption of 'bigger is better' in terms of global market presence.

Thus, in the Integration cycle, the main change risk is that a lack of brand ownership among managers of the local business units will block the organization-wide execution of the brand. This will, in reality, restrict the impact of the corporate brand to the headquarters and home market only. Of course there can be many degrees of local disengagement, from quiet ignorance to direct resistance. However, the spillover from local managerial resistance can be significant, as lack of managerial ownership will prevent the involvement of local employees and other key local stakeholders in the global execution of the brand.

Levers of Change. In the change management literature, these later stages of change address the need to consolidate improvements and institutionalize the changes at a company-wide level across markets, business units etc. (e.g. Kanter et al., 1992; Kotter, 1995). In transformational leadership, it is argued that a third act entails a 'rearchitecturing', implying both a new beginning at the individual level (i.e. enacting the brand through new scripts with renewed energy) and a reweaving of the social fabric at the organizational level (i.e. cross-functional integration and a new orchestration of communication processes) (Tichy & Sherman, 1993). For example, in order to facilitate company-wide integration, it becomes important to create stronger linkages between the success criteria for the corporate brand and individual performance, as a way for managers to ensure that the corporate brand connects individual and organizational behavior. In particular, since the classic branding model has been dominated by a 'campaign-mindset', the involvement and integration cycles are important in stressing the long term organizational implications for employees of embarking on a corporate branding strategy.

Within change management, scholars have questioned the classic notion of change processes as: 'Unfreezing – change – refreezing' assuming that change processes have a clear start and finish. Instead, many experts of change have suggested that change is a more permanent state or condition in organizations, albeit with shifting modes and challenges over time (Greiner, 1972; Kanter et al., 1992; French et al., 1994). In this conceptualization of change, the planned and emergent forces of change are seen in combination. For corporate branding, this means that the branding process does not stop at the organization-wide institutionalization of the new brand strategy. In contrast, the focus during the Integration Cycle is to maintain and expand the support for the strategic aspiration of the corporate brand, which depending on the situation of the company, may include a range of different, continuous activities.

The initiation of new and local branding cycles may well be endorsed by top management. For example, visiting senior executives from headquarters can spearhead local workshops, where people from the region or business area become engaged in the process of defining what the brand strategy means in their local context and how it should be implemented. For example, the issue of striking a balance between long-term brand building and short-term earnings in the local marketplace is often raised by local subsidiaries. There are also often different perceptions of how to give priority to classic mass market communication and more direct forms of stakeholder interaction. During integration activities, top management can encourage local managers to articulate the brand in ways that make it relevant to their employees and other stakeholders, for example through means of cascading, involving seminars, citizen activities and branding events. This will broaden the managerial responsibility for using the brand vision to influence the local organizational culture by encouraging regional managers to become leaders of change processes aimed at developing a corporate branding mindset among employees. Linkages between culture and image have to be established in the local marketplace, allowing for the development of positive synergies in the Integration cycle.

Monitoring the Corporate Brand

The focus of the *monitoring* cycle is to ensure that the company is able to measure or in other ways track the performance of the corporate brand in relation to all brand elements and the relationships between them.

Key Change Process. In most cases strategic vision and identity claims (e.g. mission and core values) define the overall criteria for assessing the performance of the brand. However, more systematic monitoring is often required in relation to key stakeholder perceptions (as manifested through organization culture and stakeholder images) and the implications for their brand related behavior (i.e. supportive or non-supportive behaviors). Although many large companies apply and develop various measurement systems, the ongoing monitoring of a corporate brand poses a set of specific challenges to measurement systems.

The basic argument of the Corporate Branding Tool-Kit is that a corporate brand is equally relevant to both internal and external stakeholders. Corporate brand monitoring should be more comprehensive than classic market tracking, in bringing together different stakeholders which have traditionally been monitored using their own measurement system. As a result, the first challenge of the Monitoring Cycle is to acknowledge the need to align the tracking of internal and external brand performance. If the existing measurements are separated, then management should push for an exchange of the knowledge provided by each measurement system (typically managed by different business functions).

For example, marketing departments often use specific measurements directed at consumer perceptions, such as Millward

Browns Brand tracking system or Young & Rubicam's Brand Asset Evaluator (BAV) (Aaker & Joachimsthaler, 2000). Corporate communication units focus more on the overall reputation of the company, applying for example the Reputation Quotient (RQ) developed by the Reputation Institute and Harris Interactive (Fombrun et al., 2000; Fombrun & Van Riel, 2000; see also www.reputationinstitute.com) along with different kinds of media tracking (e.g. tracking media coverage, perceptions among business journalists). Finally, many human resource departments measure employee satisfaction, commitment, etc., in internal systems, such as Peoplesoft or the Identification Quotient (see www.reputationinstitute.com). More often, they apply specific measurements developed by the company itself.

In monitoring their corporate brand, some companies combine general annual, external tracking systems (such as the BAV or the RQ) with smaller, more continuous brand specific measurements. For example, in building what they call their corporate 'Trustmark' (as opposed to a trademark) Johnson & Johnson monitors the impact of their numerous trust-building activities in ways that are adapted to the specific activities and local marketplaces. In the US, the company made a huge effort to change the future of nursing resulting from the critical shortage of nurses and very low enrolment at nursing schools. Johnson & Johnson's effort included different initiatives, such as image-building campaigns, partnerships with nursing schools and organizations, the creation of nursing scholarships and development of retention strategies in collaboration with the health care community. In tracking their performance, Johnson and Johnson included both changes in nursing behavior at the society level, such as the (increased) enrolment at nursing schools, and changes in application patterns among future nurses. But they also combined different ways of monitoring their performance, while executing their activities. They applied continuous tracking methods conducted by the company itself (e.g. small, weekly surveys of different stakeholders), as well as bench-marking their performance against the annual RQ and its six dimensions of reputation: Emotional appeal, products and services, workplace environment, vision and leadership, financial performance, social responsibility. The RQ has ranked Johnson & Johnson as the most reputable company in the US among the general public since the method was first applied in 2001. The company also uses the RQ as the baseline measure for their trust-building activities in the UK and China.

As a consequence of monitoring brand performance in relation to multiple stakeholders, corporate branding gaps may follow. If companies apply similar or related measurement systems to both employee and external stakeholder perceptions, that will enable managers to conduct a gap analysis of culture-image relations. For example, several companies have used the RQ both internally and externally, which paves the way for an analysis of whether the organization has the same reputation among employees and external stakeholders. Others have applied the Identification Quotient to measure employee commitment and identification, which also holds opportunities for comparison with the RQ applied to external stakeholders. However, the inclusion of gaps in relation to vision is crucial in the monitoring of a full corporate brand, as the vision sets the direction for the brand and its performance.

In principle, a deep culture-image gap may develop in organizations, because both elements are disconnected from strategic vision. It may also occur because one of the elements is much more distant from strategic vision than the other. This type of vision-image gap arose for some of companies involved in the pan-Scandinavian merger Nordea, as the visibility and image of the former national banks dropped significantly among external stakeholders for a rather long period after the merger. In other situations, employees become detached from the new vision, as was seen when British Airways© tried to implement their new multicultural brand identity (Hatch & Schultz, 2003). Novo Nordisk has an elaborate strategic vision and identity expressed in the Novo Nordisk Way of Management (see www.novonordisk.com). This has encouraged the company to systematically monitor the full corporate brand in their home market of Denmark, offering an analysis of all potential key gaps in their corporate brand. Tabel 8:2 shows a mapping of their different measurement systems related to the gaps defined by the Corporate-Branding Tool-Kit. The next challenge for Novo Nordisk is to track their full corporate brand performance in key international markets – in Europe, Japan and the US. Such monitoring, however, gets more complicated as the lack of visibility to the general public prevents more general reputation tracking and requires stakeholder specific monitoring, in their case related to diabetes.

Change Challenges. The tension most often related to monitoring the corporate brand concerns the balance between using measurement systems to assess the equity and performance of the brand, versus letting the perceived performance of the brand depend on self-contained perceptions among managers and employees. This tension may become more common due to the fast increase in available and accessible measurement systems related to brand and reputation performance.

Table 8:2 Measuring Corporate Branding Gaps at Novo Nordisk

The vision-culture gap:	
• Facilitations	International
• e-Voice	International
• Employee Reputation Quotient (RQ)	Denmark, UK, USA, Germany, China
• Identification Quotient (IdQ)	Denmark, UK (2004)
The culture-image gap:	
• Reputation Quotient (RQ)	Denmark
• Identification Quotient (IdQ)	Denmark (2004)
The image-vision gap:	
• Customer satisfaction surveys	International
• Reputation Quotient	Denmark
• Public surveys and awards	Denmark primarily

Source: Mike Rulis, Corporate Communication Manager, 2004

The risk associated with over-emphasizing brand monitoring is that most measurement systems are strongly biased towards quantitative data, and are often restricted to more general types of insights. This may lead the company to act on a foundation that does not sufficiently reflect the unique identity and special strategic context of the brand. For example, the BAV measures the brand on standardized factors such as perceived knowledge, esteem, relevance and differentiation. These factors allow tracking of the historical development of the brand and comparisons between different brands. But the BAV provides little knowledge about what the brand stands for, what it means to consumers or how well the brand identity resonates with consumers.

The other side of the tension is obviously the tendency, found in many companies, to rely on intuition and local gut feeling in perception of how well the brand is performing. The risk is that internal cultural assumptions about consumers are projected into actions. This results in the company acting upon a scattered set of perceptions of brand performance nested in the various subcultures of the organization. Even large companies often have little systematic knowledge of their reputation and brand performance. In many cases, this lack of systematic knowledge serves as an invitation to local units to avoid the changes required from a corporate brand implementation. Thus, in order to avoid the risk of side-tracking the brand, managers are faced with the need to ensure that different kinds of knowledge about the brand are distributed across functions and business units, forcing middle managers to be sensitized to brand knowledge produced outside of their own turf.

Levers for Change. Although there is a strong awareness of 'process' within change management, there is also an emphasis on the need to follow up on organization-wide performance according to specific criteria for success. Otherwise, the implementation process risks becoming trapped in internal projections and stereotypes among organization members (Kanter et al.,1992). Beer et. al. explicitly argue for the need to 'monitor and adjust strategies in response to problems in the strategic revitalization' (1990:194). In his steps towards organizational change – 'institutionalization of new approaches', the last step – Kotter argues for the need to connect new behaviors with corporation success (1995:61) and develop the means to do so.

As demonstrated in much identity research, organization members tend to react based on their perceptions of how they believe outsiders perceive the organization (e.g. Dutton & Dukerich, 1991), unless they are confronted with outsiders' actual perceptions. Likewise, employees within one subculture may act upon how they perceive the performance of their own – and other – subcultures in relation to the brand, rather than upon knowledge about actual performance. In combination, these tendencies support the need for ongoing knowledge about how the brand is perceived among different stakeholders compared with the stated purpose of the brand.

As a supplement to large-scale monitoring, qualitative ways of tracking the brand provide deeper insights into how stakeholders make sense of and attach meaning to the brand. The ambition is to develop monitoring principles which express and resonate with the identity of the brand. Some companies use ethnographic methods, including participant observations or involvement in consumers' lifestyles in order to get a deeper understanding of what the brand means to consumers. This may lead to psychographic consumer profiles and a better understanding of how the brand gets transformed by different lifestyles and becomes part of consumers' self-expression (e.g. as developed by Nissan for their new Infiniti brand). This rarely leads to quantitative measurement systems, but can substantially elaborate the different types of relationships that emerge between consumers and brands. This is, for example, described by Fournier, who uses the metaphor of human relationships to categorize various kinds of emotional relationships between consumers and brands, e.g. love and passion, self-connection, commitment, interdependency and intimacy (Fournier, 1998). South West Airlines is famous for inventing simple and cheap ways of testing their brand in relation to their stakeholders. For example, they test their brand culture in relation to future employees by placing new recruits in situations where, on a hot and sunny day, they have too choose between jumping into comfortable Bermuda shorts or continuing to wear their long trousers. From the perspective of the South West brand, only people who are bold and informal enough to dare to wear Bermudas during a recruitment process are expected to fit the culture – where playfulness, informality and extroverted character are key values.

Branding Organizational Change

The first point made in this chapter is that too many companies underestimate the organizational and managerial dynamics that corporate branding entails. It is one of the crucial lessons from the first wave of corporate branding, that corporate branding processes need special managerial attention that goes beyond the launch of the new brand identity. One of the main concerns of the second wave of corporate branding is therefore to gain a richer understanding of the challenges, tensions and opportunities in corporate branding as a strategic company-wide process. In this chapter, this dynamic has been conceptualized as five cycles of corporate branding: *Stating, organizing, involving, integrating* and *monitoring*. These cycles are proposed as an analytical framework defining concerns and activities that must be addressed by management when an organization embarks on a corporate branding strategy. However, the sequence between cycles, and the specific configurations of each cycle, most often differ according to the strategic context of the organization. For example, some employee-driven companies start out with the Involvement Cycle before the Stating Cycle; or the Stating and Integrating cycles may be conducted simultaneously in top-down driven global companies. Local Involvement Cycles are also often part of the Integration Cycle, because a global implementation of the corporate brand requires local involvement of employees and other local stakeholders. In that sense, each cycle represents important managerial and organizational activities, which in different combinations constitute the processes of building or revitalizing corporate brands. The chapter has illustrated, in a simplified way, how the cycles have commonly unfolded in different companies. In practice, the sequence and dynamic between the cycles are more fluid and interrelated than our framework suggests.

The second point is that corporate brand management can benefit from insights rooted in change management, organizational development and transformational leadership. Whereas the organizational implications of corporate branding have been underestimated by the classic marketing driven branding literature, organizational change focuses on the specific challenges involved in large-scale implementation processes and particularly offers the important inclusion of employees as the foundation for building a credible corporate brand. When corporate brand implementation is perceived as an organizational change process, it provides a more realistic understanding of the challenges and tensions confronting managers on their journey towards corporate branding. The organizational change lens also invites managers to make much better use of corporate resources by involving employees, confronting turf-issues and facing potential local resistance to brand implementation. Furthermore, lessons from organizational life-cycles suggest which type of crises are likely to happen as the company goes through transitions from one cycle to another.

As a third point, the chapter argues that corporate branding also offers valuable contributions to organizational change processes. In contrast to organizational change and development, which both have an internal focus on managers and employees, corporate branding includes external stakeholders, such as customers, suppliers, the media and political environments, as central players in the branding process. While organizational development has typically addressed ways of engaging employees in organization-wide processes, corporate branding also calls attention to corporate symbolism, market communication and exchanges between stakeholders. Finally, corporate branding originates from a unique organizational identity. This implies that organizations should strive to develop unique implementation processes that are hard to imitate – rather than to adapt to general models of corporate brand implementation.

Finally, the chapter argues that the implementation of a corporate brand reaches beyond business areas and functional departments into the domain of top management responsibility. The ability of top management to engage all employees in an organization-wide effort is a condition for the brand to be able to fully deliver its promises to the multiple external stakeholders.

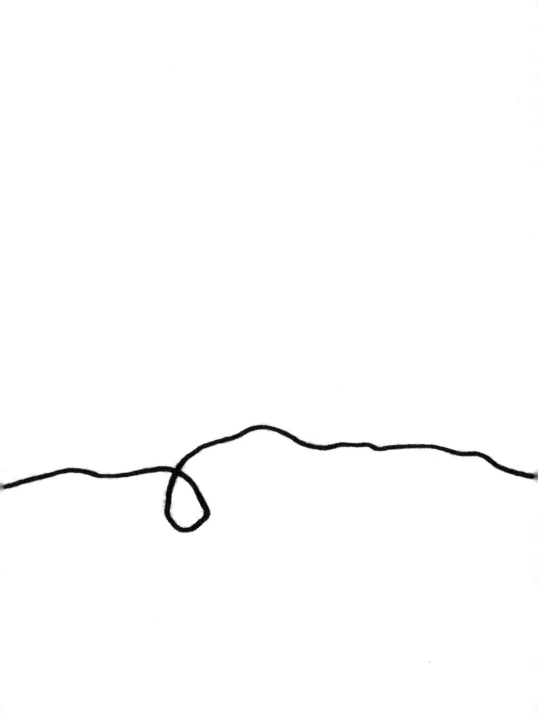

CHAPTER 9

PRINCIPLES FOR THE SECOND WAVE OF CORPORATE BRANDING

Yun Mi Antorini & Majken Schultz

As the various chapters in this book illustrate, the competitiveness and innovative force of organizations is increasingly dependent on their openness and exchanges with their environment, both globally and locally. With budgets as large as the GNP of some countries, organizations represent important institutions, which – for good or bad – play a political, social and educational role. The significance of corporate brands thus goes far beyond simply being trademarks or suppliers of products and services. Seen from this perspective, we consider corporate branding to be a process whereby the organization continually maintains and develops its *reason for being* in relation to its stakeholders and the society to which it belongs. In principle, no organization can avoid corporate branding.

We introduced this book with the argument that corporate branding currently finds itself between a first and second wave. The first wave was founded on a number of myths that locked the organization into a marketing and campaign-driven approach to corporate branding. We therefore argued that the first wave of corporate branding was only poorly able to harness the organization's competitive and innovative power due to its narrow tactical and visual focus. One of the primary suggestions of this book is, therefore, that in order for organizations to reap the benefits of corporate branding, it is vital that they go beyond the simplistic marketing and campaign-driven approach to it.

As this book has repeatedly stressed, we see potential in a *second wave of corporate branding*. The second wave of corporate branding differs from the first wave in a number of ways. Firstly, focus is expanded *from* a marketing and campaign perspective to an *integrated* and *cross-disciplinary* perspective on the creation of competitive and innovative corporate brands. In other words, the corporate brand is created *across* the organization, i.e. it draws upon many organizational functions and not just the marketing and communication functions. This shift is illustrated in table 9:1, which also summarizes the differences between the first and second wave of corporate branding.

We have observed that corporate brands rarely fail because top management's lack of commitment to the vision of the brand. Rather they fail because companies lack organization-wide cohesion across the many contact points between the organization and its different stakeholders, cf. figure 9:1. As a result, the strategic purpose is not aligned with tactical goals, as strategic interests are 'owned' by top management while the tactical interests are executed by marketing and sales functions.

Principles for the Second Wave of Corporate Branding

Table 9:1 *The First and Second Wave of Corporate Branding*

	First wave of corporate branding	Second wave of corporate branding
Basis	Corporate branding grounded in a marketing and campaign approach	Corporate branding grounded in a strategic and cross-functional perspective
Aim	Corporate branding aims to optimize transactions between the organization and consumers as part of its value creation	Corporate branding focuses on the organization's *reason for being*. Value creation arises in the interaction between the organization and its stakeholders
Internal grounding	Marketing and communications functions	All functions and business areas in the organization
Key concerns	"Share of market"	'Share of organization-stakeholder integration'
Communication goals	Information, transfer and dialog relating to products and emotional sales messages	Interaction, exchange of ideas and viewpoints, co-creating of brand meaning and manifestations
Metaphor for the role of the corporate brand	Sense giver	Facilitator: Relations between sense giving and sense making
Process	Linear	Dynamic

Despite the fact that top management is ultimately responsible for initiating, maintaining and developing corporate branding processes (Schultz, Chapter 2), the associations and expectations stakeholders attach to the corporate brand must be created across the organization as part of the move to corporate branding, cf. figure 9:1.

The following example illustrates the unfortunate consequences of separating responsibility for the corporate brand from the organization's short-term tactical goals. A few years ago, Calvin Klein® trousers began to appear in discount stores in Denmark as 'spot specials' at very low prices, over a fairly long period. One can imagine two possible explanations for this: either Calvin Klein's Danish sales function decided to clear its stocks and used discount stores as a channel, or the discount stores, acting on their own initiative, imported the products through grey channels. Whatever the actual situation, the fact was that an attractive prestige brand was put onto the market as 'spot specials' in discount stores. This meant that the Calvin Klein brand was seriously jeopardized, for the sake of fulfilling short-term sales interests. This example illustrates how important it is that an organization's long-term and strategic goals are linked to its short-term, tactical goals. It also demonstrates the importance of both perspectives being present in all relevant organizational functions.

Figure 9:1 A Cross-functional Perspective on Corporate Branding

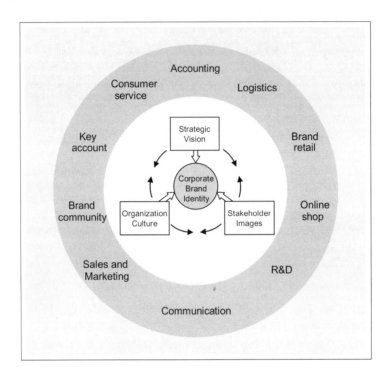

Based on these more general observations, we synthesize our approach to corporate branding in the form of five principles.

Principles for the Second Wave of Corporate Branding

The second wave of corporate branding is being driven by five basic principles. These principles can be applied to varying degrees. We argue that the better an organization is at integrating these principles, the greater the probability that it will reap the benefits from corporate branding.

Principle 1: KNOW THYSELF!

A corporate brand is characterized by a central idea. And this central idea exists as more than just an abstraction or construction. Our basic claim is that an organization is characterized by an interrelated web of identity, culture and images, which is manifested in unique practices and competencies. Together these dimensions describe what is *distinctive* about the organization, what *cannot be imitated or duplicated* by others (see Antorini & Schultz, Chapter 3 on challenging the classic notion of uniqueness).

By advancing the *Know Thyself* principle, we are arguing for a *realistic* approach to corporate branding. A realistic corporate brand is one stakeholders experience as true to the organization's distinctive character and which builds on the organization's distinctive features. We argue against the view that the corporate brand consists exclusively of aspirations and strategic vision, and claim that organizations can only achieve the full benefits of corporate branding by having a realistic attitude towards their historically embedded *identity, culture, image* and *the related practices*.

Maintaining a realistic view of 'who we are' requires that an organization is able to engage in critical self-reflection. This entails, for example, being able to make choices between the array of shifting values – saying *yes* to the values that reflect the organization's origin and can be executed with credibility – and saying *no* to politically correct or popular, but nonetheless hollow, core values.

A second area where it is important to be critical is in the use of external expertise in the development of the corporate brand. Organizations often involve communication consultants and advertising agencies in the development of their corporate brand. This involvement often generates innovative perspectives on the corporate brand which the organization would not have been able to see itself. But the process may also lead to self-seduction and the creation of unrealistic expectations of the future performance of the corporate brand. Often mood boards, projective techniques and other creative stimuli are used as ways to visually and emotionally represent the corporate brand's future position. When pursuing a realistic approach to corporate branding it is essential to be critical towards the future scenario one is agreeing to. It is important to realize that the corporate brand is based in employee behavior and stakeholder perceptions more than in visual impressions and expressiveness (See Karmark, Chapter 5 on the role of employees).

A third area where it is important to be critical is in the estimation of potential target groups for the corporate brand. All too often, development of the corporate brand is based on dubious market analyses that assume the organization is going to take over X per cent of its competitors' consumers, expand the market by Y per cent, and convince Z per cent of existing customers to become heavy users. These estimates are then used as a basis for the decision about the positioning of the corporate brand. Such an approach can result in what we call an *over-stretched corporate brand* which is disconnected from the culture and identity of the brand and not able to deliver the brand promises (see Gjøls-Andersen & Karmark, Chapter 7 on the limits of corporate brand stretch).

A realistic perception of the corporate brand's positioning and potential should instead be based on an analysis of stakeholders' specific behavior and viewpoints. Are the key stakeholders of the organization patient and forgiving when it makes mistakes? Are the organization's stakeholder relationships characterized by mutual trust and partnership, or is the brand basically viewed as a necessary evil? Do the employees trust the management, or is the organization characterized by cynicism and anomie? Do organizational members share a perception of how 'we do things around here', or is there fundamental disagreement and counter cultures? The more realistically an organization understands 'itself', the better its foundation for creating an authentic and credible corporate brand.

Principle 2: BE A FACILITATOR!

Knowing yourself is essential, but is not sufficient in an organization's pursuit of competitive and innovative advantage. As we discussed in Chapter 4 (Antorini & Andersen) with regard to the idea of co-creation (Prahalad & Ramaswamy, 2004), organizations are increasingly fusing with the market and stakeholder interests. Given that the corporate brand synthesizes the organization's reason for being, it plays an important role as a *facilitator* of this fusion. In other words, the corporate brand can be said to mediate the interaction between the organization and its multiple stakeholders.

During the first wave of corporate branding, organizations typically made use of vicarious advertisements, events, direct mails, PR, etc., to establish contact with customers. The principle of the corporate brand as a *facilitator* focuses instead on creating situations where direct interaction (either online or offline) between the organization and its stakeholders can be established. This is illustrated by the examples of IKEA, Jones Soda, and Weight Watchers in Chapter 4. Thus the second wave of corporate branding emphasizes the ongoing *vitalization* of the corporate brand, which can take place through one of the many existing, but often underexploited, contact points the organization has with stakeholders, cf. figure 9:2.

The idea of the corporate brand as a facilitator typically involves the organization redefining its location in relation to its multiple stakeholders. The traditional corporate mindset usually places the organization in the centre of events. In contrast, we describe the facilitating mindset as being rooted in the organization perceiving itself as part of a network of relationships with other institutions and stakeholders (Post, Preston & Sachs, 2002). The role of the corporate brand in this context is to facilitate these relationships, i.e. to create space for action, dialogue, idea generation, but also criticism. As in the case of the LEGO Group, where the organization – based on the corporate vision that LEGO products are for people of all ages – chose to build close relationships with adult LEGO fans. The LEGO Group's core target group is children, and in relation to this group, adult LEGO fans represent a very small group. Nonetheless, adult LEGO fans demonstrate great enthusiasm, fantastic creativity and innovative skills, as well as not insignificant buying power. The point is, the facilitating mindset enabled LEGO Group to notice and build relationships with a group of consumers that could otherwise easily have been overlooked among the organization's many priorities. Furthermore, these relationships again facilitate new contacts with other groups of consumers, as, for example, when adult LEGO fans exhibit (both in the virtual and the real world) their creations and ideas, bringing inspiration and an awareness of the LEGO brand to other people.

Principle 3: LEAD THROUGH INTERACTION!

We continue to define the role of top management as being responsible for corporate branding processes, i.e. for generating, maintaining and developing the strategic framework for the corporate brand. By 'strategic framework' we mean that top management fleshes out the organization's reason for being by seeking to align strategic vision, organizational culture and stakeholder images founded in the organization's identity (see, The Corporate Branding Tool-Kit, suggested by Hatch & Schultz in Schultz, Chapter 2). However, in contrast to the traditional and centralistic perception of the top manager, we suggest a more complex view of how the corporate brand is created and developed.

Instead, we suggest that the corporate brand is created and develops through social, and often informal, processes (Stacey, 2001). It is in the employees' *interpretation* of what the top manager sets as the vision for the corporate brand that ideas about its opportunities and limitations arise. And it is in the social interaction between people that these ideas are tested, modified, converted to narratives about the corporate brand, and hence come to life, i.e. become enacted by internal and external stakeholders.

In contrast to the first wave of corporate branding, which often made use of vicarious media to communicate the corporate brand to stakeholders, under the second wave, the corporate brand is managed in the *interaction* between people. The corporate branding process is therefore a social process that bounces back and forth within the organization as sense-making and sense-giving processes (Gioia & Chittipeddi, 1991) between the top management and employees. The process is tied together by the connections between the organization's functions and illustrates the importance of leading the brand through middle management. This interaction is illustrated in figure 9:2.

Figure 9:2 The Corporate Branding Process as Sense-making and Sense-giving

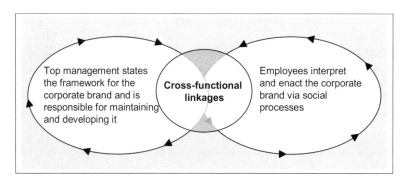

It is the role of top management to create the conditions that allow knowledge and experience about the corporate brand to be generated

Principles for the Second Wave of Corporate Branding

and shared among the functions and business areas of the organization. These conditions can be promoted by (Stacey, 2001):

- Creating flexible and flat organizational structures that promote networks and local decision making, and which prevent power struggles arising between subcultures, cf. Chapter 8
- Clearly and precisely articulating the organization's visionary and value foundation, so it can serve as a guide for individual employee decisions, cf. Chapter 2
- Management recognizing its role as an important source of inspiration that plays an active role in motivating employees to work towards the vision
- Management creating the necessary conditions for the corporate brand to be 'led from the middle', i.e. through cross-functional connections within the organization that ensure joint responsibility and broad organizational involvement
- Management removing barriers that prevent informal contacts from being established, in order to promote narratives about the corporate brand

These conditions not only represent a major managerial challenge, they also demonstrate that all the multiple competencies that relate to the organization's relationships with its environment are areas that will experience significant development under the second wave of corporate branding. In contrast to the first wave of corporate branding, where these competencies typically resided in a limited number of functions, the corporate brand is now being integrated into several organizational functions reflecting the cross-disciplinary origin of corporate brands, cf. figure 9:1.

The principle of the organization as a facilitator therefore requires a shift in mindset and an increasing openness towards competencies different from one's own, which more people in the organization must necessarily embrace. Professional expertise and insight will continue to be necessary in order to succeed, but will no longer be sufficient given the new requirement of increased integration with the organization's stakeholders. Knowledge about the organization's history, identity and culture and how social processes are developed and managed, will be just as essential. Here again, top management is responsible for creating the conditions that permit these new perceptions to be developed among relevant stakeholders.

Principle 4: EMBRACE PARADOXES

The corporate brand does *not* live in brand books and identity guidelines, it lives *through* people! In other words, simple management principles are not enough. Instead, corporate branding must be understood as a cross-disciplinary process, full of tension and paradox.

As we have argued (Schultz, Chapter 8), corporate branding seen as organizational change, gives rise to a number of conceptual paradoxes. We have highlighted seven paradoxes which are linked particularly to the leadership aspects of corporate branding moving towards the second wave, and which represent particular challenges to the organization. As table 9:2 shows, the paradoxes linked to corporate branding play out classic management paradoxes between the whole and the parts; leadership and co-determination; change and stability; and integration and over-adaptation (Quinn, 1988).

Table 9:2 Paradoxes of Corporate Branding

Think shared **VISION**	BUT...	Remember to give room to the people who give the vision vitality and power!
Think shared **CULTURE**	BUT...	Remember to challenge the culture and overcome group-think!
Think **LEADERSHIP**	BUT...	Remember to involve the organization's different subcultures and functions!
Think **CROSS-FUNCTIONAL**	BUT...	Do not forget that new ideas often require deep insights and knowledge!
Think **CHANGE**	BUT...	Do not jeopardize the organization's distinctive characteristics!
Think **CO-CREATION**	BUT ...	Do not forget in-house competencies and avoid short-term market hype!
Think **INTEGRATION** with stakeholders	BUT...	Remember the risk of hyper-adaptation to environment!

In our view, a corporate brand founded on realism will not reject these paradoxes. Instead, they will be acknowledged as part of the organization's conditions. Despite the fact that organization theorists often seek to understand organizations from *either* a stability *or* a dynamic perspective, we believe it is more fruitful to start from the premise that organizations are fundamentally *both* stable and continuously changing. We therefore believe that neither the stability nor change perspective should dominate our understanding of corporate branding. Corporate brand leadership should therefore be founded on consideration of the whole, *but also* the parts; the need for strategic direction, *but also* for co-determination; the necessity of change, *but also* of holding on to the organization's distinctive heritage; the idea of closer integration, *but also* recognition of the dangers of over-adapting products and services to the point where a focus on innovation is lost.

In relation to the second wave of corporate branding, our goal is therefore not to seek to ride roughshod over the paradoxes linked to corporate branding, but rather to encourage companies, organizations and anyone else who works with corporate branding to accept their existence. This is the only way we can counteract the development of corporate branding as a naive and unrealistic field.

Principle 5: THINK DYNAMIC!

Under the second wave, perception of corporate branding as a linear process whereby the organization defines the corporate brand in isolation is giving way to a view of corporate branding as a *dynamic process*. As figure 9:3 illustrates, the corporate branding process can be perceived as five separate cycles which, depending on the organization's life cycle, market conditions and aims, are passed through at various speeds and a varying number of times (Schultz, Chapter 8). The aim of this figure is to illustrate that the corporate branding process entails different challenges within each cycle, and that these cycles together contribute to developing and grounding the corporate brand in the organization's behavior and contact points with stakeholders.

The first cycle focuses on formulating the corporate brand's reason for being, and asks questions about identity, point of difference and strategic vision. The second cycle focuses on the organization and asks questions such as: Is the organization's structure appropriate? i.e. does it ensure that the interaction between the organization and stakeholders occurs under conditions driven by the brand? As in the case of Jones Soda, it is essential that the function giving feedback to consumers on their creative efforts and allowing the organization to optimally exploit consumer ideas is constantly adapting to changing forms of interaction.

Figure 9:3 Cycles of Corporate Branding

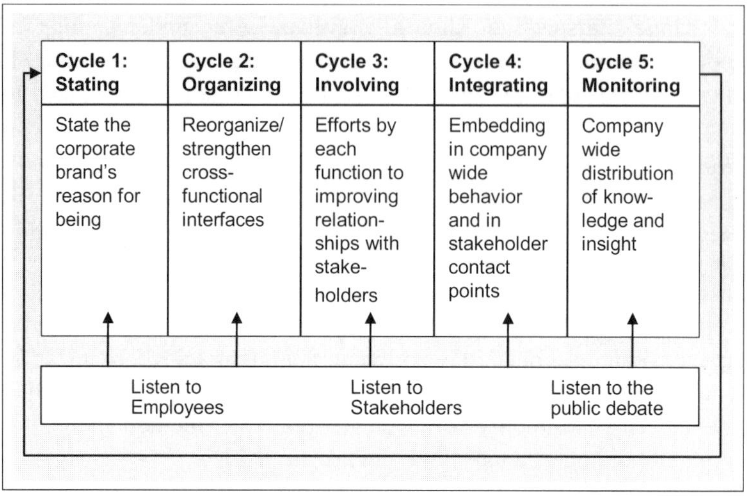

Cycle 1: Stating	Cycle 2: Organizing	Cycle 3: Involving	Cycle 4: Integrating	Cycle 5: Monitoring
State the corporate brand's reason for being	Reorganize/ strengthen cross-functional interfaces	Efforts by each function to improving relation-ships with stake-holders	Embedding in company wide behavior and in stakeholder contact points	Company wide distribution of know-ledge and insight

Listen to Employees	Listen to Stakeholders	Listen to the public debate

The third cycle aims to flesh out how each business function can develop their own way of building relationships with stakeholders, balancing the paradox between shared brand identity and adaptation to individual stakeholder needs. The fourth cycle focuses on embedding any changed practices in the organization structure and processes, embracing all stakeholder contact points. Experiments can be done using pilot projects to test new practices locally before integrating them throughout the organization. The most important thing is that knowledge about which practices most effectively engage stakeholders in the corporate brand is disseminated in the organization. The fifth cycle gathers information on these experiences and distributes it within the organization in order to measure the impact of the brand in relation to various stakeholders and improve organizational practices. Over time, new experiences will be accumulated that derive from interaction with the environment. These new experiences restart the process to some extent. Corporate branding is therefore characterized by cycles of change, and sometimes even regeneration.

Moving Towards the Second Wave of Corporate Branding

We have argued for the necessity of developing the corporate branding concept. In principle, we are back at the crossroads that the corporate branding concept faced a decade ago. Rather than continuing along the marketing and campaign-driven path, this time we choose the other path. We call this path the second wave of corporate branding. The second wave of corporate branding represents a conceptual framework through which an organization can describe its reason for being and manage its brand building as change processes. This requires a cross-functional and strategic foundation for corporate branding, and prioritizes the link between the organization and its stakeholders as being central to the organization's value creation. Based on the idea that the corporate brand is created in the dynamic interaction with stakeholders, the second wave of corporate branding requires that the people in the organization can engage in local and innovative relationships, just as the role of top management needs to be developed in order to facilitate greater integration between the organization and it's multiple stakeholders.

We conclude the book by posing ten questions to organizations moving towards the second wave of corporate branding which may provide inspiration for a new perception of corporate branding as a field of study and in practice.

10 Questions to Organizations

1. Do you know who you are as an organization? In other words, do you have a realistic perception of your identity, organizational cultures, images and special competencies?

2. Are you ready to incorporate corporate branding processes in your long-term strategies, or are you sticking to a marketing and campaign perspective?

3. Does the foundation of your corporate brand transcend all the organization's functions? Or does it (still) 'live' in the marketing and communication function only?

4. Does your vision leave room for the organization's employees to effectively perform according to its promises? i.e. is it realistic, or does it place abstract or superhuman demands on individuals?

5. Do you regularly challenge the organization's culture? Do you freely move out of your 'comfort zone' to ensure the revitalization and renewed relevance of what you stand for, or do you prefer your comfortable and well-known ways of doing things?

6. Do you actively use the knowledge that exists among your stakeholders to create an innovative and competitive corporate brand, or do the 'not invented here' mindset, organizational structures and ingrained perceptions of the organization's value creation hold you back?

7. How do you primarily use your contact points with stakeholders today? To carry out transactions or to build relationships?

8. Do you allocate resources to where the organization and stakeholders interact? Or do you (still) give priority to the vicarious media?

9. What are the most important paradoxes in your corporate brand? Do you have a common perception of these paradoxes and their implications for the organization's development?

10. Is your corporate brand managed as a campaign or as strategic development? What cycle is your brand currently in? Are you giving enough attention to the changing demands on the management and organization of corporate brands?

Bibliography

Aaker, D.A. (1991) *Managing Brand Equity*. New York: The Free Press.

Aaker, D.A. (1996) *Building Strong Brands*, New York: The Free Press.

Aaker, D.A. (1997) 'Should you take your brand to where the action is?', *Harvard Business Review* Vol. 75, pp. 135-144.

Aaker, D. A. (2003) 'The Power of the Branded Differentiator', *MIT Sloan Management Review* Vol. 45, No. 1, pp. 83-87.

Aaker, D.A (2004) 'Leveraging the Corporate Brand', *California Management Review*, Vol. 46, pp. 6-18.

Aaker, D.A. and Joachimsthaler, E. (2000) *Brand Leadership*. New York: The Free Press.

Aaker, D.A. and Keller, K.L. (1997) 'Managing the Corporate Brand: The Effects of Corporate Marketing Activity on Consumer Evaluation of Brand Extensions', *Working Paper*, Marketing Science Institute, Report No. 97-106, May.

Argyris, C. (1994) 'Good Communication That Blocks Learning', *Harvard Business Review*, Vol. 72, No. 4, pp. 77-85.

Albert, S. and Whetten, D.A. (1985) 'Organizational identity', in L.L. Cummings and M.M. Staw (eds) *Research in Organizational Behaviour* 7, pp. 263-295.

Alvesson, M. and Wilmott, H (2004) 'Identity Regulation as Organizational Control Producing the Appropriate Individual' in: Hatch, M. J. and Schultz, M. (eds) *A Reader on Organizational Identity*, pp 436-469. Oxford: Oxford University Press.

Anderson, B. (1991) *Imagined Communities*. London: Verso.

Anholt, S. (2002) 'Foreword', *Journal of Brand Management*, Vol. 9, No. 4-5, pp. 229-239.

Anholt, S. (2003) 'Branding places and nations', in R. Clifton and J. Simmons (eds) *Brands and Branding*. London: The Economist. pp. 213-226.

Anholt, S. (2004) 'Nation-brands and the value of provenance', in N. Morgan; A. Pritchard and R. Pride (eds) *Destination Branding: Creating the Unique Destination Proposition*, pp. 26-39 Oxford: Elsevier Butterworth-Heinemann.

Anonymous (1997) 'Danisco bliver politisk virksomhed' (in Danish), *Mandag Morgen*, January 3rd-20th, pp. 8-11.

Antorini, YM. and Schultz, M. (2004) 'Corporate Branding: 2. Bølge', *Mandag Morgen*, September 20th, 2004.

Argenti, P. and Foreman, J. (2004) in Schultz, M., Hatch, M.J. and Larsen, M.H.(eds) *The expressive organization: Linking identity, reputation, and the corporate brand*, pp. 233-246. Oxford: Oxford University Press.

Balmer, J.M.T. (1995) 'Corporate Branding and Connoisseurship', *Journal of General Management*, Vol. 21, No 1, pp. 24-46.

Balmer, J.M.T. (2001) 'The three virtues and seven deadly sins of corporate brand management', *Journal of General Management* Vol. 27, No. 1, pp. 1-17.

Balmer, J.M.T. and Gray, E.R. (2003) 'Corporate brands: what are they? What of them?', *European Journal of Marketing*, Vol. 37, No. 7/8, pp. 972-997.

Balmer, J.M.T. and Greyser, S. (2003) (eds) *Revealing the Corporation*, London: Routledge.

Barney, J. (1991) 'Firm resources and sustained competitive advantage', *Journal of Management* Vol. 17, No 1, pp. 99-120.

Barney, J. (1996) *Gaining and Sustaining Competitive Advantage*. New York: Addison Wesley.

Barney, J. and Stuart, A.C. (2000) 'Organizational Identity as Moral Philosophy: Competitive Implications for Diversified Corporations' in Schultz, M; Hatch, M.J and Holten Larsen, M (eds.) *The Expressive Organization*, pp. 36-51. Oxford: Oxford University Press.

Bauman, Z. (2001) *The Individualized Society.* UK*:* Polity Press.

Beardi, C. (1999) 'Interbrand Opens Foundation to Concentrate on Non-Profits', *Advertising Age*, Vol 70, No. 46, p. 120.

Beer, M., Eistenstat, R.A. and Spector, B. (1990) 'Why change programs don't produce change'; *Harvard Business Review*, November-December, pp. 158-166.

Bennett, R. and S. Savani (2003) 'The Rebranding of City Places: An International Comporative Investigation', *International Public Managemnent Review,* Vol. 4, No. 2, pp. 70-87.

Best, S. and Kellner, D. (1991) *Postmodern Theory. Critical Interrogations.* New York: The Guilford Press

Borum, F. (1995) *Organisation, power and change.* Copenhagen: Handelshøjskolens forlag.

Bousch, D. M. and B. Loken (1991) 'A Process-Tracing Study of Brand Extension Evaluation', *Journal of Marketing Research,* Vol. 28, No 2, pp. 1-28.

Boyle, M. (2003) 'Brand Killers*', Fortune Magazine,* Vol. 148, No 3, pp. 50-56.

Brannen, M.Y. (2004) 'When Mickey Loses Face: Recontextualisation, Semantic Fit, and the Semiotics of Foreignness', *Academy of Management Review*, Vol. 29, No. 4, pp. 593-616.

Broniarczyk S.M. and Alba, J.W. (1994) 'The importance of Brand in Brand Extension', *Journal of Marketing Research*, Vol. 31, No. 2, pp. 214-228.

Brown, S (1995) *Postmodern Marketing.* London: Routledge.

Brown, T.J. and Dacin, P.A. (1997) 'The Company and the Product: Corporate Associations and Consumer Product Responses', *Journal of Marketing*, Vol. 61, No. 1, pp. 68-84.

Caldwell N and Freire, J.R. (2004) 'The differences between branding a country, a region and a city: Applying the Brand Box Model', *Journal of Brand Management*, Vol. 12, No. 1, pp. 50-61.

Chatman, J. and Cha, S.E. (2003) 'Leading by Leveraging Culture' *California Management Review*, Vol. 45, No. 4, pp. 20-31.

Cheney, G. and Christensen, L.T. (2001) 'Organizational Identity: linkages between Internal and External Communication', in Jablin and Putnam (eds) *New Handbook of Organizational Communication*, pp. 231-269. London: Sage Publications.

Christensen, L.T. (2002) 'Corporate communication: the challenge of transparency', *Corporate Communications: An international Journal*, Vol. 7, No. 3, pp. 162-168.

Christensen, L.T. and Cheney, G. (2000) 'Self-absorption and self-seduction in the corporate identity game', in Schultz, M., Hatch, M.J. and Larsen, M.H. (eds) *The expressive organization: Linking identity, reputation and the corporate brand*, pp. 246-274. Oxford: Oxford University Press.

Cohen, A.P. (1985) *The Symbolic Construction of Community*. London: Routledge.

Collins, D. (2003) 'The branding of management knowledge: rethinking management 'fads'', *Journal of Organizational Change Management*, Vol. 1, No. 2, pp. 186-204.

Collins, J.C. (2001) *Good to Great*. New York: Harper Business.

Collins, J.C. and Porras, J. (1994) *Built to Last*. New York: Harper Business.

Cornelissen, J. (2004) *Corporate Communication. Theory and Practice*. London: Sage Publications.

Cova, B. (1997) 'Community and consumption. Towards a definition of the 'linking value" of products or services', *European Journal of Marketing,* Vol. 31, no 3/4, pp. 297-316.

Cova, B. and Cova, V. (2002) 'Tribal Marketing. The tribalisation of society and its impact in the conduct if marketing', *European Journal of Marketing,* Vol. 36, No 5/6, pp. 595-620.

Dacin, P.A. and D.C. Smith (1994), 'The Effect of Brand Portfolio Characteristics on Consumer Evaluations of Brand Extensions', *Journal of Marketing Research*, Vol. 31, No. 2, pp. 229-242.

Davis, S. (2000) *Brand asset management*. San Fransico: Jossey-Bass.

Davies, G. and Chun, R. (2003) 'The Use of Metaphor in the Exploration of the Brand Concept', *Journal of Marketing Management*, Vol. 19, pp. 45-71.

de Chernatony, L. (1999) 'Brand Management Through Narrowing the Gap Between Brand Identity and Brand Reputation', *Journal of Marketing Management*, Vol. 15, No 1/3, pp. 157-179.

de Chernatony, L. (2002) 'Would a brand smell sweeter by a corporate name?', in Schultz, M. and Chernatony, L. 'Special issue on corporate branding', *Corporate Reputation Review,* Vol. 4/5, pp. 114-132.

de Chernatony, L. and Segal-Horn, S. (2003) 'The Criteria for Successful Services Brands', *European Journal of Marketing*, Vol. 37, No. 7/8, pp. 1095-2019.

DiMaggio P.J. and H.K. Anheiner, (1990) 'The sociology of nonprofit organizations and sectors'. *Annual Review of Sociology* 16, pp. 137-59.

DiMaggio P.J. and W. Powell, (1983) 'The Iron Cage Revisited. Institutional Isomorphism and Collective Rationality in Organizational Fields', *American Sociological Review*, 48, pp. 147-60.

Drucker, P.F. (1989) 'What business can learn from nonprofits', *Harvard Business Review*. July/August, Vol. 67, Issue 4, pp. 88-93.

Drucker, P.F. (2001) 'Peter Drucker Interview – Unabridged' by Eric Schoenfeld in *Business 2.0*, October 2001.

Dutton, J. and Dukerich, J. (1991) 'Keeping an eye on the mirror: Image and identity in organizational adaptation', *Academy of Management Journal,* Vol 34, pp. 517-554.

Dutton, J.E., Dukerich, J.M. and Harquail, C.V. (1994) 'Organization Images and Member Identification', *Administrative Science Quarterly* Vol. 39, pp. 239-69.

Elsbach, K. and Kramer, R. (1996) 'Members responses to organizational identity threats: Encountering and countering the Business Weeks rankings', *Administrative Science Quarterly,* Vol. 41, pp. 442-76.

Fiol, C. M. (2001) 'Seeing the empty spaces: towards a more complex understanding of the meaning of power in organizations', *Organization studies,* Vol. 12, No. 4, pp. 547-566.

Fombrun, C. (1996) *Reputation: Realizing value from the corporate image*. Boston: Harvard Business School Press.

Fombrun, C., Gardberg, N.A. and Sever, J.M. (2000) 'The Reputation Quotient: A Multi-Stakeholder Measure of Corporate Reputation', *Corporate Reputation Review* Vol. 2000, pp. 241-255.

Fombrun, C and Van Riel, C. (2004) *Fame and Fortune*. New York: Prentice Hall.

Fombrun C. and Van Riel, C (1997) 'The Reputational Landscape', *Corporate Reputation Review,* Vol. 1, No. 1/2, pp. 5-13.

Fombrun, C and Rindova, V. (1999) 'Constructing competitive advantage', *Strategic Management Journal,* Vol 2, No. 8, pp. 691-710.

Fombrun, C. and Rindova, V. (2000) 'The road to transparency: Reputation management at Royal Dutch/Shell', in Schultz, M, Hatch, M.J. and Holten Larsen, M.(eds) *The Expressive Organization. Linking Identity, Reputation and the Corporate Brand*, pp. 77-97. Oxford: Oxford University Press.

Fortune (2004) 'Coke. The Real Story'. *Europe Edition, June 7 2004*.

Fortune (2004) '10 Best Companies to Work for in Europe', *January 26, 2004*.

Fournier, S. (1998) 'Consumers and Their Brands: Developing Relationship Theory in Consumer Research', *Journal of Consumer Research*, Vol. 24, pp. 343-373.

Fournier, S. (2002) *Building Brands by Building Brand Relationships*, presentation given at Brand Lab Maiden Voyage.

Fournier, S., McAlexander, J., Schouten, J. and Sensiper, S. (2000) 'Building Brand Community on the Harley-Davidson Posse Ride', *Harvard Business School case number: 9-501-015*. ECCH, Bedford: England.

Franke, N. and Shah (2003) 'How communities support innovative activities: an exploration of assistance and sharing among end-users', *Research Policy*, Vol. 32, pp. 157-178.

Frasher, S., M. Hall, J. Hildreth and M. Sorgi (2003) *A Brand for the Nation of Latvia*. Oxford: Said School of Business.

French, W. and Bell, C. (1990) *Organization development*. Englewood Cliffs: Prentice Hall.

French, W., Bell, C. and Zawacki, C. (1994) *Organizational development and transformation*. Illinios: Irwin

Giddens A. (1991) *Modernity and Self-identity. Self and Society in the Late Modern* Age. UK: Polity Press.

Gioia, D.A. and Chittipeddi, K. (1991) 'Sensemaking and sensegiving in strategic change initiation', *Strategic Management Journal*, Vol. 12, pp. 443-44.

Gioia, D.A, Schultz, M. and Corley, K (2000) 'Organizational identity, image and adaptive instability', *Academy of Management Review*, Vol. 25, issue 1, pp. 63-81.

Gioia, D.A. and Thomas, J. B. (1996) 'Identity, image and issue interpretation: Sensemaking during strategic change in academia', *Administrative Science Quarterly,* Vol. 41, pp. 370-403.

Gjoels-Andersen, P (2001) 'The Internal Dimensions of Branding' – a case study of the change of brand strategy in LEGO from a focus on the famous building brick to introducing a broad variety of LEGO products in the children's universe, *Ph.D. thesis*, Copenhagen: Copenhagen Business School.

Gotsi, M. and Wilson, A. (2001) 'Corporate Reputation Management: living the brand', *Management Decision*, Vol. 39, pp. 99-104.

Graham, Peter (1993) 'Marketing's Domain: A Critical Review of the Development of the Marketing Concept', *Marketing Bulletin*, Vol. 4, pp. 1-11.

Gray, E.R. and Balmer, J.M.T. (2001) 'The corporate brand: a strategic asset', *Management in Practice*, No. 4, pp. 1-4.

Greiner, L. (1972). 'Evalution and revolution as organizations grow', *Harvard Business Review*, Jul/Aug, Vol. 50, issue 4, pp. 37-46.

Greiner, L.E. and Malernee, K. (2005) 'Managing growth stages in consulting firms', in Greiner, L. and Poulfelt, F. (eds) *The contemporary consultant.* New York: Thompson.

Guy, M. E. and Hitchcock, J.R. (2000) 'If apples were oranges: the public/nonprofit/business nexus in Peter Drucker's work', *Journal of Management History*, Vol 6, No. 1, pp. 30-47.

Hamel, G. and Prahalad, C. K. (1994) *Competing for the Future.* Boston: Harvard Business School Press.

Hankinson, G. (2001) 'Location branding: A study of the branding practices of 12 English cities', *Brand Management,* Vol. 9, No. 2, pp. 127-142.

Hankinson, G. (2004) 'Relational network brands: Towards a conceptual model of place brands', *Journal of Vacation Marketing*, Vol. 10, No. 2, pp. 109-121.

Hankinson, P. (2002) 'The impact of brand orientation on managerial practice: A quantitative study of the UK's top 500 fundraising managers', *International Journal of Nonprofit and Voluntary Sector Marketing*, Vol. 7, No. 1, pp. 30-44.

Hankinson, P. (2004) 'The internal brand in leading UK charities', *Journal of Product and Brand Management*, Vol. 1, No. 2, pp. 84-93.

Hatch, M.J and Schultz, M. (1997) 'Relations between Organizational Culture, Identity and Image', *European Journal of Marketing,* Vol. 31, No. 5, pp. 356-65.

Hatch, M.J. and Schultz, M. (2000) 'Scaling the Tower of Organizational Identity Research', in Schultz, M., Hatch, M.J. and Larsen, M.H. (eds) *The expressive organization: Linking identity, reputation, and the corporate brand*, pp. 246-271. Oxford: Oxford University Press.

Hatch, M. J. and Schultz, M. (2001) 'Are the strategic stars aligned for your corporate brand', *Harvard Business Review,* Vol. 79, No. 2, pp. 128-134.

Hatch, M. J. and Schultz, M. (2002) 'Organizational Identity Dynamics', *Human Relations,* Vol. 55, pp. 989-1018.

Hatch, M.J. and Schultz, M. (2003) 'Bringing the Corporation into Corporate Branding', *European Journal of Marketing,* Vol 7, No. 8, pp. 1041-1064.

Hatch, M.J. and Schultz, M. (2004) *A Reader on Organizational Identity*. Oxford: Oxford University Press.

Heap, S. (2000) *NGOs engaging with business*. Oxford: INTRAC.

Hyojin, K. (2002) 'Branding of Nonprofit Organizations', *LBJ Journal of Public Affairs*, Vol. XIV, Spring, pp. 47-57.

Holt, D. B. (1995) 'How Consumers Consume: A Typology of Consumption Practice', *Journal of Consumer Research,* Vol. 22, pp. 1-16.

Holt, D. B. (2003) 'What Becomes an Icon Most?', *Harvard Business Review,* Vol. 81, No. 5, pp. 43-49.

Holt, D. B. (2004) *How Brands Become Icons. The Principles of Cultural Branding,* Boston: HBS Press.

Ind, N. (1997) *The corporate brand.* New York: New York University Press.

Ind, N. (1998) 'An integrated approach to corporate branding', *Journal of Brand Management,* Vol. 5, No. 5, pp. 323-9.

Ind, N. (2001) *Living the brand.* London: Kogan Page.

Interbrands.com, February, 2005

Isdell, E. N. (2004) *Interview with CEO E. Neville Isdell on Coca-Cola's Online Press Center,* June 22, 2004.

Jacobsen, C.R. (2003) 'IKEA giver stor lønforhøjelse', *Kommunikationsforum.dk,* May 7, 2003.

Jensen, R. (2002), *Heartstorm,* Viby J: Jyllands-Postens Erhvervsbogklub

Jick, T. (1993) *Managing change. Cases and concepts.* Illinois: Irwin

John, D.R., B. Loken & C. Joiner (1998) 'The Negative Impact of Extensions: Can Flagship Products be Diluted?', *Journal of Marketing,* Vol. 62, January, pp. 19-32.

Kamprad, I. (2004) *Interview with Theresa Howard: Ikea builds on furnishings success', USA TODAY,* December 29.

Kanter, R.M., Stein, B.A. and Jick, T. (1992) *The challenge of organizational change.* New York: The Free Press.

Kapferer, JN. (1992) *Strategic brand management -new approaches to creating and evaluating brand equity.* London: Kogan Page.

Kapferer, J.N. (2001) *Reinventing the brand – Can top brands survive the new market realities?* London: Kogan Page. (Originally published in French in 2000).

Kapferer, JN. (2004), *The New Strategic Brand Management – Creating and Sustaining Brand Equity Long Term*, 3. ed. London: Kogan Page.

Karmark, E. (2002) 'Organizational Identity in a Dualistic Subculture' – a Case Study of Organizational Identity Formation in Lego Media International, *Ph.D. thesis*, Copenhagen: Copenhagen Business School.

Keller, K.L. (2000) 'Building and Managing Corporate Brand Equity' in Schultz, M; Hatch, M.J and Holten Larsen, M (eds.) *The Expressive Organization*, pp. 115-138. Oxford: Oxford University Press.

Keller, K.L. (1998) *Strategic brand management. Building, measuring and managing brand equity*. New Jersey: Prentice-Hall.

Keller, K.L. (1997) *Strategic Brand Management: Building, Measuring, and Managing Brand Equity.* New Jersey: Pearsons Higher Education.

Klein, N. (2000) *No Logo.* London: Flamingo

Klein, N (2002) 'America's attempt to market itself abroad using advertising principles is destined to fail'. *Los Angeles Times*; Mar. 10, p. M.1

Kotler, P. (2003) *Marketing Management.* Upper Saddle River, N.J: Pearson Higher Education.

Kotler, P and Gertner, D. (2004) 'Country as brand, product and beyond: a place marketing and brand management perspective', in N. Morgan; A. Pritchard and R. Pride, *Destination Branding: Creating the Unique Destination Proposition*, pp. 40-56.

Kotler, P and Levy, S. (1969) 'Broadening the Concept of Marketing', *Journal of Marketing*, Vol. 33 (January), pp. 10-15.

Kotter, J. (1995) 'Leading Change: 'Why Transformation Efforts Fail', *Harvard Business Review,* Vol. 73, No. 2, pp. 59-67.

Kunda, G. (1992) *Engineering culture – control and commitment in a high-tech corporation.* Philadelphia: Temple University Press

Kunde, J. (2000) *Corporate Religion.* Edinburgh/London: Prentice Hall.

Lafley, A. G. (2005) 'CEO Procter and Gamble: 'It was a no-brainer', *Fortune*, February 21, 2005.

Langer, R. (2002) 'Place images and place marketing', in J. Helder and S. Kragh, *Senders and Receivers,* pp. 56-96. Copenhagen: Samfundslitteratur.

LEGO Company (1998*)* 'Strategic Intent', *Internal Company Document.*

'Lego klar til Legoland-salg', *Politiken*, March 11th 2005.

Lencioni, P. M. (2002) 'Make Your Values Mean Something', *Harvard Business Review*, Vol. 80, No. 7, pp. 113-117.

Loken, B. & D. R. John (1993), 'Diluting Brands Beliefs: When do Brand Extensions Have Negative Impact?', *Journal of Marketing*, Vol. 57, pp. 71-84.

Martin, J. (2004) 'Organizational culture', in N. Nicholson, P. Audia, and M. Pillutla, (Eds.), *The Blackwell Encyclopedic Dictionary of Organizational Behavior*, 2.ed., Oxford, England: Basil Blackwell Ltd.

Martin, J. (2002) *Organizational Culture – mapping the terrain.* California: Sage Publications Ltd.

Martin, J., Frost, J.P. and O'Neil, A.O. (in press). 'Organizational Culture: Beyond struggles for intellectual Dominance'. in Clegg, S., Hardy, C., Nord, W. and Lawrence, T. (Eds.), *Handbook of organization studies*. 2. eds. London: Sage Publications.

Martin, J., Feldman M.S., Hatch, M.J. and Sitkin, S.B.(1983) 'The Uniqueness Paradox in Organizational Stories', *Administrative Science Quarterly*, Vol. 28, pp. 438-453.

Martinović, S. (2002) 'Branding Hrvatska – a mixed blessing that might succeed: The advantage of being unrecognizable'. *Brand Management*, Vol. 9, No. 4-5, pp. 315-322.

McAlexander, J., Schouten, J. and Koenig, H. (2002) 'Building Brand Community', *Journal of Marketing,* Vol. 66, No. 1, pp. 38-54.

Mikkelsen, H. and A. Schwartenbach (2004). *The Challenges of Branding NGOs*. Unpublished Masters thesis, Copenhagen Business School.

Millar, C., Choi, C. and Chen, S. (2004) 'Global Strategic Partnerships between MNEs and NGOs: Drivers of Change and Ethical Issues', *Business and Society Review,* Vol. 109, No. 4, pp. 395-414.

Mirvis, P., Ayas, K. and Roth, G. (2003) *To the desert and back. The story of one of the most dramatic business transformations on record.* San Francisco: Jossey-Bass.

Mitchell, A. (2004) 'Getting Staff to Live the Brand: Work in Progress', *Marketing Week*, September 2nd, p. 30.

Montoya, P. (2003) *The Personal Branding Phenomenon*. Orange County: Peter Montoya Inc.

Morgan, N., Pritchard, A. & Pride, R. (2004) *Destination Branding: Creating the Unique Destination Proposition*. 2. eds. Oxford: Elsevier Butterworth-Heinemann.

Morsing, M. & Kristensen, J. (2001) 'The question of coherency in corporate branding – over time and across stakeholders', *Journal of Communication Management*, Sept. 6, pp. 24-40.

Morsing, M. & Pruzan, P. (2002) 'Values in Leadership: Perspectives, Practices and Perplexities' in Zolani, L. (eds) *Ethics in the Economy – Handbook of Business Ethics,* pp. 259-294. Germany: Peter Lang.

Muniz, A.M. & O'Guinn, T.C. (2001) 'Brand Community', *Journal of Consumer Research,* Vol. 27, pp. 412-432.

Muniz, A. M. and O'Guinn, T. C. (2005) *Marketing Communications in a World of Consumption and Brand Communities. Marketing Communication: New Approaches, Technologies and Styles.* Oxford: Oxford University Press.

Newsweek (2004) 'What's in a name? Less and less as consumers spurn big brands'*, Newsweek,* October 2004.

Nitin, N., Joyce, W. and Roberson, B.(2003) 'What really works', *Harvard Business Review,* Vol. 44, No. 1, pp. 43-52.

O'Cass, A. and Grace, D. (2003) 'An exploratory perspecive of service brand association', *The Journal of Services Marketing,* Vol. 17, pp. 452-74.

O'Guinn, T. C. & Muniz, A.M. (2005) 'Communal Consumption and the Brand', in Mick, D.G. and Ratneshwar. S. (eds) *Inside Consumption: Frontiers of Research on Consumer Motives, Goals, and Desires.* Routledge (forthcoming, 2005).

Olins, W. (1989) *Corporate Identity: Making Business Strategy Visible Through Design.* Boston: Harvard Business School Press.

Olins, W. (1999) *Trading Identities.* London: The Foreign Policy Centre.

Olins, W. (2000) 'How brands are taking over the corporation', in Schultz, M., Hatch, M.J. and Larsen, M.H. (Eds), *The Expressive Organization*, pp. 51-65. Oxford: Oxford University Press.

Olins, W. (2001) *How Brands are Taking over the Corporation*, in Schultz, M., Hatch, M.J. and Larsen, M.H. (eds) *The expressive organization: Linking identity, reputation, and the corporate brand*, pp. 246-271. Oxford: Oxford University Press.

Olins, W. (2002) 'Branding the nation – The historical context', *Journal of Brand Management*, Vol. 9, No. 4/5, pp. 241-248.

Olins, W. (2003) *On Brands*. London: Thames and Hudson.

Ooi, C.S. (2003) 'Poetics and politics of destination branding: 'Denmark. Enjoy''. *Working paper*. Copenhagen Business School.

Papadopoulos, N. & Heslop, L. (2002) 'Country equity and country branding: Problems and prospects', *Brand Management*. Vol 9, No. 4/5, pp. 294-314.

Park, C.W., M.S. McCarthy & S.J. Milberg (1993) 'The Effects of Direct and Associative Brand Extension Strategies on Consumer Response to Brand Extensions, in: L. McAllister & M. Rothschild (eds.) *Advances in Consumer Research*, 20, pp. 28-33.

Paustian, M, (2003) *Branding Filosofi*. København: Nyt fra Samfundsvidenskaberne.

Pavitt, J. (2000) 'In Goods We Trust?', in *brand.new*, London: V&A Publications.

Peters, T. (1997) 'The Brand Called You', *Fast Company*, Vol. 10 August/September, p. 83.

Peters, T. J. & Waterman, R.H. (1982) *In search of excellence – lessons from America's best-run companies*. Cambridge: Harper & Row.

Politiken (2005) 'Pendlerparty i Papegøjehaven', *Politiken,* January 30 2005.

Poole, M.S and Van de Ven, A. (1989) 'Using paradox to build management and organization theories', *Academy of Management Review,* Vol. 14, pp. 562-578.

Prahalad, C.K. & Ramaswamy, V. (2004) *The Future of Competition. Co-creating Unique Value with Customers*. USA: Harvard Business School Press.

Pratt, M. and Rafaeli, A (2005) *Artifacts in organizations: More than the cultural tip of the iceberg.* Mahwahi Erlbaum.

Quelch, J.A. and David, K. (1994) 'Extend profits, not product lines', *Harvard Business Review*, Vol. 72, pp. 153-161.

Quinn, J. B. & Cameron, K. S. (1988) *Paradox and transformation – toward a theory of change in organization and management.* Cambridge, Mass: Ballinger.

Quinn, R. E. (1988) *Beyond Rational Management. Mastering the Paradoxes and Competing Demands of High Performance.* San Francisco, CA: Jossey-Bass.

Ravasi, D. and Schultz, M. (2005) 'Responding to identity threat: Exploring the role of organizational culture'. *SCA Bocconi. Working paper.*

Regani, S. (2003) *Case: Walt Disney: The evolution of the brand.* Hyderabad: ICFAI Center for Management Research.

Rendon, J. (2003) 'When Nations Need a Little Marketing', *New York Times,* November 23, 2003. Business/Your Money, p. 23.

Ritchie, R.J.B., Swami, S. and Weinberg, C.B. (1999) 'A Brand New World for Nonprofits', *International Journal of Nonprofit and Voluntary Sector Marketing*, Vol 2, No. 1, pp. 26-42.

Rosander, M., Stiwne, D. & Granström, K. (1998) 'Bipolar groupthink: Assessing groupthink tendencies in authentic work groups', *Scandinavian Journal of Psychology*, Vol. 39, No. 2, pp. 55-129.

Schein, E.H. (1985) *Organizational culture and leadership – a dynamic view.* San Francisco: Jossey-Bass.

Schein, E.H. (1992) *Organizational culture and leadership*, 2. ed., San Francisco: Jossey-Bass.

Schein, E.H. (2004) *Organizational culture and leadership*, 3. ed., San Francisco: Jossey-Bass.

Schmitt, B. H. (1999) *Experiential Marketing. How to get customers to sense, feel, think, act, relate to your company and brands.* New York: The Free Press.

Schmitt, B. and Simonsen, A. (1997) *Marketing Aesthetics – The strategic management of brands, identity, and image.* New York: The Free Press.

Schouten, J. W. and McAlexander, J. H. (1995) 'Subcultures of Consumption: An Ethnography of the New Bikers', *Journal of Consumer Research,* Vol. 22, pp. 43-61.

Schultz D.E. & Kitchen P.J. (2004) 'Managing the Changes in Corporate Branding and Communication: Closing and Re-opening the Corporate Umbrella', *Corporate Reputation Review,* Winter 2004, Vol. 6, No. 4, pp. 347-366.

Schultz, M. (1994) *On studying organizational cultures: diagnosis and understanding.* Berlin: Walter de Gruyter and Co.

Schultz, M. (1995) *On Studying Organizational Cultures.* Berlin: Walter de Gruyter.

Schultz, M (2004) *Organizations as Brands.* Presentation given at a MBA course.

Schultz, M. and de Chernatony, L. (2002) 'Introduction. The Challenges of Corporate Branding', *Corporate Reputation Review.* Vol. 5, No. 2/3, pp. 105-112.

Schultz, M. and Hatch, M. J. (2003) 'The Cycles of Corporate Branding; The Case of the LEGO Company', *California Management Review,* Vol. 46, No. 1, pp. 6-24.

Schultz, M. and Hatch, M. J. (2005) 'A culture perspective on Corporate Branding', in Schroeder, J. and Salzer, M. (eds.) *Brand Culture.* London: Routledge.

Schultz, M. and Hatch, M. J. and Ciccolella, F. (2005) 'Living the brand through symbols and artifacts', in Pratt, M. and Rafaeli, A. (eds) *Artifacts in organizations: More than the cultural tip of the iceberg.* Mahwahi Erlbaum.

Schultz, M. and Hatch, M. J. and Larsen, M.H. (2000) 'Why the Expressive Organization?', in Schultz, M., Hatch, M.J. and Larsen,

M.H. (eds) *The expressive organization: Linking identity, reputation, and the corporate brand*, pp. 1-11. Oxford: Oxford University Press.

Schultz, M., Hatch, M.J., Rubin, J and K.S. Andersen (in press), *Novo Nordisk – Focussing the Corporate Brand,* Corporate Branding Case Series.

Schultz, M., Mouritsen, J. and Gabrielsen, G. et. al. (2001) 'Sticky Reputation', *Corporate Reputation Review,* Vol. 4, No.1, pp. 24-41.

Shaw, G. (2000) 'Planning and communicating using stories', in Schultz, M., Hatch, M. J. and Larsen, M. H. (eds) *The Expressive Organization – Linking Identity, Reputation, and the Corporate Brand*, pp. 182-196. Oxford: Oxford University Press.

Synghel, K., Speaks, M. and Berci, F. (2002) *City Branding: Image Building and Building Images*. Rotterdam: NAI Publishing

Søderberg, AM. and Mathiesen, S. (2003) *Managing Identities in a Nordic Cross-Border Merger – A Case Study of Storytelling*, Paper presented at: European Academy of Management's 3rd. Annual Conference, Milan: April 3- 5.

Thomke, S. and von Hippel, E. (2002) 'Customers as Innovators: A New Way to Create Value', *Harvard Business Review,* Vol. 80, No. 4, pp. 74-81.

Tichy, N. M. and Sherman, S. (1993) *Control your destiny or someone else will.* New York: Harper Business.

Trueman, M., Klemm, M., and Giroud, A. (2004) 'Can a City Communicate? Bradford as a corporate brand', *Corporate Communication, An International Journal*, Vol. 9, No. 4, pp. 317-330.

Upshaw, L. (1995) *Building Brand Identity*. New York: John Wiley and Sons.

Van Ham, P. (2001) 'The Rise of the Brand State', *Foreign Affairs*, Vol. 80, No. 5. September/October, pp. 2-6.

Van Maanen, J and Barley, S. (1985) 'Cultural Organization – Fragments of a Theory', in Frost et al (eds.) *Reframing Organizational Culture.* Newbury Park: Sage

Van Riel, C. (1995) *Principles of Corporate Communication.* London: Prentice Hall.

Van Riel, C. (2000) 'Corporate Communication Orchestrated by a Sustainable Corporate Story', in Schultz, M., Hatch, M. J. and Larsen, M. H. (eds) *The Expressive Organization – Linking Identity, Reputation, and the Corporate Brand,* pp. 157-182. Oxford: Oxford University Press.

Van Riel, C.B.M. & J.M.T. Balmer (1997), 'Corporate Identity: The Concept, its Measurement and Management', in *European Journal of Marketing,* Vol. 31, No. 5/6, pp. 340-355

von Hippel, E. (1988) *The Sources of Innovation.* USA: Oxford University Press.

von Hippel, E. (2001) 'Innovation by User Communities: Learning from Open-Source Software', *MIT Sloan Management Review,* Vol. 42, No. 1, pp. 82-86.

von Hippel, E. (2005) *Democratizing Innovation.* The MIT Press

Weick, K. E. (1979) *The social psychology of organizing,* 2nd ed. McGraw-Hill, Inc. New York, pp. 147-169.

Weick, K. E. (1996) 'Drop your tools: an allegory for organizational studies', *Administrative Science Quaterly,* 40th Anniversary Issue, pp. 301-313.

Weick, K. E. (2002) 'Puzzles in Organizational Learning: An Exercise in Disciplined Imagination', *British Journal of Management,* Vol. 13, pp. 7-15.

Wetlaufer, S. (2000), 'Reinventing Disney', in *Strategic Direction,* Sep. 16, p. 9.

Whetten, D. and Godfrey, P. (1998.) (eds) *Identity in Organizations. Building theory through conversations.* Thousands Oaks: Sage Publications.

Woodliff, J. and Deri, C. (2001) 'NGOs: The New Super Brands', *Corporate Reputation Review*, Vol. 4, No. 2, pp. 157-164.

Websites:

http://www2.coca-cola.com/ourcompany/enduringstory.html
www.reputationinstitute.com
www.interbrand.com
www.brandstudies.com
www.expressiveorganization.com